FrontPage® 2003 For Dummies®

FrontPage Toolbars You'll Use Most Often

The Standard toolbar

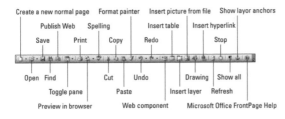

Create a new normal page · Format painter · Insert picture from file · Show layor anchors
Publish Web · Spelling · Insert table · Insert hyperlink
Save · Print · Copy · Redo · Stop

Open · Find · Cut · Undo · Drawing · Show all
Toggle pane · Paste · Insert layer · Refresh
Preview in browser · Web component · Microsoft Office FrontPage Help

The Formatting toolbar

Numbering
Increase font size · Decrease indent
Italic · Align right · Outside borders
Style · Font · Font size · Align left · Font color

Bold · Center · Highlight
Underline · Justify · Bullets
Decrease font size · Increase indent

The Pictures toolbar

Insert picture from file · More brightness
Bring forward · More contrast · Format picture · Rectangular hotspot
Auto thumbnail · Rotate left 90° · Resample · Polygonal hotspot
Flip Horizontal · Line style · Color · Restore

Text · Format picture · Select · Highlight hotspots
Position absolutely · Less brightness · Bevel · Circular hotspot
Send backward · Less contrast · Set transparent color
Rotate right 90° · Flip vertical

The Tables toolbar

Distribute rows evenly
Center vertically · Autofit to contents
Insert rows · Delete cells · Table autoformat combo
Show layout tool · Draw table · Split cell · Fill down

Eraser · Align top · Fill color · Fill right
Draw layout table · Merge cells · Table autoformat
Insert columns · Align bottom · Distribute columns evenly

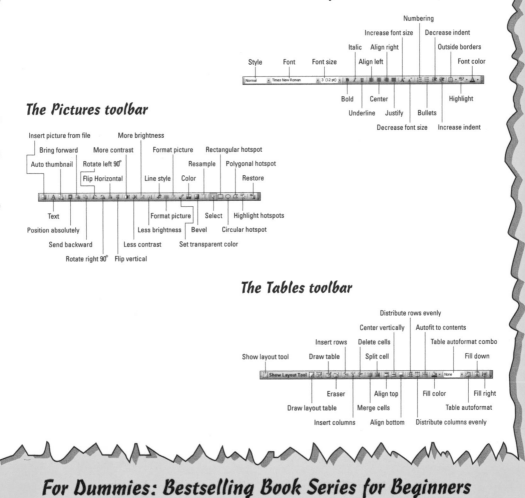

FOR DUMMIES
BESTSELLING
BOOK SERIES™

FrontPage® 2003
For Dummies®

Cheat Sheet

The FrontPage Buzzword Translator

FrontPage doesn't just come with a bucketful o' features; the program includes its very own set of obscure buzzwords! Check out the following terms:

- **Web site:** A collection of linked Web pages and files that's visible on the World Wide Web or an internal corporate network.

- **Web page:** An individual Web site file, written in HTML. Web pages (along with other types of files) make up the content of a Web site.

- **HTML:** Short for *HyperText Markup Language,* HTML is a set of simple text codes that defines the structure of a Web page. If you want to create Web pages, you need either to learn HTML or to use a program such as FrontPage, which cranks out the HTML for you.

- **URL:** Stands for *Uniform Resource Locator,* the technical name for an Internet site address. The URL for Microsoft's Web site is www.microsoft.com.

- **Web server:** A special type of program that knows how to deliver (serve) Web pages on request. The computer on which the Web server program is installed also is called a Web server.

- **Parent Web site:** What FrontPage calls a top-level Web site. If you visit the Web site at www.microsoft.com, for example, you're looking at Microsoft's parent Web site.

- **Subsite:** What FrontPage calls a second-level Web site, or a complete Web site that lives in a folder on the same server as the parent Web site. If you visit the FrontPage Web site at www.microsoft.com/frontpage, for example, you're looking at the frontpage subsite.

- **Link bars:** Also called *navigation bars,* these rows of hyperlinks enable visitors to easily get around your Web site.

- **Themes:** Coordinated sets of graphics, colors, and text effects you can apply to your site to give it polish and style.

- **Web components:** Unique FrontPage tools you can add to your site. Web components simplify Web publishing tasks or add dynamic features to your Web site.

- **FrontPage Server Extensions:** A set of auxiliary programs, installed on the Web server, that enables certain FrontPage-specific features to work.

Where to Go for More Help

If you have a burning question this book doesn't answer, turn to the following resources for more help:

- **FrontPage Help system:** Sometimes you just can't beat the help that comes with FrontPage. To access Help, choose Help⇨Microsoft FrontPage Help.

- **The Microsoft FrontPage Web site:** This site contains lots of helpful articles, related links, and other tidbits. See www.microsoft.com/frontpage.

- **Microsoft Support Online:** Home of the mammoth Microsoft Knowledge Base, a searchable database of answers to all sorts of software-related questions. See support.microsoft.com.

- **Microsoft FrontPage Newsgroup:** People just like you are posting problems and sharing solutions on the FrontPage Usenet newsgroup. Point your news reader to microsoft.public.frontpage.client and join the fun!

- **Real, live tech support people:** Your licensed copy of FrontPage comes with access to Microsoft support engineers who can help you through persistent tough spots. Check the documentation that comes with FrontPage for contact information.

For Dummies: Bestselling Book Series for Beginners

by Asha Dornfest

Wiley Publishing, Inc.

FrontPage® 2003 For Dummies®

Published by
Wiley Publishing, Inc.
111 River Street
Hoboken, NJ 07030
www.wiley.com

About the Author

On her first day of college, **Asha Dornfest** took a bold step: She replaced her broken typewriter with a PC.

Asha didn't consider herself a geek; her computer was simply a tool to help her write papers and reports. But by her senior year, she came to regard her computer with a sense of kinship.

After graduation, Asha trudged into the real world with a liberal arts degree and decent computer skills. (Which do you think got her a job?) She enjoyed showing people how computers could simplify their lives, when the things weren't making life more difficult, that is.

In 1994, Asha discovered the Internet. Soon after, she and her husband Rael started a Web design business in their dining room and began hawking their electronic wares. Mind you, this venture began during the Web-publishing Stone Age when many people had never even heard of the World Wide Web. A savvy friend quipped that *For Dummies* books about Web publishing may one day hit the shelves. Asha scoffed.

Today, Asha writes about Web publishing and other topics. She welcomes visitors to her virtual home at www.ashaland.com.

Dedication

To my lovely Mirabai, who arrived just as this book was going to print.

Author's Acknowledgments

I'd like to thank all the people who made *FrontPage 2003 For Dummies* run so smoothly. Special thanks to Project Editor Nicole Sholly, Acquisitions Editor Steve Hayes, Technical Editor Jim Kelly, and Copy Editor Jean Rogers.

Once again, the Microsoft FrontPage team put together an excellent beta program. I am especially grateful to John Jansen and Terry Crowley for timely answers to my sometimes-niggly questions.

My thanks to Studio B Productions for advocacy and support.

Finally, to my family and friends . . . thank you for showing me what's important every day.

Publisher's Acknowledgments

We're proud of this book; please send us your comments through our online registration form located at www.dummies.com/register/.

Some of the people who helped bring this book to market include the following:

Acquisitions, Editorial, and Media Development

Project Editor: Nicole Sholly

Acquisitions Editor: Steve Hayes

Copy Editor: Jean Rogers

Technical Editor: Jim Kelly

Editorial Manager: Kevin Kirschner

Permissions Editor: Carmen Krikorian

Media Development Specialist:

Media Development Manager: Laura VanWinkle

Media Development Supervisor: Richard Graves

Editorial Assistant: Amanda Foxworth

Cartoons: Rich Tennant, www.the5thwave.com

Production

Project Coordinator: Maridee Ennis

Layout and Graphics: Amanda Carter, Carrie Foster, Lauren Goddard, Joyce Haughey, Stephanie D. Jumper, Lynsey Osborn, Heather Ryan, Jacque Schneider, Shae Wilson

Proofreaders: Carl William Pierce, Christine Sabooni, Kathy Simpson, Charles Spencer

Indexer: TECHBOOKS Production Services

Publishing and Editorial for Technology Dummies

 Richard Swadley, Vice President and Executive Group Publisher

 Andy Cummings, Vice President and Publisher

 Mary C. Corder, Editorial Director

Publishing for Consumer Dummies

 Diane Graves Steele, Vice President and Publisher

 Joyce Pepple, Acquisitions Director

Composition Services

 Gerry Fahey, Vice President of Production Services

 Debbie Stailey, Director of Composition Services

Table of Contents

Introduction

● ●

*N*ot so long ago, the Internet was the domain of geeks, academics, and soda-fueled computer jocks. Today, surfing the Web is almost as automatic as dialing a phone or flipping through the Yellow Pages. The Internet has become such a constant presence in home and work life that having your own Web site is not unlike having a cell phone number or an e-mail address: not exactly mandatory, but just about.

And yet, even though so many folks want a home page to call their own, actually creating the Web site, getting the thing to look and work the way you want, and then getting it online is still a daunting task.

Thankfully, FrontPage 2003, the latest incarnation of Microsoft's popular Web site creation tool, brings Web publishing down to earth. Without knowing HTML (the language used to create Web pages), you can use FrontPage to build and manage a beautiful and sophisticated Web site.

FrontPage is a hefty piece of software. And like a lot of powerful software, FrontPage is easy to use — *after* you figure out what all those buttons and menus do.

Enter *FrontPage 2003 For Dummies*.

About This Book

In this book, I concentrate on the information you need to build a well-designed, attractive, easy-to-navigate Web site. I figure you're not interested in becoming a FrontPage expert; you want to get up to speed with FrontPage quickly and easily so that you can get your project under way *now*. And why not have a little fun while you're at it?

FrontPage 2003 For Dummies is a reference book, so you don't need to start at Chapter 1; just flip to the section that tells you what you want to know. If you're new to Web publishing, you may want to skim the book to get a sense of what building a Web site entails, and then read the stuff that looks interesting. If you're adventurous, fire up FrontPage, click the buttons, play with the menus, and grab the book when you get stumped.

Conventions Used in This Book

I use a few text conventions throughout the book:

- ✔ A notation like "Choose File➪Open" is a condensed version of "from the File menu, choose the Open command."
- ✔ When I say, "Press Ctrl+N," I mean, "While holding down the Ctrl key on your keyboard, press the N key."
- ✔ E-mail address and Web site addresses appear in this `computese font`. If a Web address is really long, or I want to show you a bit of HTML code, it will appear on its own line, like this:

  ```
  This is a line of code.
  ```

FrontPage often gives you more than one way to tackle a task. For example, the following actions might all accomplish the same thing:

- ✔ Choosing a menu item
- ✔ Clicking a toolbar button
- ✔ Pressing a keyboard shortcut
- ✔ Right-clicking an item and then choosing an option from the pop-up menu that appears

In this book, I generally tell you the easiest way to carry out a particular task. If you prefer to use an alternate method, by all means, go ahead.

Foolish Assumptions

FrontPage 2003 For Dummies helps you jump right into using FrontPage. I therefore make a few assumptions about who you are and what you already know how to do:

- ✔ **You've developed a cordial relationship with your computer and its associates: the mouse, keyboard, monitor, and modem or network connection.** You ask the computer nicely to do things by pressing keys and clicking the mouse, and it usually complies. You're comfortable with the basic workings of Windows, such as using the Start menu, double-clicking items, getting around the Windows desktop, clicking buttons on toolbars, and choosing commands from menu bars.
- ✔ **You have an Internet connection through your workplace, school, an Internet Service Provider (ISP), or an online service, and you've spent**

some time surfing the Web. You don't necessarily understand how the Internet works, but you have a staff person at your ISP, company techie, or nerdy neighbor to call when you have a problem.

✔ **You have FrontPage sitting in a box in a highly visible location on your desk so that passersby will see it and think how technically savvy you are.** If you're brave, you've installed FrontPage on your computer.

✔ **You've never tried your hand at Web publishing.** If you've tried Web publishing, you've never done it with FrontPage. If you have worked with FrontPage, you were perplexed after fiddling with the program, rushed to the bookstore, and are reading this book right now.

How This Book Is Organized

FrontPage 2003 For Dummies contains all the information you need to create great-looking Web sites with FrontPage 2003. FrontPage is no small topic, so I divide the subject into easily chewable parts.

Part I: Getting Friendly with FrontPage

Part I introduces you to FrontPage and helps you become comfortable with the program's interface and basic functions.

Part II: Web Page Construction Basics

Part II familiarizes you with the fundamentals of Web design and page creation. You discover how to work with text, create hyperlinks, add pictures, and build grid tables. You also find out how to create interactive forms that let your visitors communicate with you.

Part III: Pump Up Your Web Site!

Part III shows you how to turn nice, basic Web pages into impress-your-friends-and-coworkers showpieces. You become familiar with layout tables, the professional Web designer's most important tool. You find out how to embellish your Web site with graphical themes, multimedia, and Dynamic HTML. You get to know Web components — sets of ready-made tools you can plop into your Web site. Finally, if you want to take a peek under the hood, you can ease yourself into working with FrontPage 2003's HTML tools.

Part IV: Taking Your Web Site to a New Level

Part IV shows you how to take advantage of FrontPage's site management capabilities. You also discover how Dynamic Web Templates can save you time when you're ready to update your site. You find out how to control access to your Web site and use FrontPage workgroup and collaboration features. Finally, you discover how to make your Web site visible on the World Wide Web.

Part V: The Part of Tens

The Part of Tens helps you venture beyond FrontPage when you're ready to see what else is out there. You find out about ten FrontPage add-ins that extend the program and give it new capabilities. You also read about ten Web sites that I think no Web publisher should miss.

Icons Used in This Book

Icon-studded paragraphs and sidebars highlight special information.

This icon points out important details you don't want to forget.

Here, you find a timesaving FrontPage shortcut. Or you may receive a design tip you can use to add oomph to your Web site. Or perhaps you get a pointer to relevant information on the Web.

Your computer doesn't explode when you see this icon. The icon alerts you to a potential FrontPage or Web publishing sticky spot.

The information flagged with this icon is for those of you who want to dig a little deeper into the technical aspects of Web publishing. For the code-curious among you, watch for this icon to find an HTML shortcut or tip. If you don't care to learn the HTML or just want to get that Web site published, skip this stuff.

This is a sidebar

Text tucked inside a gray-shaded box is called a *sidebar.* These sidebars highlight extra information that's related to the topic being covered.

Where to Go from Here

Enough preamble . . . it's time to get that Web site started!

My hope is that this book helps you develop the confidence and skills to create whatever Web site you envision. Onward, ho!

Part I
Getting Friendly with FrontPage

The 5th Wave — By Rich Tennant

"YOU KNOW KIDS — YOU CAN'T BUY THEM JUST ANY WEB AUTHORING SOFTWARE."

In this part . . .

Facing the task of mastering a new piece of software feels a little bit like walking into a party and not recognizing anyone. The scariest moment occurs after you launch the program for the first time and stare at all those unfamiliar buttons and menu items.

In this part, you get acquainted with FrontPage. I make some introductions, pass around a few refreshments, and pretty soon you'll feel right at home.

Chapter 1

Weaving a FrontPage Web Site

*W*ith so many people jumping on the Web publishing bandwagon, you can easily feel like you've been left in the dust. Just a few years ago, many of us used our computers as glorified typewriters and calculators. Today, regular folks are hitching the dusty old desktop machine to a modem or network connection and are cranking out publications with worldwide impact. What happened?

The World Wide Web happened. Now that the Web is part of everyday life, computers are no longer isolated islands of correspondence, recipes, and personal finance records. Your computer can now hook you into a world of information and communication possibilities. The writing's on the wall: The Web is here to stay, and everybody who's anybody wants to be a part of the excitement.

So where does that leave you? If you're edging your way into the dot-com world (or being dragged in, kicking and screaming, by your employer or your kids), you're in for a pleasant surprise: With a little help, creating a Web site with FrontPage 2003 is easy and fun.

In this chapter, you get your feet wet with FrontPage. You fire up the program and get started on a new Web site. You find out how to import an existing Web site into FrontPage, and how to open, close, and delete Web sites.

Exactly What Is Web Publishing?

Before you hang your shingle as a FrontPage Web publisher, it helps to understand what you're actually doing when you create and publish a Web site.

No doubt, you've already seen a Web site. Web sites are the places you visit as you make your way around the World Wide Web. Some folks refer to their Web sites as their *home pages*. FrontPage often refers to Web sites simply as *sites*. As a book is made up of individual pages, a Web site is made up of individual files called *Web pages*. Web pages contain the text, pictures, and other content you see when you visit a Web site.

As you construct a Web site, you create Web pages and then string the pages together using *hyperlinks*. Hyperlinks are the highlighted words and pictures inside the page that visitors can click to jump to a different location, page, or Web site. Hyperlinks can also initiate a download or pop open an e-mail window.

After your site is complete, you *publish* it. In other words, you make the site visible to the rest of the world on the World Wide Web (or, if you're working on an internal company site, the company's intranet). This isn't automatic. For a Web site to be live, you must transfer the site's files from your computer to a *Web server,* a host computer that runs special Web server software and that's connected to the Internet 24 hours per day.

If you're working on an intranet site, the publishing process is similar, except that only those with a password to access the intranet can view your site. An *intranet* is an internal company network based on the same type of technology as the Internet, with access restricted to people within that company. Intranet sites generally contain information useful to company insiders, such as policies, collaborative tools, and department announcements.

Many people gain access to a host Web server by signing up for an account with an Internet service provider (or *ISP*) that makes Web server space available to its users. Others use a Web server maintained by their workplace or school. Yet another option is to sign up with one of the many hosting companies that offer server space for free (see Chapter 17 for pointers to some of these companies).

Creating Your First FrontPage Web Site

If you read the previous section of this chapter, you have a general idea about how Web publishing works. You don't need more than a fuzzy sense at this point — the process will become clearer as you tinker with FrontPage. And what better way to get started than to create your first Web site?

If this feels like getting thrown into the deep end before learning to swim, relax. As you get acquainted with FrontPage, you can change any aspect of your Web site or just delete the Web site and start over.

To create your first FrontPage Web site, follow these steps:

1. **Launch FrontPage by choosing Microsoft Office FrontPage 2003 from the Start menu. (The exact location of the FrontPage icon depends on choices you make when installing FrontPage and on the version of Windows you have on your computer.)**

   FrontPage launches. Your screen should look like Figure 1-1. A new, blank Web page named new_page_1.htm appears in the program's main window with its cursor blinking patiently.

   (If this is the very first time you're launching FrontPage, a dialog box appears encouraging you to activate your program. You can click the Cancel button to make the dialog box disappear for now, but it will pop up again each time you launch FrontPage. Sooner or later, you'll have to take the extra few seconds to activate FrontPage; just follow the directions in the dialog box when the time comes.)

2. **Insert some text into the page — that is, start typing.**

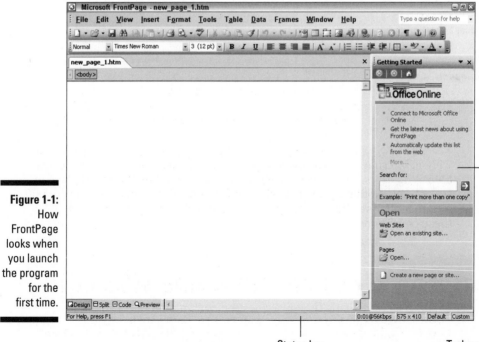

Figure 1-1:
How
FrontPage
looks when
you launch
the program
for the
first time.

Status bar   Task pane

3. **On the Standard toolbar near the top of the FrontPage window, click the Save button.**

    The Save As dialog box appears, as shown in Figure 1-2. The dialog box prompts you to save your new Web page in the My Web Sites folder (which is located inside the My Documents folder on your hard drive). When you installed FrontPage, the Setup program created the My Web Sites folder as the default saving location for your FrontPage Web sites.

    Note: If you share a computer with other people and use the Windows system of users and passwords to maintain separate settings, the My Documents folder is located inside the Documents and Settings folder, in a subfolder identified by your user name.

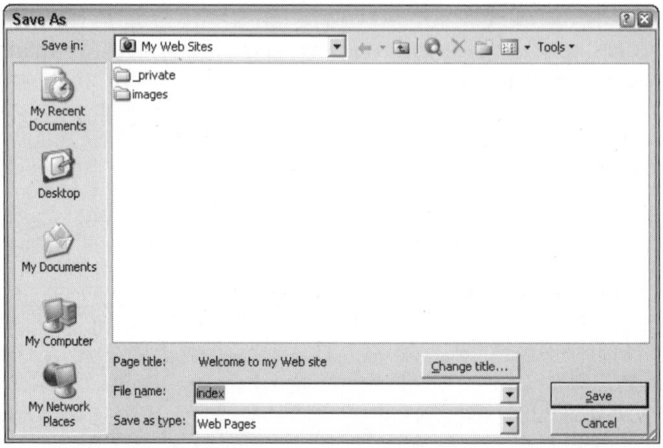

Figure 1-2:
The Save As
dialog box.

4. **Don't change the default filename (**index**) visible in the dialog box's File Name text box.**

    Most Web servers look for the file named *index* to identify the Web site's default page, also known as the site's *home page*.

    When you save the page, FrontPage automatically adds the .htm extension to the filename. I talk more about how to name Web pages in Chapter 2.

5. **To change the page title, click the Change Title button.**

    The Set Page Title dialog box appears.

6. **In the dialog box's Set Page Title text box, enter a new title.**

    Choose a title that describes the content and purpose of the page (something like My First Web Site: Home Page). In Chapter 2, I go into more detail about how to choose a good page title.

7. **Click OK to close the Set Page Title dialog box.**

   The Save As dialog box becomes visible again.

8. **Click the Save button.**

   The Save As dialog box closes, and FrontPage saves the page. If it's not already visible, the Folder List appears and displays a list of the folders and files that make up your first Web site (see Figure 1-3).

Congratulations — you've just laid the groundwork for your first FrontPage Web site! From here, you can do one of three things:

- Add more content — text, pictures, and anything else you want to display in your Web site — to the page you just started. The chapters in Part II show you how.

- Fill out your Web site with more new Web pages. I explain how to create new pages in Chapter 2.

- Set your first Web site aside and create a completely new Web site (read on for details).

Create a new normal page

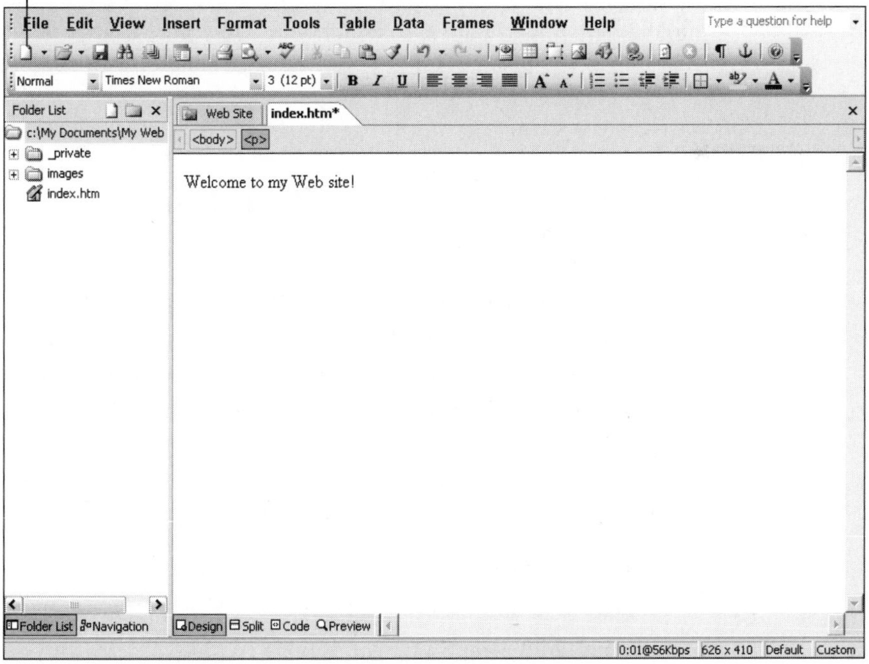

Figure 1-3:
Your first
Web site.

Creating Additional Web Sites

When you're ready to go beyond the initial site you created when you first launched FrontPage, you're at the point where the program confuses many folks. After all, the notion of creating a new Web site *before* creating individual Web pages seems backward. Surely one must first create the pages, then "bind" those pages together to form a site, right?

Not exactly. FrontPage prompts you *first* to create a Web site, and *then* to fill the site with the pages and other files that make up the site's content. This sequence of events makes sense when you know what the program is doing behind the scenes. For FrontPage, the first step in creating a new Web site is creating a folder and earmarking it as the future storage location for all the pages and files that will make up the site. After FrontPage creates that folder, the program is ready for you to begin work building your Web site, whether that's by creating new Web pages, importing existing pages from another location, or whatever. (I discuss the nitty-gritty of site-building in future chapters; I mention this now only to familiarize you with the big-picture workings of FrontPage.)

When you're ready to create a new Web site, FrontPage provides you with a comfortable balance of direction and flexibility. If you want help getting started, use a Web site template or wizard to crank out a boilerplate Web site, complete with linked pages, to which you add your own text and graphics. If you bristle at the prospect of an off-the-rack Web site, you can easily build your own site from scratch.

Creating a Web site by using a template or wizard

Templates lay the groundwork for "canned" Web sites you can customize to suit your own needs. Admittedly, sites created with FrontPage templates lack the flair of custom-designed Web sites, but if you're not sure where to begin, they give you a good place to start.

FrontPage comes with four templates:

- ✔ **Customer Support Web Site:** This site is geared toward companies who want to provide Web-based product support. Site visitors can read product news, have questions answered, brainstorm with other users, view catalogs, and more.

- ✔ **Personal Web Site:** Use this template to jump-start your personal home page. This template contains space for a photo collection, personal information, and a list of favorite sites.

✔ **Project Web Site:** This site tracks the status of a project and includes space for project team members, status reports, schedules, an archive, a search form, and a discussion forum.

✔ **SharePoint Team Site:** Sites created with this template (as well as the templates visible in the Packages tab of the Web Site Templates dialog box) must be published on a host server that supports SharePoint Services. I briefly discuss SharePoint in Chapter 17.

A *wizard* takes you through the site-creation process by presenting you with a series of dialog boxes that prompt you to select different options. FrontPage comes with wizards for its most elaborate Web site templates:

✔ **Corporate Presence Wizard:** The Corporate Presence Wizard sets up a corporate Web site complete with graphics. Depending on the options you choose, the site may contain anything from a product catalog to a discussion forum to company contact information.

✔ **Discussion Web Wizard:** The Discussion Web Wizard creates an interactive site where visitors post comments and read others' replies about a given topic.

FrontPage comes with two additional wizards: the Import Web Site Wizard and the Database Interface Wizard. I introduce you to the Import Web Site Wizard later in this chapter.

The Database Interface Wizard helps you hitch your site to a Microsoft Access, Microsoft SQL Server, or Oracle database. The implications are powerful: Visitors can add to or change database records using their Web browsers, and much more.

FrontPage contains other tools for working with databases as well; however, creating database-driven Web sites with FrontPage is an intermediate-to-advanced task and goes beyond the scope of this book. Fortunately, the FrontPage Help system contains detailed instructions about working with databases, including the system requirements for the host server. To access Help, press F1.

To create a new Web site by using a template or wizard, follow these steps:

1. **With FrontPage running, choose File⇨New.**

   The task pane appears at the right of the FrontPage window, as shown in Figure 1-4. The contents of the task pane change depending on what you happen to be doing. Because you just asked FrontPage to help you create a new Web site, the task pane displays its array of New Page and New Web Site tools and shortcuts.

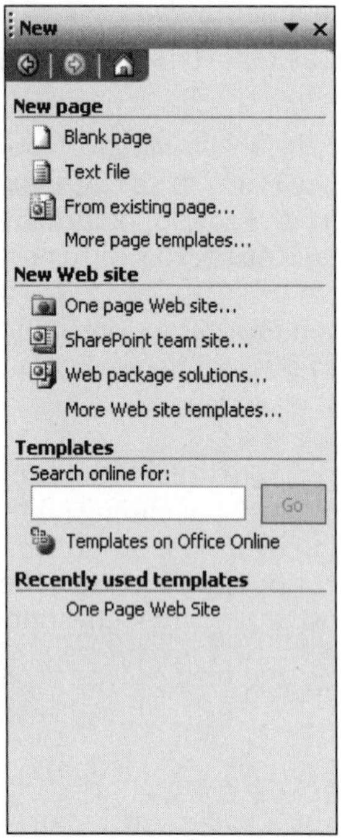

New

New page
- Blank page
- Text file
- From existing page...
- More page templates...

New Web site
- One page Web site...
- SharePoint team site...
- Web package solutions...
- More Web site templates...

Templates
Search online for:

[   ] [Go]

- Templates on Office Online

Recently used templates
- One Page Web Site

Figure 1-4:
The task
pane.

2. **In the task pane's New Web Site section, click More Web Site Templates.**

   The Web Site Templates dialog box appears.

   Quick shortcut for next time: On the Standard toolbar, click the downward-pointing arrow next to the Create a New Normal Page button. From the menu that appears, choose Web Site. This action pops you straight into the Web Site Templates dialog box.

3. **In the dialog box's General tab, click the template or wizard you want to use.**

4. **In the Specify the Location of the New Web Site text box, enter the location of the new Web site, or click the Browse button to choose a location from a folder list.**

   By default, FrontPage saves new Web sites inside a subfolder of the My Web Sites folder (which is located inside the My Documents folder, generally on the C drive). To save the Web site in a different folder on your hard drive or local network, enter the folder's file path. If you're not sure how file paths work, refer to the sidebar "File path 101," later in this chapter.

   If you click the Browse button in this step, the New Web Site Location dialog box appears. In this dialog box, navigate to the location in which you want FrontPage to create the new site, and then click the Open button. The dialog box closes, and the Web Site Templates dialog box becomes visible again. The path to the location you chose appears in the Specify the Location of the New Web Site text box.

If you save your new Web site inside a folder that already contains files, the files themselves are not affected, but FrontPage treats the files as part of the new Web site. If, however, you choose a folder that already contains a FrontPage Web site, FrontPage prompts you to choose a different location.

Note: To keep your Web site distinct (and your hard drive well organized), I recommend saving the site in its own unique folder.

5. **In the Web Site Templates dialog box, click OK.**

   If you chose a template in Step 3, the dialog box closes, and FrontPage creates the new Web site in the location you specified.

   If you chose a wizard in Step 3, after the dialog box closes, the introductory wizard dialog box appears. Answer the wizard's questions and then click Next to move on. If you change your mind about a decision you made earlier in the process, click the Back button as many times as you need to and change your settings. When you reach the final wizard dialog box, click the Finish button to complete the Web site.

(If another Web site is already open in FrontPage when you create a new Web site, the new Web site appears in a separate FrontPage window.)

After FrontPage creates the new Web site, the site's rather daunting array of files and folders appears in the Folder List. A duplicate file list also appears in the main portion of the FrontPage window inside a tabbed area called *Web Site*. Try not to be put off by the sheer number of files you see; they fit together nicely and make sense when you open the site's home page (named index) and start looking around. Chapter 2 shows you how to open pages, and the chapters in Part II tell you everything you need to know about adding and changing Web page content. In Chapter 15, I explain the workings of the Web Site tab in detail.

File path 101

When you create a Web site in FrontPage, the program prompts you to save the site's pages in a folder on your hard drive. You specify the location of the folder using a notation called a *file path*. The file path describes the location of a file or folder by listing the name of the drive on which the file is stored, followed by the name of the folder (or, in the case of a single file, the filename). If the folder or file is stored inside another folder, that folder name is preceded by a backslash (\). So, for example, instead of describing the location of a file by saying "the file named index.htm that's stored inside the My Web Sites folder inside the My Documents folder on the C drive," you can just say C:\My Documents\My WebSites\index.htm.

Another piece of the puzzle: FrontPage Server Extensions

Certain templates and wizards make use of unique FrontPage features, such as keyword site searches and interactive discussion groups. For these and several other fancy features to work properly, the host Web server on which you eventually publish your Web site must have *FrontPage Server Extensions* installed. FrontPage Server Extensions is a set of programs that works together with the host Web server. Although you can just as easily publish FrontPage Web sites on servers that don't have FrontPage Server Extensions installed, you can't take advantage of certain extra-cool FrontPage goodies. Throughout the book, I point out features that require the assistance of FrontPage Server Extensions (most don't), and I cover FrontPage Server Extensions in more detail in Chapter 17.

Creating a Web site from scratch

Templates and wizards can be helpful, but frankly, the sites they generate lack personality. You'd probably spend more time customizing a template-based site than you would building a site from the ground up.

In a from-scratch Web site, you supply the design and content. Here's how to begin:

1. **With FrontPage running, choose File⇨New.**

   The task pane appears (refer to Figure 1-4).

2. **In the New Web Site section of the task pane, click One Page Web Site.**

   The Web Site Templates dialog box appears with the One Page Web Site template already selected.

3. **In the Specify the Location of the New Web Site text box, enter the location of the new Web site, or click the Browse button to choose a location from a folder list.**

4. **After you've chosen the Web site's location, click OK in the Web Site Templates dialog box.**

   The dialog box closes, and FrontPage creates a new Web site. Take a look at the Folder list and notice the site contains only a single page: the home page, and it's empty at that, ready for you to furnish as you see fit.

   (If another Web site is already open in FrontPage when you create a new Web site, the new Web site appears in a new FrontPage window.)

The stage is now set for you to begin construction on your masterpiece.

Importing an Existing Web Site into FrontPage

If you want to use FrontPage to maintain and update a Web site that was originally assembled using a different program or coded by hand, you must first import that site into FrontPage. The easiest way to accomplish this task is by using the Import Web Site Wizard, a handy tool that does most of the work for you.

How the wizard works depends on the location of the site you want to import.

Importing a site from a location on your computer or network

If the site you want to import lives on your hard drive or local network, you simply need to point the Import Web Site Wizard at that location so that it can grab the site's files.

To do so, follow these steps:

1. **With FrontPage running, choose File⇨New.**

   The task pane appears.

2. **In the New Web Site section of the task pane, click More Web Site Templates.**

   The Web Site Templates dialog box appears.

3. **In the dialog box's General tab, click Import Web Site Wizard.**

4. **In the Specify the Location of the New Web Site text box, enter the location of the new Web site, or click the Browse button to choose a location from a folder list.**

   This "new" Web site will contain all the content you are about to import; in other words, it will end up as a copy of the original Web site.

5. **After you've chosen the new Web site's location, click OK in the Web Site Templates dialog box.**

   The dialog box closes, and the Import Web Site Wizard — Welcome dialog box appears (see Figure 1-5).

6. **Select the File System option.**

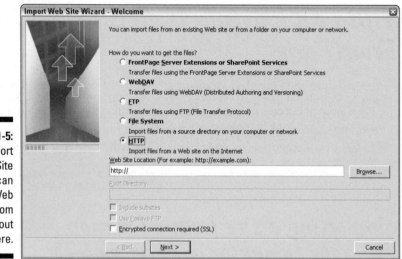

Figure 1-5:
The Import
Web Site
Wizard can
grab Web
sites from
just about
anywhere.

7. **In the Web Site Location text box, specify the location of the Web site you want to import.**

   Type the folder's path or click the Browse button to navigate your file system or network.

8. **If the site you want to import contains subsites, and you want to import them, mark the Include Subsites check box.**

   A *subsite* is a fully functional Web site that lives inside a folder in the Web site you're importing. (I talk in detail about subsites in Chapter 15.)

9. **Click Next.**

   The Choose Your Destination Web Location dialog box appears. The location you specified in Step 4 appears in the Local Copy Location text box. You can stick with this location, or you can enter a new file path here (you must uncheck the Add to Current Web Site check box to access the file path).

10. **After you've chosen a location for the imported Web site, click Next.**

    The Congratulations dialog box appears, letting you know you're almost done.

11. **Click Finish.**

    The Import Web Site wizard closes, and the Remote Web Site view appears inside the main FrontPage window (see Figure 1-6).

    You delve into the Remote Web Site view in Chapter 17, because this is the same part of the program you use to eventually publish your finished site on the Web. In this case, however, FrontPage uses the Remote Web Site view to show you, file by file, the import process (essentially a fancy way of copying files and folders from one place on your hard drive or network to another). The left side of the window displays the file system of the saving location you selected in Step 4, and the right side displays the file system of the site you're importing. Items with arrows next to them will be imported. To keep a page from importing, right-click the file's icon, and from the pop-up menu that appears, choose Don't Publish. The arrow is replaced by a stern red X.

12. **In the lower-right corner of the FrontPage window, click the Publish Web Site button.**

   FrontPage imports the site. To open the site's pages, double-click their icons in the Folder List.

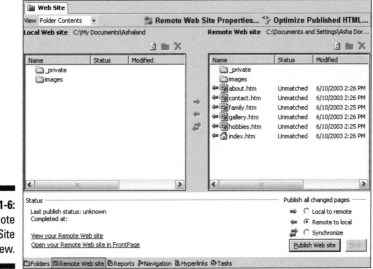

Figure 1-6:
The Remote
Web Site
view.

Even though the button says "Publish Web Site," you're not actually *publishing* your site (that is, making it live on the Web for all to see). Publishing involves a few more steps, which I describe in Chapter 17.

Importing a site from the Web

FrontPage knows how to grab a site directly from the Web — quite a time-saver if you've already published a site using a different program, or if you're inheriting a site that's already up and running.

When you import a site from the Web, it helps to know something about the host Web server's features. Does the server run the HTTP or FTP protocol? Does the server have FrontPage Server Extensions or SharePoint Services installed? If your answer to these questions is "uhhhhhm," or you can't get a hold of the server's administrator to find out, not to worry; FrontPage is smart enough to figure out a few things on its own.

To import a site from the Web, first activate your Internet connection, and then do this:

1. **With FrontPage running, choose File⇨New.**

   The New task pane appears.

2. **In the New Web Site section of the task pane, click More Web Site Templates.**

   The Web Site Templates dialog box appears.

3. **In the General tab, click Import Web Site Wizard.**

4. **In the Specify the Location of the New Web Site text box, enter the location of the new Web site, or click the Browse button to choose a location from a folder list.**

   This "new" Web site will contain all the content you are about to import; in other words, it will end up as a copy of the original Web site.

5. **After you've chosen the new Web site's location, click OK in the Web Site Templates dialog box.**

   The dialog box closes, and the Import Web Site Wizard — Welcome dialog box appears.

6. **Select the option that corresponds to the type of host server on which the site is stored.**

   • If you're importing a site from a host Web server outfitted with FrontPage Server Extensions or SharePoint Services, choose the FrontPage Server Extensions or SharePoint Services option.

   • If host Web server supports neither FrontPage Server Extensions nor SharePoint, or if you're not sure, choose the HTTP option.

   Note: FrontPage also knows how to import Web sites from FTP servers and WebDAV-enabled Web servers. FTP servers are servers which are set up for file transfer, not Web hosting, but which sometimes serve as storage locations for Web sites nonetheless. WebDAV enables users to collaboratively manage and edit files on remote servers.

7. **In the Web Site Location text box, specify the Web address of the Web site you want to import.**

   The address looks something like `http://server.address.com`.

8. **If the site you want to import contains subsites, and you want to import them, mark the Include Subsites check box.**

   A *subsite* is a fully functional Web site that lives inside a folder in the Web site you're importing. (I talk in detail about subsites in Chapter 15.)

   Don't forget to turn on your Internet connection.

9. **Click Next.**

   - If you chose the FrontPage Server Extensions or SharePoint Services option, the Enter Network Password dialog box appears. In the dialog box, type your user name and password (you chose these when you signed up for an account with your ISP) and then click OK. The dialog box closes, and the Choose Your Destination Web Location dialog box appears (read on for details).

   - If you chose the HTTP option, the Choose Your Destination Web Location dialog box appears. The file path you chose in Step 4 appears in the Local Copy Location text box. You can stick with this location, or you can enter a new file path here (you must uncheck the Add to Current Web Site check box to access the file path).

10. **After you've chosen a location for the imported Web site, click Next.**

    The next dialog box that appears depends on the server type you chose in Step 6.

    - If you chose the HTTP option, the Set Import Limits dialog box appears. This dialog box enables you to control how much of the Web site you want FrontPage to import. To limit the levels of sub-folders FrontPage imports, select the Import the Home Page Plus Linked Pages X Levels Deep check box and, in the accompanying text box, enter the number of levels. To limit the amount of total file space taken up by the downloaded files, select the Import a Maximum of X Kilobytes check box and, in the accompanying text box, enter a number of kilobytes. To tell FrontPage to import only the site's Web pages and image files, select the Import Only HTML and Image Files check box. When you're done, click Next.

    - If you chose the FrontPage Server Extensions or SharePoint Services option, you are presented with the reassuring Congratulations dialog box, leading you to believe that you're finished with the import process (guess what — you're not).

11. **Click Finish.**

    If you chose the HTTP option, the Import Web Site Wizard performs its magic and, in a moment (or several if the site's big), your Web site appears in FrontPage. You're done! Stop reading this section!

    If you chose the FrontPage Server Extensions or SharePoint Services option in Step 6, the Import Web Site Wizard closes, and the main FrontPage window becomes visible again, with its Remote Web Site view showing (refer to Figure 1-6).

    What you're essentially doing now is *reverse publishing* from the remote computer (the host Web server) to your local computer. The left side of the window displays the file system of the saving location you selected in Step 4, and the right side displays the file system of the site you're importing. Items with arrows next to them will be imported. To keep a page from importing, right-click the file's icon, and from the pop-up menu that appears, choose Don't Publish. The arrow is replaced by a red X.

    When you're ready, in the lower-right corner of the FrontPage window, click the Publish Web Site button, and watch as FrontPage sucks the files right into your local file system. Phew.

Open, Sesame!

You don't need a special incantation to open a FrontPage Web site. Each time you launch FrontPage, the program automatically opens the last Web site you were working on. FrontPage also saves shortcuts to recently opened Web sites in the Getting Started task pane, as well as in the File⇨Recent Sites menu item. If you don't see the site you want there, follow these steps:

1. **With FrontPage running, choose File⇨Open Site.**

   The Open Site dialog box appears. This dialog box displays the folders on your computer or local network.

2. **In the dialog box, navigate your hard drive or network to the location of the folder that contains the Web site you want to open.**

   Folders containing FrontPage Web sites are marked with little globe icons.

3. **Click Open.**

   The Open Site dialog box closes, and the selected Web site opens in FrontPage.

If you open more than one Web site at the same time, FrontPage opens subsequent Web sites in new windows, enabling you to jump back and forth between the sites by clicking their respective buttons in the Windows taskbar, or by pressing Alt+Tab.

 Opening a subsite of the current site is a snap: In the Folder List, double-click the subsite's folder. (If the Folder List isn't visible, on the Standard toolbar, click the Toggle Pane button or choose View➪Folder List.) You can tell if a folder inside a FrontPage Web site contains a subsite because the subsite's folder is marked with a globe icon.

Closing a Web Site

To close a Web site, close the window in which the site is displayed (click the little X button in the upper-right corner of the window). If you haven't yet saved changes to the site's pages, FrontPage prompts you to do so. After FrontPage saves any changes, the window closes.

If you have only one Web site open and want to close the site but leave FrontPage running, choose File➪Close Site.

Deleting a Web Site

Remove those dusty old Web sites lurking in the corners of your computer. You're rewarded with a tidy hard drive and lots of free disk space.

To delete a Web site that's currently open in FrontPage, follow these steps:

1. **In the Folder List, click the Web site's top-level folder and then press the Delete key.**

   The Confirm Delete dialog box appears and warns you that deleting a Web site is a permanent action (in other words, you can't decide after you delete your Web site that you want it back — it's kaput).

2. **In the dialog box, select the Delete This Web Site Entirely option and then click OK.**

   The dialog box closes, and FrontPage deletes the Web site.

 When you delete a Web site, you delete its subsites as well.

Screaming . . . er, calling for help

By now, I'm sure you've developed an inkling of the power and complexity of FrontPage. (No doubt that inkling motivated you to buy this book!) Never fear: Help is as close as your mouse. Choose Help➪Microsoft FrontPage Help (or press F1) to access a nicely organized set of FrontPage crib notes, plus related links to Web-based resources. Or type a question into the text box sitting in the upper-right corner of the FrontPage window, and Help will do its best to find an answer.

For a reminder about the purpose of a particular button, pause your mouse pointer over the button; in a moment, a yellow ToolTip appears.

If you still can't find answers to your question, check out the Cheat Sheet at the front of the book for more places to go for help.

To delete a subsite, first open the parent Web site in FrontPage. In the Folder List, click the subsite's folder icon and then press Delete. In the Confirm Delete dialog box that appears, click Yes.

You can also delete FrontPage Web sites by deleting their folders using Windows Explorer. The benefit here is that deleted sites go into the Recycle Bin, so you *can* retrieve them if you later change your mind.

Exiting FrontPage

When you're done with Web-building for the day, closing up shop takes only a second or two. To exit FrontPage, choose File➪Exit. If any of the site's pages are currently open and unsaved, FrontPage prompts you to save the pages, and then the program closes.

Chapter 2

Basic Web Page Tasks

· ·

· ·

My artistic period took place between the ages of six and ten, when my teachers set aside part of each school day for creative time. I drew pictures, wrote poems, and perfected my finger-painting technique.

As I got older, my artistic ability dwindled to scribbling on cocktail napkins. Then I discovered Web publishing and entered my renaissance. I no longer work with construction paper or tempera paints; I now use FrontPage to create stacks of colorful Web pages.

In this chapter, you become familiar with basic Web page operations: creating, opening, previewing, and saving pages. If you already feel comfy doing these basic tasks and are ready to tinker with page content and design tools, turn to the chapters in Part II.

Creating a New Web Page

FrontPage can whip out a Web page in milliseconds. One click of a button, and FrontPage presents you with a new, empty Web page ready for filling. If the prospect of an empty page intimidates you, let FrontPage supply a ready-made layout, or use an existing page as the new page's starting point.

Although people often use the terms "Web site" and "Web page" interchangeably, with FrontPage, *Web pages* are the individual page files (the files that end in .htm or .html). A *Web site* is a related collection of individual Web pages.

Creating blank pages

To create a blank page, click the Create a New Normal Page button on the Standard toolbar. If a Web site is currently open in FrontPage, after you save the page, it is added to the site. If no Web site is currently open, FrontPage prompts you for a location when you save the page.

When you create a new, empty page, the Layout Tables and Cells task pane also appears (see Figure 2-1). This feature (which I predict you will grow to love and rely upon) enables you to choose a layout before you add text, pictures, and other content to the page. Choosing the layout first is an optional step, but, as I hope to convince you in Chapter 9, it's a must for well-designed pages.

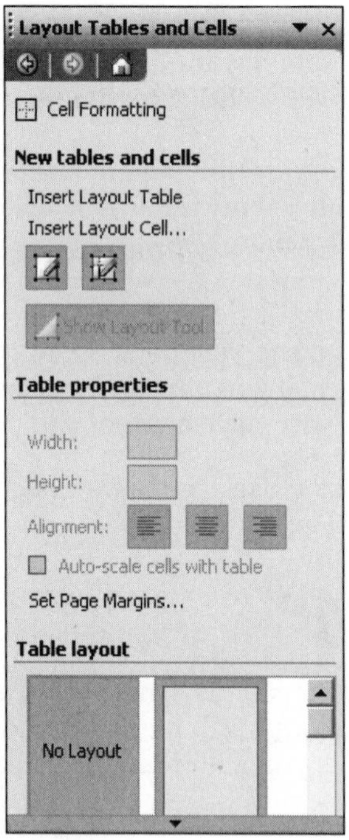

Figure 2-1:
The Layout Tables and Cells task pane.

To choose a layout, in the task pane's Table Layout area, scroll down to peruse your options, and if you see a layout you like, click it. After you click, your formerly empty page is outfitted with an empty layout table, ready to be filled with text, pictures, or whatever else you like. In Chapter 9, you learn all you need to know about working with layout tables, including how to fiddle with the preset layouts FrontPage provides, or how to create your own.

If you're just getting started with FrontPage, you may find it easier to forego the layout tables for now, play with the tools and features detailed in Part II of the book, and then add a layout table to your page later. However, as you become more comfortable with FrontPage, you will find starting your empty pages with layout tables saves a lot of time and cut-and-paste frustration.

Creating a new page based on an existing page

FrontPage can grab the content from an existing page to use as the starting point for a new page. If your site will contain lots of similarly laid out pages, this feature will slash your workload. Just follow these steps:

1. **If you intend to add the new page to an existing FrontPage Web site, open the Web site. If not, or if you're not sure, skip to Step 2.**

2. **Choose File⇨New.**

   The New task pane appears.

3. **In the New Page section of the task pane, click From Existing Page.**

   The New from Existing Page dialog box appears.

4. **In the dialog box, navigate to the location of the file you want to use as the starting point for the new page. When you find the file, double-click it.**

   The New from Existing Page dialog box closes, and a new page based on the file you selected appears in FrontPage.

Another option if you find yourself creating lots of similarly laid-out pages is to create a FrontPage template to use as your starting point. It's easy to save a page as a template that you can then use over and over; I explain how in the "Saving a page as a template" section later in this chapter. (Incidentally, FrontPage comes with a number of preinstalled page templates, but the pages they create are so basic they end up saving you little time or effort.)

Opening a Web Page

If you already have Web pages hanging around on your hard drive, you can easily open them in FrontPage. Whether or not the pages are part of a FrontPage Web site doesn't matter; FrontPage willingly opens any Web page. In fact, FrontPage can open pages that aren't even stored on your computer; the pages may live somewhere on your local network or in the wilds of the World Wide Web. FrontPage can even open non-Web page files that are part of your Web site (such as graphic files or Microsoft Office documents) by launching the appropriate program for that type of file.

Opening a page that's part of the current Web site

FrontPage gives you several ways to open pages and files that make up your Web site. I list the easiest methods here.

A note about Web site security

Opening Web pages stored on other Web servers brings up the topic of security. After all, if people can use FrontPage to open any page anywhere, what's to keep them from fooling around with someone else's Web site files (aside from their consciences)?

Web servers keep files safe by using an identification system of user names and passwords. If you want to make changes to files stored on a particular server, the server's administrator must give you a unique user name and password that you must enter before you can proceed. In other words, although anyone with FrontPage can open just about any Web page, only those folks with password access can actually make changes to the pages sitting on the server and have those changes be visible on the World Wide Web.

(You can set up password protection for your own FrontPage Web sites; I discuss the topic in Chapter 17.)

For FrontPage to be able to work with the server's password system, the server must be running a set of programs called FrontPage Server Extensions. Without FrontPage Server Extensions, FrontPage doesn't know how to access the server's list of authorized user names and passwords.

Therefore, you may use FrontPage to edit only live pages that are stored on servers to which you have password access and those servers must be running FrontPage Server Extensions. I discuss FrontPage Server Extensions in more detail in Chapter 17.

First, open the Web site that contains the page you want to open (if you're not sure how to open a Web site, see Chapter 1). Next, double-click a page or file icon in the Folder List. If the Folder List isn't visible, choose View⇨Folder List.

To open a page that's part of a subsite inside the currently open Web site, double-click the subsite's folder in the Folder List. The contents of the subsite pop open in a new window. From there, you can proceed as usual to open one of the subsite's files. (What's a subsite, you ask? Check out Chapter 15.)

You can open one page at a time, or you can open several pages and move between them by clicking their tabs at the top of the main FrontPage window.

Opening a page stored on your computer or network

You may want to open a page that's part of a FrontPage Web site, but not the Web site that's *currently open* in FrontPage. No problem. You can even open a Web page that isn't part of a FrontPage Web site — FrontPage isn't particular.

To do so, follow these steps:

1. **On the Standard toolbar, click the Open button.**

   The Open File dialog box appears, displaying a list of files and folders contained in the Web site currently open in FrontPage. If no Web site is currently open, the dialog box displays the contents of the last folder you viewed.

2. **In the dialog box, navigate to the location of the file you want to open.**

   The page may be stored anywhere on your computer or network.

3. **In the dialog box's file list, click the file and then click the Open button.**

   The Open File dialog box closes, and the page opens.

   If the page is part of a FrontPage Web site, FrontPage opens the Web site as well, and the Web site's files and folders appear in the Folder List.

Opening a page from the World Wide Web

FrontPage enables you to open any Web page stored on just about any Web server in the world. This feature is useful if you want to open a Web page directly from the World Wide Web or from your company *intranet* (an internal company network based on Internet technology, but accessible only to company insiders).

To open a page stored on a remote Web server, follow these steps:

1. **Activate your Internet or network connection.**

2. **Click the Open button on the Standard toolbar.**

   The Open File dialog box appears.

3. **In the dialog box's File Name text box, type the file's Web address.**

   A Web address (also known as a *URL*) looks similar to the following address:

   ```
   http://www.server.com/file.html
   ```

4. **Click Open.**

   The Open File dialog box closes. If the file is part of a Web site stored on a Web server that supports FrontPage Server Extensions, the Enter Network Password dialog box appears. In the dialog box, type your user name and password and then click OK. The dialog box closes, and FrontPage opens both the page and the Web site.

   When you open a Web site stored on a server to which you have password access, you are working on the *live version* of the Web site, meaning that your changes are visible to the world as soon as you save the page.

   If the host Web server doesn't support FrontPage Server Extensions, FrontPage opens a copy of the page for you to edit (not the live page itself). When you later save the page, FrontPage prompts you to choose a saving location on your own computer or network. (See the nearby sidebar, "A note about Web site security," for more about FrontPage Server Extensions.)

Converting Other Documents into Web Pages

Because much of your Web site's content may already exist in other formats, document conversion is one of the most lovable FrontPage features. FrontPage can convert the following popular document formats into Web pages in the blink of an eye:

Document Type	File Extension(s)
Microsoft Word document	DOC
Microsoft Works 4.0 document	WPS

Document Type	File Extension(s)
WordPerfect 5.*x* and 6.*x* document	DOC, WPD
Microsoft Excel and Lotus 1-2-3 documents	XLS, XLW, WK1, WK3, WK4
Windows Write files	WRI
RTF (Rich Text Format) documents	RTF
Plain text documents	TXT

If you have information stored in a file format other than those listed here, FrontPage does its best to recover text from any file format.

Conversion considerations

To convert or not to convert? It's a worthwhile question because you have several options when deciding how to include non-Web page files in your Web site. Here's a quick rundown:

✔ **Using FrontPage to convert the file into a Web page works well for text files, simply formatted word-processing files, or files in which all you need is static data.** If you just want to grab content from a file to dump into a Web page, this is the way to go.

✔ **Importing the file into your Web site in its native format makes more sense for long or complex documents, such as reports or publications, or if you want users to have access to dynamic information in a document (such as equations and functions in a spreadsheet worksheet).** The upside is that visitors can open the documents on their own computers as long as they have programs that know how to read the documents. The downside is that non-Web page files can be quite large and therefore take a long time to download. (For details on how to import files into a FrontPage Web site, see Chapter 15.)

✔ **Many Web sites make formatted documents available as PDF files.** PDF files look just like snapshots of the original files, but download quickly because the files are compact. Visitors can install a free PDF viewer (called Adobe Acrobat reader, available at www.adobe.com) to look at and print the file. This is a good way to make a complex document — such as a brochure — easy for your visitors to download. However, you must buy a separate program called Adobe Acrobat to be able to create PDF files.

Microsoft Office (2000 and later) users have some additional options. Word, Excel, and PowerPoint can each save documents as Web pages, and often work better for complex or highly formatted documents (see each program's Help system for details). Office 2000 (and later) also contains a feature called *Office Web components,* which enables Office users to embed in Web pages some of the Office functionality many know and love, including spreadsheets, PivotTables, and charts. For more information about Web components, see Chapter 12.

When you use FrontPage to convert a word-processing or RTF file into a Web page, FrontPage maintains much of the document's text and paragraph formatting by converting the formats to the closest HTML style. By the way, RTF stands for *Rich Text Format,* a format all kinds of word-processing programs can read. Folks often use RTF when they want to share formatted documents with others who are using different types of software or computer systems.

FrontPage can also convert spreadsheet worksheets into Web pages. If you've never worked with a *spreadsheet,* it's a type of program that simplifies numerical calculations. Lotus 1-2-3 and Microsoft Excel are spreadsheet programs beloved by number crunchers everywhere. Spreadsheet *worksheets* (what the program calls its documents) are arranged in rows and columns of information.

Unless you use Office Web components, when you use FrontPage to convert a worksheet, the resulting Web page contains static numbers, and you lose the ability to use functions and equations. Office Web components come with specific system requirements; I discuss them in Chapter 12.

Text documents contain no formatting whatsoever. No bold or italics, no tables, no curly quotes (" ") — just regular old characters and spaces. FrontPage can convert a text document to a Web page in one of the following ways:

- ✔ **One formatted paragraph:** FrontPage stuffs all the document's paragraphs into a single paragraph, to which the program applies the Formatted style. In a Web page, the Formatted style appears as a monospaced font — in most Web browsers, the font appears as Courier. If your text document contains rows and columns of information separated by spaces or tabs, this style is a good choice.

- ✔ **Formatted paragraphs:** FrontPage maintains the separation between individual paragraphs and applies the Formatted style to each one.

- ✔ **Normal paragraphs:** You use this option most often. FrontPage applies the Normal style to each paragraph in the document. The Normal style is the default style for Web page text. The Normal style appears as a proportional font — most browsers display Times.

- ✔ **Normal paragraphs with line breaks:** FrontPage applies the Normal style to the document's paragraphs and retains line breaks. Use this style if you want your document's line breaks to remain intact.

- ✔ **Do not convert:** If the text file contains HTML tags, this option tells FrontPage to treat the tags as valid HTML and not to place the tags into the body of the Web page.

If you don't want to convert an entire document, you can cut or copy data from other programs and then paste the data into an open page in FrontPage.

Now that you know your options for converting documents into Web pages, here's how to proceed:

1. **In FrontPage, create a new page.**

   I discuss how earlier in this chapter.

   If you want to place converted content inside an existing Web page, open that page and place the cursor where you want the content to appear.

2. **Choose Insert➪File.**

   The Select File dialog box appears.

3. **In the dialog box's Files of Type list box, choose the type of file you want to convert, and then navigate your computer or network to the location of the file.**

4. **In the dialog box, double-click the file.**

   The Select File dialog box closes, and one of the following three things happens:

   - If FrontPage knows how to proceed, it converts the document's content and places the content into the Web page. (You can skip the rest of the steps in this section.)

   - If the document is a text file, the Convert Text dialog box appears. This dialog box offers you five ways to convert text, which I describe earlier in this section. Proceed to Step 5.

   - If FrontPage needs guidance, it asks your permission to install a file converter. If you decide to proceed, you'll need to grab your FrontPage or Office program CD, as the file converter must be installed from there. Follow the dialog boxes for directions.

5. **In the Convert Text dialog box, select the option you want to use, and then click OK.**

   The dialog box closes, and FrontPage proceeds to convert the document's content according to your preference.

FrontPage's conversion features can't reliably handle certain word-processing special effects, such as annotations, footnotes, and embedded objects.

If in doubt, try the conversion. If you don't like the way FrontPage converts your document, close the page without saving it. Because your original document remains safely unchanged, you can choose a different conversion method later.

Previewing a Page

As you create pages in FrontPage, the pages look similar to how they appear as viewed with a Web browser. In techno-speak, this similarity is called *WYSIWYG* (pronounced *wizzy wig*), which stands for *What You See Is What You Get*.

Even so, previewing your pages is a good idea. Previewing gives you a more accurate representation of how your pages will appear to your visitors after the site has been published. FrontPage enables you to quickly preview your pages by using FrontPage's built-in Preview view or by opening the pages in a separate Web browser, such as Microsoft Internet Explorer, Netscape Navigator, or Opera.

Previewing pages using the FrontPage Preview view

Preview view shows you how your page would look and act in a Web browser — specifically, the version of Microsoft Internet Explorer you have installed on your computer. Unlike previewing your page with a separate browser, you don't need to first save the page to preview it, which is handy for on-the-fly previewing. The Preview view also has the advantage of living inside FrontPage, so you don't need to launch a separate program or switch between windows to preview your pages.

Preview To see how your page looks in Preview view, click the Preview icon at the lower-left corner of the main FrontPage window. When you're ready to leave Preview and edit the page again, click the Design icon, which is located in the lower-left corner. (Design view is where you do all of your page editing; you can't make changes to a page while looking at it in Preview view. The chapters in Part II detail Design view's capabilities.)

The Preview view works only if you have Microsoft Internet Explorer 3.0 or later installed on your computer. FrontPage doesn't have a browser built into its midst; it uses Internet Explorer to display what's visible in the built-in Preview. Therefore, if you don't have the program installed, FrontPage has no way of rendering a page preview.

Furthermore, the Preview view can't accurately display working versions of certain FrontPage Web site effects.

Monitors and windows: Size does matter

In the world of print design, readers don't get to determine the page sizes of the books or reports they read. Barring differences in visual acuity, what one reader of a print document sees is pretty much identical to what every other reader sees. Not so in Web design. The size of the "page" (if you can call an electronic Web document that) is determined by two things: the visitor's monitor resolution (how many pixels a monitor can display) and the size of the visitor's browser window. Both of these factors vary from user to user. Therefore, you can never be sure what "size" your Web page will be when it appears on your visitors' screens. You can, however, get a sense of what your page looks like in different situations. The FrontPage Preview In Browser function helps in this regard,

as does the built-in ruler and grid (choose View➪Ruler and Grid➪Show Ruler, and View➪Ruler and Grid➪Show Grid). So does a tiny feature you may have not even noticed yet. In the lower-right corner of the FrontPage window, you see two numbers separated by an X. Click those numbers to reveal a menu containing a range of pixel values that simulate, in Design view, several resolutions and browser window sizes. For example, the menu item *600 x 300 (640 x 480, Maximized)* shows how a page would look if viewed in a maximized browser window on a monitor with 640 x 480 resolution. As you design your pages, keep an eye on this feature in order to be sure your pages look good to a wide range of visitors.

Previewing pages using a Web browser

For the extra few seconds of lag time while the program launches, I recommend previewing your pages in an honest-to-goodness Web browser. By using a Web browser to preview your pages as you work, you get the most accurate representation of what your visitors will see when they check out your Web site.

Even better, if you have more than one Web browser installed on your computer, you can choose which browser you'd like FrontPage to launch. You can also select different window sizes so that you can see how your page looks to visitors who have monitors set to a resolution different from yours.

Because FrontPage makes previewing your pages in several browsers so easy, consider downloading and installing more than one browser program (preferably ones that can display different features) if you have the room on your hard drive. The insight you gain about how different pages may look in different browsers is worth the extra bit of effort that installing the extra browsers requires. (Of course, you're able to see how your pages look inside Windows-based browsers only; keep in mind that pesky display variations occur across operating system platforms as well. So after you've published your finished site, ask your Mac- and Unix-using friends to give the site a once-over to be sure everything's kosher.)

For an overview of the display capabilities of different Web browsers, visit Webmonkey's Browser Chart at `hotwired.lycos.com/webmonkey/reference/browser_chart/`. You can download different Web browsers from Download.com at `www.download.com`.

For more information about browser-specific Web publishing effects, see Chapter 3. For tips on how to account for browser-specific differences in your site's design, refer to Chapter 4.

 To preview your page in your default Web browser, click the Preview in Browser button on the Standard toolbar.

To choose the browser in which you want to open and preview a page or to control the window size, follow these steps:

1. **Choose File⇨Preview in Browser.**

   The Preview in Browser menu expands to display a range of preview options, as shown in Figure 2-2. Each browser installed on your computer appears in the list, along with several standard resolution values.

   A monitor's *resolution* refers to the number of pixels the monitor can display on-screen. The larger the number, the higher the resolution of the picture and the more "real estate" a monitor can display.

Figure 2-2:
The Preview in Browser menu.

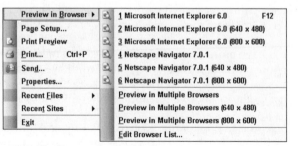

2. **From the menu, choose the name of the browser and the resolution size you want to use.**

   If you haven't yet saved your page, a Microsoft FrontPage dialog box pops up prompting you to do so. In the dialog box, click Yes to save the page. After saving the Web page, FrontPage opens your page in the browser and window size of your choice.

To edit the page, return to FrontPage by clicking the Microsoft FrontPage button in the Windows taskbar (or press Alt+Tab to switch between open windows). Make any changes you want and then save the page. To view changes, click the Preview in Browser button again or switch back to your browser and click the browser's Reload or Refresh button.

Saving a Page

Your Web publishing masterpiece is only as grand as the last time you saved your pages. So save your work often. My fingers instinctively press Ctrl+S to quickly save my work every time I finish writing a particularly brilliant sentence.

You can save a page as part of the Web site currently open in FrontPage, elsewhere on your hard drive or network, directly on the World Wide Web, or as a FrontPage template.

 If you've made lots of changes to your page but haven't yet saved the changes, you can erase all the changes and revert to the previously saved version of the page. To do so, click the Refresh button on the Standard toolbar. After FrontPage asks if you want to revert to the previously saved version of the page, click Yes.

Tips and tricks for naming files

Here are a few tips to keep in mind as you consider what to name your Web pages:

✔ **Filename:** Keep your filenames short and sweet. I recommend sticking to one-word names that use only lowercase letters. This saves your visitors from having to type a long, involved filename when they want to view the page in a Web browser.

✔ **Home page filename:** The host Web server, on which you will eventually publish your finished Web site, determines your home page filename. Most Web servers recognize the filename index.htm or index.html as the Web site's home page (index.htm

is the default home page name FrontPage uses), but a few servers recognize different names. Before you publish your Web site, ask your system administrator or a helpful person at your ISP which home page filename you should use.

✔ **Filename extension:** Should you use the HTM or HTML filename extension? It's up to you — they're interchangeable. FrontPage automatically appends the .htm extension to whatever filename you choose, but if you prefer to use HTML, when you save the file, add .html to the filename you specify. You can also change the filenames of existing pages; I explain how in Chapter 15.

If you can't remember which open pages you've saved recently, glance at the pages' tabs in Design view. On a tab, a filename followed by an asterisk (*) indicates that you haven't saved changes to a page yet. To quickly save all your open pages, choose File⇨Save All.

Saving a page on your computer or network

Most often, you save new pages inside FrontPage Web sites, but you can just as easily choose another location, such as anywhere on your computer or local network.

To save a page on your computer or local network, follow these steps:

1. **Click the Save button on the Standard toolbar.**

   The Save As dialog box appears (see Figure 2-3).

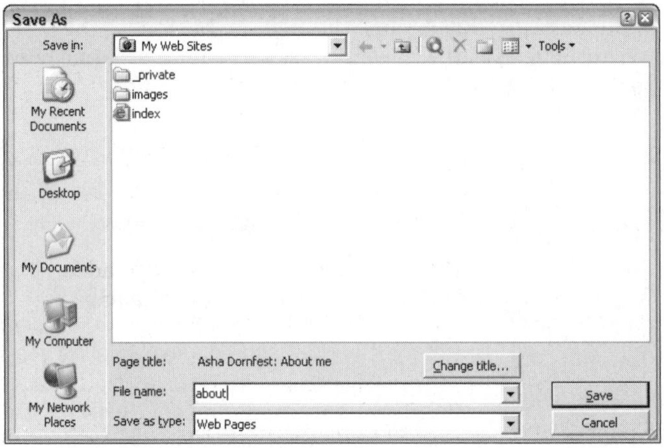

Figure 2-3: The Save As dialog box.

If you're saving an existing page, no dialog box appears — the command just saves your changes. If you want to save the page in a different location, choose File⇨Save As to display the Save As dialog box.

By default, FrontPage saves pages as follows:

- If a Web site is currently open in FrontPage and you create a new page, FrontPage prompts you to save the new page as part of that Web site.

- If no Web site is currently open in FrontPage and you create a new page, FrontPage prompts you to save the page in the My Web Sites folder.

- When you make changes to an existing page, FrontPage saves the changes in the same location, *except* if you originally opened the page from a sité on a different Web server on which you don't have authoring access. In that case, FrontPage prompts you to save the page in a location on your computer or network.

2. **If you want to save the page in a different location, in the Save In list box, navigate to the location on your computer or network.**

3. **To change the page title, click the Change Title button in the dialog box.**

   The Set Page Title dialog box appears.

   When you view a Web page in a Web browser, the title appears in the browser's *title bar* — the colorful strip at the very top of the browser window. Page titles also appear in search indexes (such as Yahoo!) and in visitors' lists of browser bookmarks. The title should sum up the page's content in a way that's meaningful to visitors. For example, whereas the title *My Home Page* could apply to millions of different pages all over the World Wide Web, *Asha Dornfest's Home Page* tells the visitor exactly what to expect.

4. **In the Set Page Title dialog box's Page Title text box, type a new title, and then click OK.**

   The dialog box closes and the Save As dialog box becomes active again.

5. **If you want to change the page's filename, enter a new name in the File Name list box.**

   If you don't specify a filename extension, FrontPage adds `.htm` to the end of the name you enter here when you save the page.

6. **Click Save.**

   The dialog box closes, and FrontPage saves the page.

   If the page you're saving contains pictures, the Save Embedded Files dialog box appears. I explain how to use this dialog box in the sidebar "Saving pages containing pictures," elsewhere in this chapter.

If you open a page from one location and then save the page to a different location, FrontPage saves a copy of the edited page. The original, unchanged page remains in its original spot.

Saving pages containing pictures

If you save a page that was originally opened from a location outside the current Web site and that page contains graphics, FrontPage is smart enough to ask if you want to save the associated graphic files as well. If FrontPage didn't take this extra step, the pictures in the page wouldn't show up because no associated graphic files would be available to display. (You discover the mechanics of Web graphics in Chapter 6.)

When you save a page containing pictures, in addition to saving the page, FrontPage pops open the Save Embedded Files dialog box. This dialog box enables you to save the graphic files as well as to change the graphics' filenames and specify the folder in which the graphics are stored. You can also click the Picture Options button in the dialog box to specify details about the graphic file's format details. After you specify your preferences, click OK to save the graphics.

Saving a page as a template

You can save any page as a page template. This feature saves countless hours if you create lots of pages with standard layouts. Even better, if you are working with a Web design team, you can create shared templates that everyone on the team can access.

1. **With the page you want to save as a template open in FrontPage, choose File⇨Save As.**

   The Save As dialog box appears.

2. **In the Save as Type list box, choose FrontPage Template, and then click Save. (It's at the bottom of the list.)**

   The Save As dialog box closes, and the Save As Template dialog box appears.

3. **In the Save As Template dialog box, type a descriptive title in the Title text box.**

4. **In the Name text box, type a filename.**

   Just type a short word — FrontPage automatically applies the appropriate filename extension (.tem) to the filename you enter.

5. **In the Description text box, type a short description of the template's function.**

6. **To create a shared template that other site authors can use when they're working on the Web site, select the Save Template in Current Web Site check box.**

7. Click OK.

The dialog box closes, and FrontPage saves the page as a template. (The page visible in FrontPage is a regular Web page, so any additional changes you make are not saved as part of the template.)

If the page that you're saving contains pictures, the Save Embedded Files dialog box appears. Earlier in the chapter, I explain how to use this dialog box.

To create a new page based on the template you just created, follow these steps:

1. Choose File⇨New.

The New task pane appears.

2. In the New Page section of the task pane, click More Page Templates.

The Page Templates dialog box appears.

3. In the dialog box, click the My Templates tab to make the templates you've created visible.

4. Double-click the template that you want to use.

The dialog box closes, and a new page based on the template you selected appears in FrontPage.

Unlike with Microsoft Word document templates, you cannot attach a FrontPage Web page template to an already existing page. You must use the template as the starting point for a new Web page.

Part II

Web Page Construction Basics

The 5th Wave   By Rich Tennant

"As a web site designer I never thought I'd say this, but I don't think your site has enough bells and whistles."

In this part . . .

Mastering FrontPage is one thing. Understanding how to construct a great-looking, easy-to-navigate Web site is another. Part II helps you do both.

In this part, you discover how to build Web pages from the ground up. You delve into the inner workings of the FrontPage Design view, your tool for doing everything from creating hyperlinks to adding interactive forms to your Web site.

Chapter 3

Web Design Fundamentals

*T*he desktop-publishing revolution taught wannabe designers a lesson: Buying a big, fat desktop-publishing program doesn't guarantee professional-looking newsletters and reports. The crucial ingredient — design sense or a "good eye" — isn't built into the software.

In the same way, creating great-looking Web sites requires a thorough understanding of FrontPage's capabilities *and* an eye for what makes a Web site work. This chapter gets you thinking about design so that you can build a site that's easy to navigate, loads quickly, and looks fantastic.

Clients and Servers 101

To understand Web design, you first need to understand the basic relationship between clients and servers on the Web. The client-server relationship is the yin and yang that makes the Internet work.

A *server* is any computer that contains and distributes information. A *client* is the program that retrieves and processes or displays that information. Web servers store and serve Web pages, and Web clients (better known as *Web browsers*) display the pages on your screen. Clients and servers are useless without each other, much like separate halves of a piece of Velcro.

If you're unclear about the client-server relationship, think of your television. After you turn on your TV, the device hunts for signals from a broadcast station, assembles the signals into *Will and Grace,* and displays the show on your TV screen. In this example, the broadcast station is the server, and your

TV set is the client. Without the signals sent by the broadcast station, your TV is an empty box. By the same token, without TVs to pick up and display these signals, broadcast stations have no purpose. Figure 3-1 illustrates the client-server relationship.

When you publish a site on the Web, you place all the site's linked files on a Web server. The server waits patiently, listening for client requests from the Internet or company intranet. As soon as the server receives a request (for instance, a visitor types the file's address into his or her browser and presses Enter), the server springs into action and delivers the requested file. How the file looks after appearing on your visitor's screen depends in large part on the particular features of the visitor's computer and Internet setup, such as the choice of browser software, operating system, and size and resolution of the monitor.

Return to the TV analogy for a moment. The broadcast station (the server) spits signals into the ether, which your TV (the client) picks up and translates into *Will and Grace* (the file). You're watching the same show as everyone else. What you see on your HDTV set, however, looks different from what your neighbor sees on the little old black-and-white TV in her kitchen (see Figure 3-2).

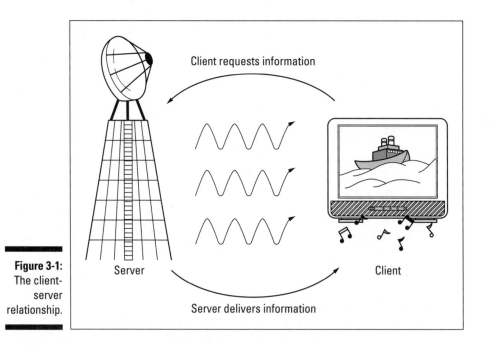

Figure 3-1:
The client-server relationship.

Client requests information

Server

Server delivers information

Client

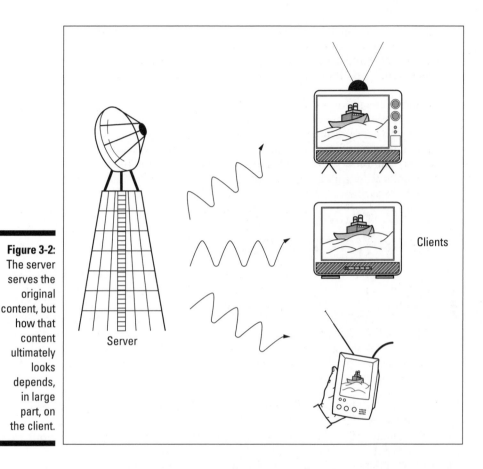

Figure 3-2:
The server serves the original content, but how that content ultimately looks depends, in large part, on the client.

In a fit of mischief, you adjust the color and contrast setting on your TV, and Grace's face turns green. She doesn't turn green all over America, just on your set — and the broadcast station can't do a thing about it.

The moral of this story is that you have only so much control over how your Web site looks after it ends up on your visitors' screens. Read on if you want to discover more about the specific differences between clients and how to accommodate those differences in your site's design.

Cross-Platform Mania

Designing for the Web is often compared to taming a large, hairy beast. Whereas print design enables you to control how the finished product looks down to the finest detail, Web design can be, at times, a crapshoot. Why?

Because the Web is a *cross-platform medium*, which means that people browse the Web by using any number of hardware devices, software programs, and operating systems. Each piece of the platform affects how Web sites ultimately look after the sites show up on the visitor's screen.

The challenge (or, as those less tactful may say, pain-in-the-butt) is to design sites that account for platform variations and still manage to look good. Doing so is not difficult after you accept a few truisms about the Web as a publishing medium. You soon realize that the Web design beast, although still big and hairy, is just a teddy bear after you come to know it.

Web truism #1: Your visitors use different computers

Just as people drive to work in buses, Bugs, and BMWs, folks cruise the Net with all sorts of computers and devices. Some drive old clunkers with tiny monitors. Others speed along with turbo-charged processors and a big, full-color display. The beauty of the Web is that the vehicle doesn't matter — whether you use a Mac, a PC, a Unix workstation, a television, or even a cell phone — all you need is a Web browser and an Internet connection, and you're ready to roll. The problem, however, is that Web sites look different depending on the visitor's hardware setup.

A particular Web site viewed on different computers doesn't necessarily look so different that you wouldn't recognize the site, but elements such as color, text alignment, and font size are all affected (in varying degrees) by your visitor's monitor size or resolution and choice of operating system. I created my personal site on a PC running Windows, for example, and I gave my page a lovely lemon-yellow background color. To my chagrin, a designer friend — a Mac user — looked at my page with his Web browser and told me that my page was a sickly green. (Fortunately, this problem was easy to fix — I share the secret in Chapter 6.)

Web truism #2: Your visitors use different browsers

Not only do your visitors use different computers, they also use different programs to browse the Web. As with platform differences, Web pages appear slightly different in each Web browser — and even in older versions of the same browser.

The vast majority of the Web-surfing population uses some version of Netscape Navigator or Microsoft Internet Explorer, the big guns in the browser field. The rest use other browsers, such as Lynx (a text-only browser), browsers designed to accommodate disabilities, or foreign-language browsers (to name a few).

Browser-specific design effects further complicate the situation. In an effort to encourage folks to use their products, Netscape and Microsoft each use technology that produces special design effects — but only if viewed by the companies' own browsers and, even then, only by the most recent version. If you're one of the unfortunate few using another browser, or you use an older version of Internet Explorer or Navigator, too bad.

Fortunately, FrontPage gives you some level of control over browser-specific effects as you design your Web site. I show you how to use this feature in Chapter 4.

Web truism #3: Your visitors connect to the Internet at different speeds

Speed is an obsession on the Internet. A few seconds spent waiting for a Web site to appear on-screen feels like an eternity. Seconds stretch into agonizing minutes for those of your visitors using slow Internet connections.

What causes a Web site to load at tortoise speed? Some factors are beyond your control, such as the speed of the Web server that hosts the Web site or the amount of traffic clogging the network at that particular moment.

Other factors directly relate to the design of the Web site itself. Graphics are the most common culprit. Big pictures with lots of colors take a long time to load and aren't always worth the time spent waiting. In Chapter 6, I include tips on how to keep your Web graphics loading quickly.

The length of a Web page also affects its speed. Pages containing several screens full of text load more slowly than shorter pages.

Other sloths include multimedia goodies, such as sounds, videos, and embedded miniprograms called Java applets or ActiveX components. These extras, so loved by designers with lightning-fast Internet connections, are the bane of regular folks surfing with a dial-up modem. Therefore, if you decide to include multimedia in your Web site, keep in mind its effect on your Web site's load time. I show you how to work with FrontPage multimedia features in Chapter 13.

Web truism #4: Your visitors come from diverse cultures

Consider your visitors' cultural backgrounds to be as central to your design as platform differences. Differences in language and outlook affect how your visitors experience your Web site just as much as their choice of computer or browser. Beyond its appearance, your site must speak to people of different cultures, nationalities, and value systems. Keep a diverse audience in mind as you build your site. By making sure that each page is easy to navigate and is clearly written, you make your site accessible to the largest audience possible.

FrontPage has sophisticated foreign language capabilities, both in the program's interface and in the program's ability to create Web pages that contain different languages. For details, refer to the Help system coverage by choosing Help⇨Microsoft FrontPage Help.

Five Steps to a Brilliant Web Site

If you read the preceding section, you're now aware of the Web-design truisms, and you can account for these factors as you design your site. The following sections describe how to do so in five easy steps.

Give your site a purpose

As I write this book, my purpose isn't to document the Internet or even to explain every nook and cranny of FrontPage. My purpose is to show you how to use FrontPage to quickly create a beautiful Web site — and have fun at the same time.

Your site needs a similar clarity of purpose to be effective. Focus on what you want your site to accomplish: Do you want to educate your visitors? Do you want to sell them a product? Do you just want to share your warped vision of the world? After you decide what you want your site to do, make the purpose clear to your visitors right away so they know what to expect if they decide to stay for a while.

Remember your visitors

Establishing a purpose can be daunting unless you concentrate on your most important visitors: your *target audience.* Just as *Seventeen* targets teenyboppers and *Wired* targets technology addicts, your site must target people with specific interests.

Visualize your target audience. No, don't try to divine your visitors' hair color or astrological signs. Ask yourself: "Are they technically savvy? How old are they? What kind of information do they want?" The more answers you come up with, the better you can communicate your message to your visitors.

Cultivate an image

Elvis, Nike, and Madonna all have something your Web site needs: an image. Your site's image is everything it says without words — in advertising and design lingo, its *look and feel*. So think about how you'd want your target audience to describe your site — "friendly," "cutting edge," "useful," "bizarre" — and choose your site's tone, graphics, and layout accordingly. To give your site a quick graphic makeover, consider a FrontPage theme (see Chapter 11 for details).

Make your site easy to navigate

If you've ever driven a car in San Francisco, you know it's not what one would call a user-friendly city. One-way streets, nosebleed hills, and elusive parking make driving in San Francisco a daunting experience for the first-time visitor. (Of course, you can always double-park while you hop out for a cappuccino, which makes up for the hassles.)

Your Web site should be just the opposite. Your site must be easy to navigate the very first time around. Guide your visitors with clearly categorized information and thoughtfully placed links. (Navigation bars with hyperlinks to other pages in your site — which FrontPage calls *link bars* — help your visitors, too; check out Chapter 5 for details.) Break information into manageable bits, keeping pages short and easy to read. If your visitors get lost, give them a map containing links to all the pages in your site or, even better, set up the site so that visitors can search your site for keywords. (You can perform this task by using the Web Search component, which I describe in Chapter 12.)

Plan for the future

Web sites, like little babies, grow. It's inevitable. As time goes on, you're bound to add new pages and even new sections to your site. Build some growing room into your site's organization. Minimize repetitive tasks by creating page templates (see Chapter 2 for details). Use shared borders and Dynamic Web Templates to automate the inclusion of standard elements in your pages. (You can read about shared borders in Chapter 5 and Dynamic Web Templates in Chapter 16.) Most importantly, keep the growth of your Web site in perspective by refining your site's purpose and by remaining focused on your target audience.

The Web loves to talk about itself, hence the enormous number of Web sites devoted to the topic of Web design. Here are a few I like:

- ✔ Webmonkey at `hotwired.lycos.com/webmonkey`
- ✔ Builder.com at `builder.com.com` (you read it correctly, that's *two* dot-coms)
- ✔ Web Review at `www.webreview.com`

Or if you're looking for some good books on the topic of Web design, check out *Web Design For Dummies,* by Lisa Lopuck (Wiley Publishing, Inc.), or *The Non-Designer's Web Book,* 2nd Edition, by Robin Williams and John Tollett (Peachpit Press). Another good choice: *Don't Make Me Think: A Common Sense Approach to Web Usability,* by Steve Krug and Roger Black (Que).

Chapter 4

Tweaking Your Text

*Y*ou didn't buy this book just to find out how to use FrontPage. Figuring out FrontPage is a means to an end; your ultimate goal is to create a spectacular Web site. In this and the following chapters, I show you how to build beautiful pages using FrontPage's Design view.

Design view contains a gazillion tools and commands that control various aspects of a Web page. In this chapter, I concentrate on the tools that affect the main ingredient of a page: text.

What Does Design View Do?

You use Design view to add stuff to the individual pages that make up your Web site.

Before programs like FrontPage hit the scene, you had to create and work with Web pages by fiddling with HTML. HTML stands for *HyperText Markup Language,* which is a set of codes that defines the layout and structure of a Web page. These codes (called *tags*) control how the page looks and acts. Figure 4-1 illustrates a bare-naked Web page with its HTML tags in full view. As you surf the Web, your Web browser translates HTML tags into the nice, neat Web page you see on-screen (see Figure 4-2).

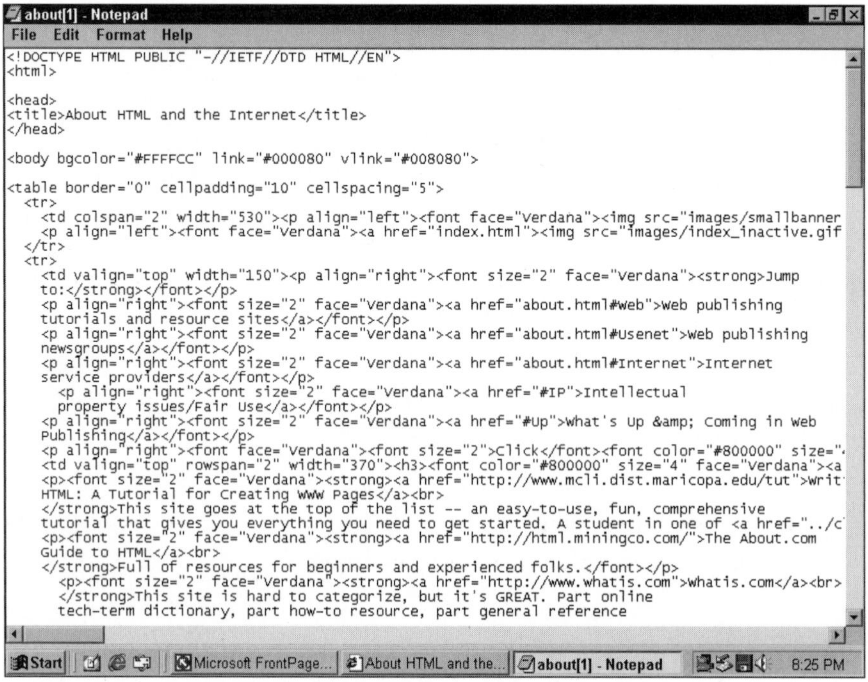

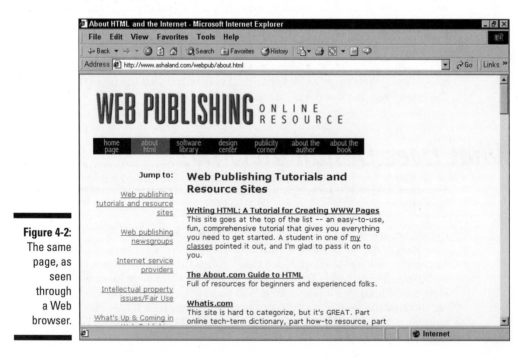

Figure 4-1:
Please avert
your eyes:
This page's
HTML
tags are
showing.

Figure 4-2:
The same
page, as
seen
through
a Web
browser.

Until recently, you had to know HTML to create a Web page. Although memorizing tags is not difficult, doing so does take time. Because most of us would rather frolic on the beach than spend weekends in front of the computer, the process of learning HTML (along with programming the VCR) stayed tucked away in the techie zone.

That is, until programs like FrontPage came along. Design view does the HTML grunt work for you, freeing your brain cells for creative tasks. You get to choose menu items and click buttons, and Design view generates all the HTML behind the scenes — which means you can create sophisticated Web pages without sacrificing beach time.

Adding Text to a Page

Words, letters, numbers, characters. Text. It seems rather prosaic alongside the World Wide Web's flashy graphics and interactive effects. Yet text is the most important part of each page that you create because the text makes up the majority of the content. You may dazzle your visitors with cutting-edge visuals and multimedia tricks, but the content — fresh, interesting, useful information — is what keeps people coming back for more.

Enough with the lecture. I promised to get you started on a Web page, didn't I? Okay, so launch FrontPage and open your Web site, create a new blank page (or open an existing page), and start typing. (If you're not sure how to launch or get around in FrontPage, flip through the chapters in Part I.)

If you want more room to type, you can increase your screen real estate by hiding the Folder List. To toggle the current setting, press Alt+F1.

FrontPage shares many attractive features with its Microsoft Office siblings. Table 4-1 shows you some of the buttons that can save you a lot of time.

Table 4-1	Timesaving Buttons on the Standard Toolbar	
Button	**What It Is**	**What It Does**
	Undo button	Enables you to take back mistakes, up to the last 30 actions.
	Redo button	Enables you to redo anything you've undone.
	Cut button	Cuts stuff (text, images, just about anything you can select with the pointer).

(continued)

Table 4-1 (continued)

Button	What It Is	What It Does
	Copy button	Copies stuff.
	Paste button	Pastes stuff. If you want more control over how FrontPage formats the text you are about to paste into your document, choose Edit➪Paste Special.
	Spelling button	Checks your spelling and enables you to correct spelling mistakes.
	Format Painter button	Enables you to copy formatting from one piece of text and then apply that formatting elsewhere.

In addition, the following features may tempt you to give your computer a big, affectionate squeeze:

✔ **Office Clipboard:** The Office Clipboard enables you to cut, copy, and paste multiple items between Office programs. To turn on the Office Clipboard (which lives in the task pane), choose Edit➪Office Clipboard.

✔ **Drag and drop:** You can drag and drop text, graphics, and other elements to different locations on pages.

✔ **Find and Replace:** The Edit➪Find command enables you to jump directly to the location of a character, word, or phrase. You can even replace all instances of that character/word/phrase with another character/word/phrase by using the Edit➪Replace command. Both the Find and the Replace functions work inside a single page or across the entire Web site. These functions can even sift through the pages' HTML tags (a useful feature if you're HTML-literate). To search for a document across Web sites or other Office applications, choose File➪File Search.

✔ **Thesaurus:** The built-in Thesaurus (accessible by choosing Tools➪ Thesaurus) instantly boosts your vocabulary by thousands of words.

✔ **Spell checking:** Click the Spelling button to take care of last-minute typo cleanups. If you activate the spell checker while in Design view, Front Page spell checks the open page. If you're currently looking at the contents of the Web Site tab, FrontPage offers to spell check the entire Web site in one go. FrontPage also knows how to check spelling as you type. Red squiggly lines appear inside the page beneath words that are either misspelled or unrecognizable to FrontPage. To correct a mistake, right-click the word and then choose the correct spelling from the pop-up menu that appears. If the word is spelled correctly but is unfamiliar to FrontPage, add the word to the FrontPage dictionary by right-clicking the word and then choosing Add to Dictionary. (To turn on and off automatic spell checking, choose Tools⇨Page Options. On the General tab of the Options dialog box that appears, select the Check Spelling as You Type check box. Click OK to close the dialog box.)

✔ **Customizable toolbars:** You can show, hide, rearrange, and customize any of the FrontPage toolbars. To show or hide toolbars, choose View⇨ Toolbars, and then choose the name of the toolbar you want to show or hide (in the Toolbars list, check marks indicate toolbars that are currently visible). To customize your toolbars, click the down arrow on the right side of the toolbar, and then choose Add or Remove Buttons and then the name of the toolbar. From the pop-up menu that appears, choose the buttons you want to show or hide. You can also *float* toolbars; pass the pointer over the left edge of the toolbar until the pointer turns into a crossed arrow. Click and drag the toolbar anywhere inside the Front Page window, and then drop it. To dock the toolbar back in its original position, double-click the title bar on the top of the toolbar.

✔ **Right-click pop-up menus:** FrontPage contains shortcuts to commonly used commands in pop-up menus that appear after you hover the pointer over an element (a piece of text, a hyperlink, a graphic, anything) and click the right mouse button. The pop-up menu that appears contains commands pertaining to the element you just right-clicked.

✔ **Tool Tips:** If you can't remember a toolbar item's function, move your pointer over the item and then keep it there; in a moment, a Tool Tip appears telling you the item's name.

✔ **Personalized desktop setup:** The Tools⇨Customize command gives you access to all sorts of options for setting menu commands, toolbars, and other desktop settings just the way you like them.

Keeping Site Accessibility in Mind

Now, before you get too far along in your Web-building adventures, is a good time to give some thought to your site's accessibility. If you read Chapter 3, you know that designing for the Web means taking into account big variations in your audience; their hardware, software, and cultural and other differences all play a part in how you set up your site. No doubt you want your site to be visible and understandable to the widest possible audience, and FrontPage gives you tools to help make this possible.

Choosing a Web server and browser platform

FrontPage enables you to choose a Web browser platform for which you want to optimize your site, and you can also pick and choose among browser-specific design effects. You need to think about this now — *before* you embark on site-building — because, based on your choices, FrontPage makes decisions about how it carries out text formatting and other design tasks. Furthermore, FrontPage makes available in its menus and toolbars only those effects that will work in your chosen platform.

You'll find a handy table that summarizes browser support for different Web design effects at `hotwired.lycos.com/webmonkey/reference/browser_chart`. (Be sure to check out the charts for non-Windows browsers as well; you'll find links to these charts on this page.)

You can also specify the type of host Web server on which you'll eventually publish your site. This feature is most helpful if you intend to publish your site on a Web server that doesn't support FrontPage Server Extensions or SharePoint Services, because it automatically disables effects that require those features to work. (I talk in detail about what FrontPage Server Extensions and SharePoint Services are and do in Chapter 17.)

Note: You might need to give your ISP or system administrator a call to find out what features your host server supports.

So before you begin building your site, follow these steps to control how FrontPage uses platform-specific effects:

1. **Choose Tools⇨Page Options.**

   The Page Options dialog box appears. (Even though the command is called Page Options, the compatibility settings apply to the entire Web site, including the site's subsites.)

2. **Click the Authoring tab to make that group of options visible.**

3. **In the FrontPage and SharePoint Technologies section, choose options that correspond to the type of host server you'll use to publish your site.**

   If the host server supports both FrontPage Server Extensions and SharePoint Services, from the list box, choose Default.

   If the server supports FrontPage Server Extensions, but not SharePoint Services, with Default visible in the list box, de-select the SharePoint Services and VML Graphics check boxes.

   If your host server does not have FrontPage Server Extensions or SharePoint Services installed, from the list box, choose None.

No matter what features your host server supports, if you exclusively use FrontPage to create and manage your site, you can select the check box next to Author-time Web Components (both Navigation and Shared Borders). These FrontPage-specific features are not affected by the host server or by what browser your visitors use.

4. **From the Browsers list box, choose the name of the Web browser group for which you want to design.**

   FrontPage only lists two Web browsers — Internet Explorer and Netscape Navigator — because these browsers account for the majority of the Web browsing population.

5. **From the Browser Versions list box, choose the browser version number for which you want to design.**

   Later versions of both browsers support more design features than earlier versions.

   You can also select or deselect check boxes next to specific technologies you want to include or exclude.

6. **Click OK.**

   The Page Options dialog box closes, and FrontPage saves your settings.

From now on, FrontPage makes available only those effects that work with the platform you've chosen. All other effects appear dimmed in FrontPage menus and dialog boxes, or disappear from the interface altogether.

In my experience, not all browsers display certain effects the same way, even though FrontPage says otherwise. For example, even though both Internet Explorer and Netscape Navigator (versions 4.0 and later) support JavaScript and Cascading Style Sheets (CSS), each browser displays the effects slightly differently. Therefore, if you use browser-specific effects in your Web site, be sure to thoroughly preview your page by using more than one Web browser. If you're not sure how to preview a page, see Chapter 2.

Checking your site against accessibility guidelines

Web browser and server differences aren't the only variations to consider when creating your site. Making your site accessible also means taking into account those of your visitors with disabilities or who speak different languages. Although it is near impossible to accommodate 100 percent of your visitors, familiarizing yourself with accepted accessibility guidelines will help a lot.

Both the World Wide Web Consortium (W3C) and the Federal government have come up with guidelines. The W3C, a consortium of Web-savvy organizations and businesses, creates universal standards for Web content and design. The W3C's Web Content Accessibility Guidelines (WCAG) explain how to make Web sites understandable to the majority of Web visitors. These guidelines are mainly geared toward people with hearing, visual, or mobility challenges, but they effectively make Web sites more usable for everyone. The guidelines are divided into priorities, with Priority 1 items being the most important guidelines to follow, Priority 2 still important, and Priority 3 a good idea, but certainly not as important as the first two groups.

The Access Board, an agency of the federal government of the United States, has also created accessibility standards specifically for Web sites (and other information technology resources) developed, used, or maintained by a U.S. federal agency. These standards fall under Section 508 of the Rehabilitation Act, passed by the U.S. Congress in 1988.

I recommend perusing the guidelines so you can keep them in mind as you create your site. These are meaty documents, but a look-through could actually save you lots of time as you consider how to design your site. The WCAG is available at www.w3.org/TR/1999/WAI-WEBCONTENT-19990505/, and a quick checklist is available at www.w3.org/TR/1999/WAI-WEBCONTENT-19990505/full-checklist.html. For more about Section 508 standards, see www.access-board.gov/sec508/summary.htm.

FrontPage knows about both sets of accessibility standards, and can scan your site to be sure it conforms to one or both sets. Unlike server and browser compatibility options (see the preceding section), however, this tool is better used *after* you have created your site because it scans your Web site and then proposes design changes based on what it finds. Therefore, this tool is best used as a final check before you publish your site. I explain how to publish your site in Chapter 17.

To check your Web site against accessibility standards, do this:

1. **With a Web site open, choose Tools⇨Accessibility.**

   The Accessibility dialog box appears.

2. **In the Check Where section of the dialog box, select the radio button next to the group of pages you want FrontPage to check.**

   You can check the entire site in one go, or you can select specific pages.

3. **In the Check For section of the dialog box, select the check boxes next to the accessibility standards you want to use.**

4. **In the Show section of the dialog box, select the check boxes next to the types of information that you want to appear in the report.**

   I suggest checking all three for good measure.

5. **Click the Check button (at the bottom of the dialog box).**

   FrontPage checks the selected document(s) against the accessibility standards you chose, and then lets you know it's finished by popping up a Microsoft FrontPage dialog box telling you so (click OK to close the dialog box).

The Accessibility dialog box is still visible, but now, the main part of the dialog box contains cryptic messages flagging the various trouble spots in your document(s), as shown in Figure 4-3. Each problem is identified by line number, which refers to the page's HTML. (You can see the HTML line numbers by looking inside the document's Code view, which I talk about in Chapter 14.)

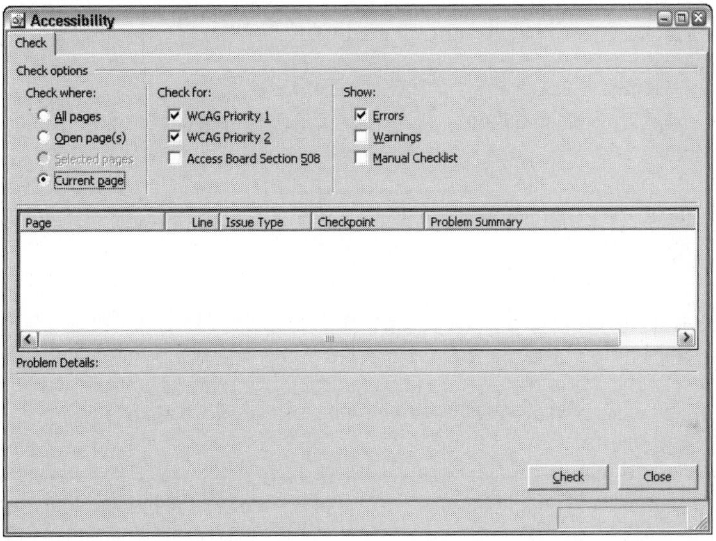

Figure 4-3:
FrontPage can suggest design and content changes based on accessibility guidelines.

To save the accessibility report, in the Accessibility dialog box, click the Generate HTML Report button, and then click Close. After the dialog box closes, you see a new page visible in FrontPage titled *Accessibility Report Template*. To save the page, press Ctrl+S.

The Accessibility Report lists the filenames of the documents FrontPage checked, along with a description of each potential problem. Some of these descriptions will make little sense if you don't know HTML, while others propose easy content or formatting changes. Make whatever changes you can, and then generate the report again to see how your site checks out.

If you're unable to comply with every guideline, don't worry too much. Whatever measures you can take to increase your site's accessibility will help.

Foolin' with Fonts

In FrontPage lingo, *font* refers to how text looks on your Web page. Character-istics such as bold or italics, size, color, and typeface all make up a charac-ter's font. Characters — the thingies that appear on-screen after you press keys on the keyboard — can be an unruly bunch. FrontPage comes with an arsenal of font tools (shown in Table 4-2) that can rein in those rowdy . . . er, characters.

Table 4-2	Formatting Toolbar Buttons That Control Font Changes	
Button	*What It Is*	*What It Does*
U	Bold button	Creates bold text.
B	Italic button	Creates italic text.
I	Underline button	Creates underlined text.
A	Increase Font Size button	Makes text bigger.
A	Decrease Font Size button	Makes text smaller.
ab	Highlight button	Colors the background of selected text (similar in effect to a highlighter pen).
A	Font Color button	Changes font color.

Using font tools

You'll find all your font tools in the Font dialog box and on the Formatting toolbar. The Font dialog box contains every tool you need to control your characters. The options in this dialog box enable you to change the font, style, color, size, and effect of text in your page. To access the Font dialog box, choose Format➪Font.

The Formatting toolbar contains buttons for the text tools you use most often. Table 4-2 gives you a rundown of the Formatting toolbar buttons that control font changes. If the toolbar isn't already visible, choose View⇨ Toolbars⇨Formatting.

You can use font tools in either of the following ways:

✔ Type a bunch of text, select the text that you want to format, and then turn on the appropriate tool, either by choosing an option in the Font dialog box or by clicking a button on the Formatting toolbar.

✔ Turn on the tool first, type the formatted text, and then turn off the tool when you're done.

You can apply more than one font format to a piece of text. You can, for example, make a word both bold and italic at the same time.

 The Format Painter button on the Standard toolbar enables you to copy formatting from one piece of text and then apply that formatting elsewhere. To do so, select the text that contains the formatting you want to copy, click the Format Painter button, and then select the text to which you want to apply the formatting. To apply the formatting to more than one clump of text, select the text that contains the formatting you want to copy, double-click the Format Painter button, select the text to which you want to apply the formatting, and then click the Format Painter button to deselect the tool when you're finished.

To turn off all font styles as you type, press Ctrl+Spacebar. To remove all font styles from a selected chunk of text, choose Format⇨Remove Formatting.

Changing fonts

Usually, when folks talk about a document's font, they're referring specifically to its *typeface,* or the style and shape of the characters. The right choice of font sets the tone for your document and makes the text easy to read.

 If you use custom fonts in your Web pages, your visitors' computers must also have these fonts installed in order for your text to appear correctly on their screens. If your visitors don't have a particular font on their machines, any text you format in that font appears to them in their browsers' default font. For example, if you use the Tolkien font in your pages and a visitor who doesn't have Tolkien installed on her machine browses your page, she sees your page's text in Times (the default font for most browsers).

To change text font, on the Formatting toolbar, choose a new font from the Font list box.

The thrill of themes

One of the sexier features in FrontPage 2003 is its extensive collection of graphical themes. *Themes* are coordinated sets of fonts, colors, graphics, and backgrounds that you can apply to your Web site. Chapter 11 goes into detail about themes, but I mention them here because they affect each of the text-tweaking tricks that I cover in this chapter. For example, if you create a new Web page that is formatted using a theme, it will already have a set font. If you insert a horizontal line, a custom-designed graphic line appears in place of the standard gray stripe. Keep these variations in mind as you progress through this chapter.

To set the default font for FrontPage, choose Tools⇨Page Options. In the Options dialog box that appears, click the Default Fonts tab, and then select the desired fonts from the Default Proportional Font and Default Fixed-Width Font list boxes. Click OK to close the dialog box.

Being bold (or italic or underlined or . . .)

Bold and italic text makes up the foundation of the font-formatting team. You pull these formats out like a trusty hammer every time you build a page.

In addition to bold and italic, you have a bunch of other text effects at your disposal, such as subscript, superscript, strikethrough, and small caps. One effect deserves special mention: the *Blink* effect. Blink, a Netscape-specific effect, causes text to flash on and off like a faulty neon sign outside a cheap motel. Trust me — the instances are very few where the Blink effect is anything but tacky.

To apply a font effect, do one of the following things:

- ✔ Click the appropriate button on the Formatting toolbar.

- ✔ Choose Format⇨Font to open the Font dialog box. Choose a style from the Font Style list, or select the check box next to the effect you want (if any). If you're not sure how a particular effect looks, select the check box to see a preview of the effect in the Preview area of the dialog box. When you're done, click OK.

The Overline, Capitalize, Small Caps, and All Caps font effects come courtesy of CSS (Cascading Style Sheets) commands. Browsers that are unable to display style sheets can't display these effects. Additionally, older browsers are unable to display the Strikethrough effect because it's a relatively new addition to HTML. I talk more about style sheets in Chapter 14.

As you add text and formatting to your page, notice the line of HTML tags growing near the top of the Design view window. This handy tool is called the *Quick Tag Selector* because it gives you easy access to the page's HTML without having to venture into the Code view. I talk in detail about the Quick Tag Selector in Chapter 14, but I sprinkle a few HTML tricks throughout the book so that you can give this feature a spin. To hide or show the Quick Tag Selector, choose View⇨Quick Tag Selector.

Changing text size

Text size in print documents is measured in absolute units called *points* or *picas*. Because of the way HTML works, text size in Web pages is based on a relative system of *increments*.

HTML text sizes range in increments from 1 (the smallest size) to 7 (the biggest). In FrontPage, the point-size equivalents for each increment range from 8 points (for size 1) to 36 points (for size 7). The catch: The number of points each increment value turns out to be when viewed with a Web browser is determined by *each visitor's individual browser settings,* not by FrontPage.

Here's where you run into some cross-platform prickles, because you can't assume that all of your visitors' browsers are set to display text sizes the same way. For example, by default, FrontPage creates Web pages with size 3 text, which Design view displays as 12-point type. A nearsighted visitor browsing your site, however, may have set her Web browser to display size 3 text as 18-point type. (This scenario is a good illustration of the client-server relationship at work. Refer to Chapter 3 for more information.)

The moral of this story: Although you can control the increment size of the text on your page, you can't control each increment's point-size equivalent as it appears in visitors' Web browsers. The visitor controls his or her own browser settings.

To change text size, on the Formatting toolbar, choose a size from the Font Size list box, or click the Increase Font Size or Decrease Font Size buttons until you're happy with what you see.

Another way to change text size is to use the Heading paragraph style. I show you how to use paragraph styles later in this chapter.

This HTML trick enables you to work around the problem of browser settings affecting text size. By adding a bit of CSS (Cascading Style Sheets) syntax to selected HTML tags, you can set text size using points rather than increments. To do so, select the text you want to change, and then choose the closest font size from the Font Size list box. In the Quick Tag Selector, move your cursor over the `<font>` tag, and then click the down arrow that appears to its right. (If the `<font>` tag isn't visible in the Quick Tag Selector, click anywhere outside the selected text to deselect it, and then click on it again.) From the pop-up menu that appears, choose Edit Tag. The Quick Tag Editor appears with the entire tag `<font size="x">` (with *x* being the size increment you chose) visible. Click inside the tag, and add the following bit of CSS syntax so that the tag looks *exactly* like this:

```
<font size="x" style="font-size:ypt">
```

(In this line of code, *y* is the number of points.) When you are done, in the Quick Tag Editor, click the green check button. The Quick Tag Editor closes, and the text changes accordingly (if it doesn't, follow the steps again, making sure the tag looks exactly as I have written, including white space and quote marks).

Changing text color

You can dress up your text in any color of the rainbow (plus a few fluorescent shades that don't appear in nature). Color gives your text panache, calls attention to important words, and, if coordinated with the colors of the page's graphics, unifies design.

To change the color of selected text, click the down arrow attached to the Font Color button to display a list box of standard colors, as shown in Figure 4-4. Click the desired color swatch to apply that color to your text.

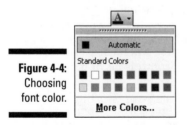

Figure 4-4:
Choosing
font color.

Cascading Style Sheets wizardry

Cascading Style Sheets (or CSS) enable you to sidestep many of the limitations inherent in Web design. A *style sheet* is a collection of formatting and style instructions that tell the Web browser how to display the page.

FrontPage contains built-in support for style sheets, so you can create virtually any font or paragraph style you like (with caveats, of course). See Chapter 14 for details.

If you don't see a standard color you like, you can choose from a palette of 135 browser-safe colors. (I explain what I mean by *browser-safe* in Chapter 6.) You can even grab colors from any object on your screen, such as a graphic or an icon. To do so, follow these steps:

1. **Click the down arrow next to the Font Color button and then click More Colors.**

   The More Colors dialog box appears, as shown in Figure 4-5.

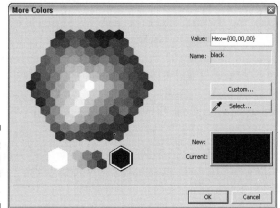

Figure 4-5:
The More
Colors
dialog box.

2. **In the dialog box's color palette, click the color you like.**

   Or, if you would rather grab a color from an existing object, click the Select button. The pointer turns into a little eyedropper. Move the eyedropper over an object on your screen that contains the color you want to use (the active color appears in the New box), and then click to select the color.

3. **Click OK.**

   The More Colors dialog box closes, and FrontPage applies the selected color to your text.

Each time you apply a color to your page, FrontPage adds that color to the Document's Colors section in all color-related list boxes. You run into these list boxes whenever you add or change an element's color in your page, such as hyperlinks (covered in Chapter 5) or table borders (covered in Chapter 7). This thoughtful extra makes applying colors elsewhere in your page easy, and it helps you keep an eye on your page's overall color scheme.

To change the body text color for the entire page, choose Format⇨Background to display the Formatting tab of the Page Properties dialog box. From the Text list box, select the color swatch you like, and then click OK.

Changing character spacing

FrontPage makes it easy to increase or reduce the amount of blank space separating selected characters. To do so, follow these steps:

1. **Choose Format⇨Font to display the Font dialog box.**

2. **In the dialog box, click the Character Spacing tab to make the options visible.**

3. **From the Spacing list box, choose Expanded or Condensed.**

4. **In the accompanying By box, enter the number of pixels by which FrontPage will expand or contract the selected text.**

   Note: The Position options in this dialog box enable you to control the amount of space between regular text and superscript or subscript text.

5. **Click Apply to see how the spacing change looks before closing the dialog box, or click OK to close the dialog box and apply the character spacing.**

The character spacing options come courtesy of Cascading Style Sheets (CSS) commands. Browsers that are unable to display style sheets won't display these effects.

Creating Stylish Paragraphs

Unlike font effects, which you can apply to individual letters and words, paragraph styles operate on entire paragraphs. Use paragraph styles if you want to make widespread changes throughout your page.

A FrontPage paragraph differs from the paragraph as defined by your composition teacher. To FrontPage, every time you press the Enter key, you create a new paragraph. Even if you type only one word and then hit Enter, FrontPage considers the word a paragraph.

FrontPage contains the following paragraph styles:

✔ **Normal:** The default style for paragraphs. Nothing fancy — just regular old left-aligned paragraphs with a proportional font. (The Times font appears in most Web browsers.)

✔ **Formatted:** Creates paragraphs with a fixed-width font (Courier for most browsers).

✔ **Address:** A holdover from the olden days of Web design (around 1993). Back then, the Address style was used to designate the page creator's e-mail address so visitors could get in touch. Today, folks format their contact information any number of ways, so the Address style has, for the most part, become obsolete. Besides, the style creates italic text just as the italic font style does, so why use the old clunker?

✔ **Headings:** Help identify clumps of information inside a page. Large headings, usually located at the top of the page, identify what the page is all about, and smaller headings, sprinkled throughout, divide the page's information into manageable bits. Headings in Web pages come in six sizes. Strangely enough, Heading 1 is the largest size, and Heading 6 is the smallest.

✔ **Lists:** Group related bits of information together by using bullets, numbers, or special text formatting. I discuss lists in the next section of this chapter.

Table 4-3 shows you all the buttons in the Formatting toolbar that control paragraphs.

Table 4-3	Formatting Toolbar Buttons That Control Paragraphs	
Button	*What It Is*	*What It Does*
	Align Left button	Aligns paragraph text along the left page margin.
	Center button	Centers paragraph text.
	Align Right button	Aligns paragraph text along the right page margin.
	Justify button	Aligns paragraph text along the left and right page margins.
	Numbering button	Creates a numbered list.
	Bullets button	Creates a bulleted list.
	Decrease Indent button	Restores indentation you've previously increased.
	Increase Indent button	Places a bit of white space on either side of a paragraph, at the left and right margins. Good for setting off quoted text.
	Outside Borders button	Adds borders to the selected paragraph.

Practicing safe styles

I remember the first time I used a word processor. I was seduced by the millions of text styles at my disposal and proceeded to use most of them in my first document. (I think it was a letter to a pen pal.) The finished product looked like a cut-and-paste ransom note you might see in an old private-eye movie. The text was readable, but it was a gaudy mess.

I'm not suggesting that you lack restraint. I relate the example only to illustrate how moderate use of font and paragraph styles enhances a page's readability and visual appeal, whereas overuse sends your readers screaming to a new Web destination.

For example, consider limiting font and color choices in your Web site. Choose a single font for headings, and perhaps one more font for body text. Keep your hyperlinks a single color so that visitors can easily identify clickable bits of text (I show you how to change hyperlink colors in Chapter 5). In general, keep in mind that "less is more."

To change the style of a paragraph, follow these steps:

1. **Place the cursor inside the paragraph you want to format, or select more than one paragraph.**

2. **On the Formatting toolbar, choose the style you want from the Style list box.**

Whenever you press the Enter key, FrontPage thinks you want to create a new paragraph. If you simply want to create a new line without creating a new paragraph, use a line break instead. To create a line break, press Shift+Enter.

To distinguish between line breaks and new paragraphs in your page, click the Show/Hide ¶ button on the Standard toolbar. Line breaks are flagged with left-pointing arrows.

The list of lists

Lists. I love 'em and hate 'em. I love 'em because lists promote the illusion that I'm in control. I hate 'em because lists show me just how much work I still need to do.

Lists in Web pages, on the other hand, do nothing but make life easier by organizing your page's information so that your text is easy to read and understand.

Bulleted and numbered lists

Bulleted lists are not lists that were attacked with an assault weapon. Such lists are groups of items, each of which is preceded by a solid dot, called a *bullet.* A *numbered list* looks like a bulleted list, except that numbers stand in for the bullets. Numbered lists are great if you need to present a series of ordered steps.

To create a bulleted or numbered list, follow these steps:

1. **Place the cursor in the page where you want the list to begin.**

2. **Click the Bullets button or the Numbering button.**

    A bullet or number appears at the beginning of the first line.

3. **Type the first list item and then press Enter.**

    A bullet or number appears on the next line.

4. **Type your second list item (and so on).**

5. **After you're done adding items to your list, press Enter twice to end the list.**

You can convert existing paragraphs into bulleted or numbered lists by selecting the paragraphs that you want included in the list and then clicking the Bullets button or the Numbering button.

To split a long list into two separate lists, click at the end of a list item and press Enter twice. The list splits into two lists and, in the case of numbered lists, renumbers itself automatically.

If the plain dots or numbers sitting in your lists don't appeal to your aesthetic senses, you can dress 'em up. The List Properties dialog box enables you to change the shape of your bullets or replace the dreary black spots with pictures. If you want to give a numbered list a makeover, you can use the List Properties dialog box to apply Roman numerals or change the list's starting number.

To access the List Properties dialog box, click within the list you want to format, and then choose Format⇨Bullets and Numbering.

Here's another idea: Apply a theme to your Web site. Each theme has its own set of graphic bullets. I show you how to use themes in Chapter 11.

List-in-a-list

Sometimes a simple list doesn't cut it. Say you need something more sophisticated, such as a multilevel outline or a numbered list with bullets following certain items (similar to the one shown in Figure 4-6). No problem!

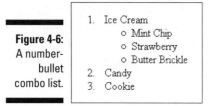

Figure 4-6:
A number-
bullet
combo list.

To create such a fancy-shmancy combo list, follow these steps:

1. **Create a bulleted or numbered list.**

   The list should contain every item, regardless of level.

2. **Highlight the item or items you want to move down (or up) a level, and then click the Increase Indent (or Decrease Indent) button twice.**

   The list items move down (or up) a level.

3. **To change the items' numbering or bullet style, with the items still highlighted, click the Bullets or Numbering button.**

   For more bullet and number style options, instead of clicking Bullets or Numbering, right-click the selection and choose List Properties from the pop-up menu. Choose the numbering or bullet style you want from the List Properties dialog box, and then click OK to close the dialog box.

Adjusting paragraph alignment, indenting, and spacing

By default, FrontPage paragraphs (with the exceptions of headings and lists) are single-spaced, line up with the page's left margin, and contain no indentation (that is, no extra space exists between the margin and the paragraph). Also, a little bit of space precedes and follows each paragraph. You can change these default paragraph settings one of two ways: the easy-but-basic way, and the slightly-more-involved-but-with-greater-control way.

✔ **Easy-but-basic way to change paragraph alignment:** Click inside the paragraph (or select multiple paragraphs) and then click the Align Left, Center, Align Right, or Justify button. (Justify **creates** paragraphs with neat-and-tidy text that lines up along the left and right margins.)

✔ **Easy-but-basic way to indent a paragraph:** Click inside the paragraph (or select multiple paragraphs) and then click the Increase Indent button. You may click the button as many times as you want to achieve the desired effect. To decrease the level of an indented paragraph, click the Decrease Indent button.

✔ **Slightly-more-involved-but-with-greater-control way to change paragraph alignment, indentation, and spacing:** Go through the steps that follow:

1. **Click inside the paragraph (or select multiple paragraphs).**

2. **Choose Format➪Paragraph.**

   The Paragraph dialog box appears.

3. **From the Alignment list box, choose the alignment option you want.**

4. **From the list boxes in the Indentation section, specify the amount of indentation (in pixels) you want.**

   The Before Text list box controls indentation along the left margin, and the After Text list box controls indentation along the right margin. The Indent First Line list box enables you to apply a different indentation setting to the first line of the paragraph.

5. **From the list boxes in the Spacing section, specify the amount of spacing (in pixels) you want.**

   The Before list box controls the amount of space before the paragraph; the After list box controls the amount of space after the paragraph; the Word list box controls the amount of space between words in the paragraph; and the Line Spacing list box controls (you guessed it) the space between the lines in the paragraph.

6. **Click OK.**

   The Paragraph dialog box closes, and FrontPage applies the formatting to the selected paragraph(s).

The options in the Paragraph dialog box come courtesy of CSS commands. Browsers that are unable to display style sheets won't display these effects.

If you want more control over the placement of your paragraphs than the Paragraph dialog box can give you, consider using a layout table (see Chapter 9), or positioning (see the sidebar called "Puttering with positioning," also in Chapter 9).

Adding borders and shading

Want to surround the selected paragraph with a box? Or give the paragraph a colorful background so it visually jumps off the page? These effects and more await you in the Borders and Shading dialog box.

Adding a border

To quickly add a border to the selected paragraph, click the down arrow next to the Border button and choose a border style you like. For a little more control, do this:

1. **Click inside the paragraph (or select multiple paragraphs) and then choose Format⇨Borders and Shading.**

   The Borders and Shading dialog box appears, as shown in Figure 4-7.

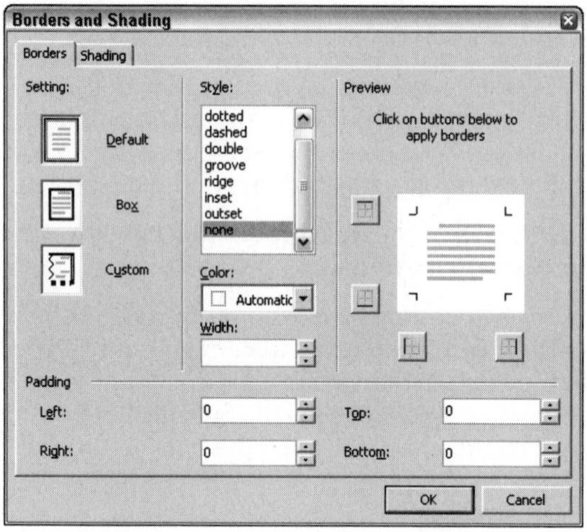

Figure 4-7: The Borders and Shading dialog box.

2. **In the Setting area of the dialog box, click the option that corresponds to the type of border you want.**

3. **In the Style box, click the name of the border style you want.**

4. **Choose a border color from the Color list box.**

   If you choose More Colors, the More Colors dialog box appears. I explain how to use the More Colors dialog box in the earlier section, "Changing text color."

5. **Enter a border width (in pixels) in the Width box.**

6. **To turn on or off individual borders, in the Preview area, click the button that corresponds to the border you want to change.**

7. **To add empty space between the paragraph text and the surrounding border, enter pixel values in boxes in the Padding area of the dialog box.**

8. **Click OK to close the dialog box and apply the border settings.**

Adding shading

In FrontPage, *shading* refers to the paragraph's foreground and background attributes. The paragraph's foreground attribute is its text color, and its background attributes are the color or picture that sits behind the selected paragraph's text.

 To quickly apply a background color to selected text, click the Highlight Color button. To add more complex shading, do this:

1. **Click inside the paragraph (or select multiple paragraphs) and then choose Format⇨Borders and Shading.**

   The Borders and Shading dialog box appears.

2. **In the dialog box, click the Shading tab to make those options visible.**

3. **To change the paragraph's background color, choose an option from the Background Color list box.**

4. **To change the paragraph's foreground (text) color, choose an option from the Foreground Color list box.**

5. **To place a picture in the paragraph's background, in the Background Picture text box, type the graphic file's path, or click Browse to select the file from a folder location.**

   If you click Browse, the Select Background Picture dialog box appears. If you're not sure how to use this dialog box, I give you directions in Chapter 6.

6. **To control how the picture repeats in the paragraph background, select an option from the Repeat list box.**

   By default, the picture repeats itself over and over until it fills the selected paragraph's background area. Repeat-X causes the picture to repeat horizontally, and Repeat-Y causes the picture to repeat vertically. No-Repeat causes the picture to appear only once.

7. **To change the position of the picture relative to the paragraph, choose options from the Vertical Position and Horizontal Position list boxes.**

   For example, if you choose a vertical position of top and a horizontal position of left, the image appears in the top-left corner of the paragraph's background.

   Note: The Attachment list box controls whether the background image moves when the visitor scrolls down the page (by default, the image appears fixed in place with the text scrolling on top). Because the effect is only visible in Microsoft Internet Explorer, I recommend leaving the default setting as it is.

8. **Click OK to close the dialog box and apply the shading settings.**

The options in the Borders and Shading dialog box and the Highlight Color effect come courtesy of CSS commands. Browsers that are unable to display style sheets won't display these effects. Furthermore, browsers that support CSS don't always display borders and shading consistently. If you decide to use these effects, be sure to preview your Web site with more than one browser make and version.

Inserting Comments

You can insert explanatory text and reminders to yourself (or to other members of your Web-building team) in the form of comments. *Comments* are notes that appear only in FrontPage, and not to a visitor views the page with a Web browser. To insert a comment, follow these steps:

1. **Place the cursor in the page where you want the comment to appear.**

2. **Choose Insert⇨Comment.**

   The Comment dialog box appears.

3. **In the Comment text box, type your comment and then click OK.**

   The dialog box closes, and the comment appears in your page as colorful text.

To edit a comment, double-click the comment. To delete a comment, click the comment and then press the Delete key.

Keep in mind that comments aren't *completely* invisible; your visitors can see the comments if they look at your page's underlying HTML tags. If you want to keep your comments completely private, you can tell FrontPage to remove comments before you publish your site. I explain how in Chapter 17.

Inserting Horizontal Lines

Horizontal lines are thin gray stripes that run the width of your Web page. How do they fit into a chapter about tweaking text, you ask? Because, as is true of font and paragraph styles, horizontal lines help group together bunches of related information. (Work with me here.) You can use a horizontal line if you need a quick way to divide your Web page into different sections. You can even change the line's width and height for a little variety.

Keep in mind that overusing horizontal lines wreaks design havoc. A line or two can provide a much-needed visual break. Too many lines make your page look as though it's trapped behind bars.

To insert a horizontal line, place the cursor in the page where you want the line to appear and choose Insert➪Horizontal Line. To customize how the line looks, follow these steps:

1. **In the page, double-click the horizontal line.**

   The Horizontal Line Properties dialog box appears.

2. **In the Width area of the dialog box, type a value into the text box and then click the Percent of Window or Pixels radio button.**

   You can indicate the width as a percentage of the width of the browser window, or you can specify an absolute number of pixels.

3. **In the Height text box, type the line's height (its thickness) in pixels.**

4. **In the Alignment area, click the Left, Center, or Right radio button.**

5. **Choose a color from the Color list box.**

6. **If you want the line to appear solid instead of engraved, select the Solid Line (No Shading) check box.**

7. **Click OK to close the dialog box and insert the line into the page.**

To delete a horizontal line, click the line and then press the Delete key.

Chapter 5

Getting Your Visitors from Here to There with Hyperlinks

*H*yperlinks are the gems that make surfing the Web so addictive. Click a link, and you find yourself somewhere else — maybe on another page in your Web site or, just as easily, on a page stored on a server in Sri Lanka or Cheyenne. Too bad Web surfing doesn't earn frequent flyer miles.

The heady nature of Web travel may lead you to believe that hyperlinks are difficult to create. Relax and discover how easily you can hitch your Web site to the global conga line known as the World Wide Web.

The Hyperlink Two-Step

Hyperlinks are bits of text or pictures that act as springboards to other locations. Hyperlinks between pages and files in a Web site *(internal hyperlinks)* transform the site from a jumble of separate files into a cohesive unit. Hyperlinks to locations outside the Web site *(external hyperlinks)* connect the site to the rest of the World Wide Web.

After you launch FrontPage and open the Web site and/or the page you want to edit, creating a hyperlink is a two-step process. Here are the basic steps (the rest of this chapter fills in the details):

1. **In the page, select the thing you want to transform into a hyperlink.**

   I call this "thing" the *hyperlink source* — it's the object people click. A hyperlink source can be a character, a word, a phrase, or a picture. (Chapter 6 explains how to insert a picture into your page.)

2. **Connect the hyperlink source to the place you want visitors to end up after they click the hyperlink.**

   From now on, I call this location the *hyperlink destination.* A hyperlink destination can be a spot in the same page, another page or file inside the same Web site, or a different site on the Internet. A hyperlink destination can also point to an e-mail address or initiate a file download.

Keep practicing these steps, and you can soon do the hyperlink two-step with the best of 'em.

Linking to a Web page or file

Most often, when you create a hyperlink, you already have the link's destination in mind. As long as you know that destination's location — whether it's a page inside the same Web site or a different Web site altogether — you're ready to roll.

To link to an existing page or file, follow these steps:

1. **In the page, select the object you want to turn into a hyperlink (the hyperlink source).**

   Highlight a bit of text, click a picture, double-click a word — whatever.

2. **On the Standard toolbar, click the Insert Hyperlink button.**

   The Insert Hyperlink dialog box appears, as shown in Figure 5-1.

3. **Click the Existing File or Web Page icon in the dialog box's Link To section (if it's not already selected) to make those options visible.**

4. **Depending on location of the page or file to which you want the hyperlink to lead, specify the hyperlink destination:**

   • If the destination file is part of the currently open Web site, in the dialog box's file list, click the file. If the file is stored inside a folder or a subsite, double-click the folder or subsite to open it and then click the file.

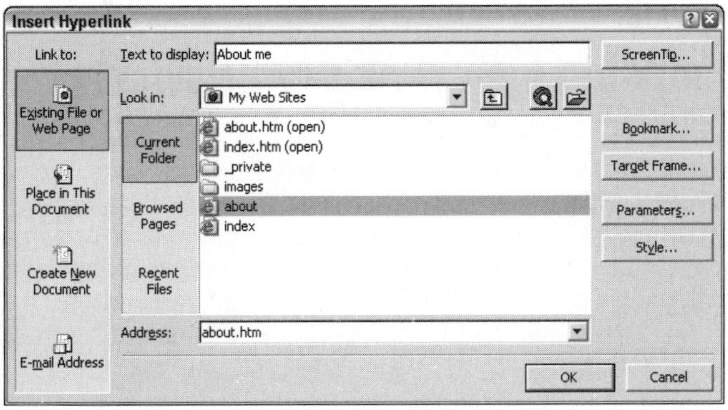

Figure 5-1:
The Insert Hyperlink dialog box.

When a page is currently open in Design view, *two* instances of that page appear in the dialog box's file list. You can click either icon in this step.

- If the destination file is located on the World Wide Web, type its address (also known as its *URL*) in the Address box. A World Wide Web URL looks similar to the following addresses:

```
http://www.server.com
http://www.server.com/filename.htm
http://www.server.com/foldername/filename.htm
```

If you can't remember the URL, in the dialog box, click the Browse the Web button (it looks like a globe with a magnifying glass on top) to launch your Web browser. Surf to your destination, switch back to FrontPage by clicking FrontPage's button in the Windows taskbar, and — huzzah! — the URL appears in the Address box.

- If the page or file is elsewhere on your hard drive or network, read the sidebar, "Linking to a file stored on your computer or local network," for a heads-up about potential problems with this type of hyperlink. If you're sure you want to create the link, in the dialog box, navigate to the location of the file and then click it.

5. **Click OK.**

   The dialog box closes, and a hyperlink is born.

If the hyperlink source is text, that text now displays the proud markings of a link: underlining and color.

You can still apply font and paragraph styles — bold, italic, and so on — to text hyperlinks as you can to regular text. You can also get rid of the default underlining that appears when you transform regular text into a hyperlink. To do so, click inside the link, and then click the Underline button on the Formatting toolbar.

Choosing hyperlink words wisely

Hyperlinks immediately attract attention. There-fore, choose the clearest, most meaningful text for promotion to linkhood. Avoid the temptation to create links that say things such as "Click here to see a picture of Harold, my pet ferret." (The underlined words are the hyperlink in the previous sentence.) Instead, choose text that clues the visitor in on what's sitting at the other end of the hyperlink. If you want to immortalize Harold the ferret in your home page, you're better off using the following link text: "See a picture of Harold, my pet ferret."

If the hyperlink source is a picture, the image itself looks no different than before its transformation. Trust me — the image is now a *graphic hyperlink*. If you want proof, pass your pointer over any text or graphic hyperlink, and the link destination appears in the status bar at the bottom of the FrontPage window.

To differentiate graphic hyperlinks from regular pictures in your Web pages, you can give graphic hyperlinks a border. The borders of graphic hyperlinks are the same color as text links, giving visitors a visual cue to click the pic-ture to jump elsewhere. (The effect doesn't always look so good, but at least you know your options.) I show you how to add borders to pictures in Chapter 6.

Instant hyperlink shortcut! Drag an icon from the Folder List and drop it into the page currently open in Design view. (If the Folder List isn't visible, click the Folder List button on the Standard toolbar or choose View➪Folder List.) FrontPage creates a link to the selected destination page, using the destina-tion page's title as the hyperlink text.

If you type a URL or an e-mail address inside the body of your page and then press the spacebar or Enter, FrontPage automatically turns the URL/address text into a hyperlink to that location or address.

Keep in mind that the steps in this section apply to links leading to *any* type of file, not just Web pages. For example, say you want to create a hyperlink that, when clicked, enables visitors to download a file. No problem. Simply import the item (in this case, the file you want to make available for down-load) into your Web site (see Chapter 15 for details), and then create a hyper-link leading to that item. When a visitor clicks that link, if the visitor's Web browser doesn't know how to open that file type, the browser automatically prompts the visitor to download the file (try it and see).

Linking to an e-mail address

The quickest way to help your visitors get in touch with you is to include a link to your e-mail address inside each page in your site. That way, if visitors have comments (or, dare I say it, complaints), they can click this link to pop open an e-mail window, preaddressed to you, from their Web browsers. From there, they can fire off messages in seconds.

For e-mail links to work, the visitor's browser must either have a built-in e-mail component or be able to hook up with a separate e-mail program.

The no-brainer approach to creating a link to your e-mail address is to type your e-mail address in the page followed by a tap on the spacebar or Enter key. FrontPage automatically transforms the address text into a link. Otherwise, do this:

1. **In the page, select the hyperlink source.**

2. **Click the Insert Hyperlink button to open the Insert Hyperlink dialog box.**

3. **In the dialog box's Link To section, click the E-mail Address icon.**

   The contents of the Insert Hyperlink dialog box change accordingly.

4. **In the E-mail Address text box, type an e-mail address.**

   The address should look something like this: `name@address.com`. When you start typing your address, FrontPage automatically tacks `mailto:` to the beginning. That's okay.

5. **Optionally, in the Subject text box, type a subject line for the e-mail message generated by this link.**

6. **Click OK.**

Linking to a file stored on your computer or local network

FrontPage enables you to create a link from your Web page to a file stored elsewhere on your computer's hard drive. The problem is, when you publish your finished Web site on a host Web server, the link no longer works because the location of the hyperlink destination file is specific to your computer's file system, not the Web server's.

Sometimes this feature comes in handy, such as if you're creating a local Web presentation to be displayed only on your computer or local network (not on the World Wide Web). If you decide to use this option, proceed with care, and double-check the link after you've published your site to be sure the link works properly.

To instantly place a link to your e-mail address at the bottom of every page in your site, place the mailto link inside a *shared border*. I show you how to use shared borders later in this chapter.

Another way to encourage visitor feedback is to provide an interactive form. I show you how in Chapter 8.

Editing Hyperlinks

Just as you can change your hair color, you can easily change your hyperlinks. You can change the text that makes up the link, the destination to which the link leads, its appearance, and even how it behaves.

Changing a hyperlink's text or destination and adding a ScreenTip

A visit to the Edit Hyperlink dialog box enables you to change the text that makes up a hyperlink, change its destination, or add a ScreenTip. A *ScreenTip* is a caption-like label that pops up when the visitor passes the cursor over the link (similar to the Tool Tip that appears when you hover your cursor over a toolbar button in FrontPage).

ScreenTips appear only to those of your visitors using Microsoft Internet Explorer 4.0 and later.

To change a hyperlink's text or destination or to add a ScreenTip to a hyperlink, follow these steps:

1. **In the page, click the hyperlink that you want to change.**

 2. **Click the Insert Hyperlink button to open the Edit Hyperlink dialog box.**

3. **To change the hyperlink text visible in the page, type new text in the Text to Display text box.**

4. **To change the link's destination, click a different file in the file list or type a different URL in the Address list box.**

   Refer to the "Linking to a Web page or file" section, earlier in the chapter, for detailed instructions on how to specify a link's destination.

5. **To add a ScreenTip, click the ScreenTip button to display the Set Hyperlink ScreenTip dialog box. Type the ScreenTip text into the appropriate text box, and then click OK.**

The Edit Hyperlink dialog box becomes visible again.

6. **Click OK to close the dialog box.**

Note: The steps outlined in this section work only on hyperlinks that are *not* part of a FrontPage link bar. I talk more about link bars later in this chapter.

Displaying a hyperlink's destination in a new browser window

You may have experienced this trick during your own Web wanderings: You click a link inside a Web page, and, instead of replacing the contents of the current browser window, the hyperlink destination shows up in a second browser window.

This effect comes in handy for several situations. Some Web site creators program all their external links (links that point to locations outside the Web site) to pop open new windows when clicked, so visitors get a clear visual cue when they "leave" the site. Other designers use this effect to display supplementary information without replacing the contents of the original window (a good example would be a product catalog with a link leading to a size chart that appears in its own window).

To cause the hyperlink destination to appear in a new browser window, do the following:

1. **In the page, click the hyperlink you want to change.**

2. **Click the Insert Hyperlink button to open the Edit Hyperlink dialog box.**

3. **In the dialog box, click the Target Frame button.**

   The Target Frame dialog box appears. (You'll use this dialog box often if you decide to use *frames* in your site — hence the name "Target Frame." I tell you all about frames in Chapter 10.)

4. **In the dialog box's Common Targets list box, click New Window, and then click OK.**

   The Target Frame dialog box closes, and the Edit Hyperlink dialog box becomes visible again.

5. **Click OK to close the dialog box.**

Note: The steps outlined in this section work only on hyperlinks that are *not* part of a FrontPage link bar. I talk more about link bars later in this chapter.

Changing hyperlink color

Hyperlinks stand out from regular text because hyperlinks appear in a different color from their ordinary text siblings, and they are usually underlined. The default hyperlink color is blue, but you can change the link's color so that the hyperlink coordinates nicely with the site's color scheme.

Hyperlinks actually have three distinct colors: the default color, the active color, and the visited color. These colors appear when a visitor views the page in a Web browser:

- **Default color:** The link's color before the visitor follows the hyperlink trail. When a visitor arrives at your page for the first time, all the page's links appear in the default color, because the visitor hasn't yet followed any of the links.

- **Active color:** The color the link becomes "mid-click." The active color lets visitors know they are indeed activating that particular link.

- **Visited color:** The color the link changes to after a visitor follows a link and then returns to the page. The visited color lets visitors know which links they've already followed and which ones they haven't yet explored. (Each individual visitor's browser keeps track of which links that person has followed inside each page.)

You can select unique hyperlink colors for each page you create. You also can apply a theme to your Web site; each theme contains a nicely coordinated set of hyperlink colors. (I cover themes in Chapter 11.)

To select link colors for a page, follow these steps:

1. **With the page open in Design view, choose Format⇨Background.**

   The Page Properties dialog box appears with the Formatting tab visible. The current link color settings appear in the list boxes labeled Hyperlink, Visited Hyperlink, and Active Hyperlink, as shown in Figure 5-2.

2. **Choose a new color from one or all the list boxes corresponding to each hyperlink state.**

   If you choose More Colors, the More Colors dialog box appears. I explain how to use the More Colors dialog box in Chapter 4.

   Note: If the current Web site page is formatted with a theme, the hyperlink colors are listed as "automatic" because themes contain a preset palette of text and hyperlink colors. To change the theme's hyperlink colors, you must customize the theme itself, which I explain in Chapter 11.

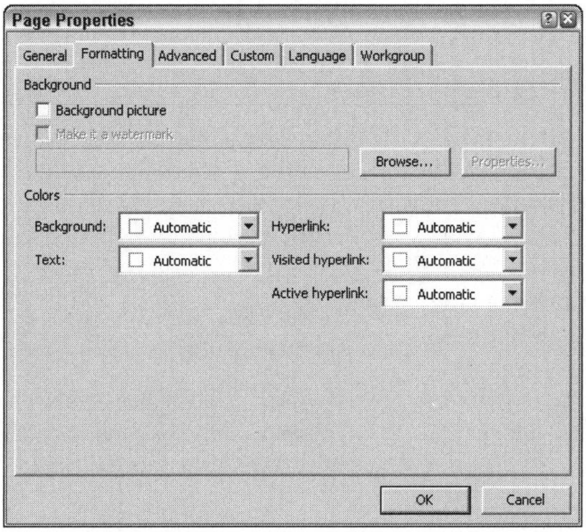

Figure 5-2:
The
Formatting
tab of the
Page
Properties
dialog box.

3. **Click OK.**

The dialog box closes, and the page's links change color.

To see how the active and visited colors look, preview the page in a Web browser.

Wise advice about hyperlink colors

The steps in the "Changing hyperlink color" section change the hyperlink colors for all the hyperlinks *in the current page.* You could use the Font Color button to change the colors of individual hyperlinks, but color changes made this way show up only in recent versions of advanced browsers. Besides, maintaining a consistent link color minimizes confusion amongst your visitors, so they can more easily ascertain what's clickable and what's just decoration. Therefore, if you do change your hyperlink's colors, keep the same color scheme for all the pages in your site.

You could open each page in your site and follow the steps outlined in the "Changing

hyperlink color" section — a fine option for a site containing five pages. But what if your site contains fifty pages? A hundred? Consider creating a separate *style sheet* for your site that specifies hyperlink colors, and then link the style sheet to each of your pages. That way, if you decide later to change the hyperlink color (or any number of other stylistic attributes) throughout your site, you simply update the style sheet, and the changes are reflected throughout your entire site automatically. Powerful stuff. If you're interested, you can get started with style sheets in Chapter 14.

Creating a table of contents

A table of contents displays the titles of all your site's pages in a hierarchical list, with links to each page. The table of contents also lists any external links that you add to your site's navigation structure. (See Chapter 15 for information about the purpose of a navigation structure.) Visitors love tables of contents for the bird's-eye view they provide, but even the best-intentioned Web designer dreads creating a table of contents for a big Web site, especially if he or she is constantly adding and changing pages.

Here's where the Table of Contents Web Component swoops in to the rescue. FrontPage can crank out a fully linked table of contents and updates it if pages change.

To create a table of contents, do the following:

1. **In the page, place the cursor where you want the table of contents to appear.**

2. **Choose Insert⇨Web Component.**

   The Insert Web Component dialog box appears.

3. **In the dialog box's Component Type list box, click Table of Contents.**

4. **In the dialog box's Choose a Table of Contents list box, click For This Web Site, and then click the Finish button.**

   The Table of Contents Properties dialog box appears.

5. **In the Page URL for Starting Point of Table text box, type the filename of the page that you want to appear at the top of the table of contents.**

   Alternatively, click the Browse button to select a page from a list of files in your Web site. By default, FrontPage specifies the site's home page as its starting point.

6. **From the Heading Font Size list box, choose the heading size for the first item in the table of contents.**

Choosing a relatively bold heading (such as Heading 1 or Heading 2) sets the first item apart from the rest so that the item acts as a title for the table of contents.

7. **If you want each page in your site to appear in the table of contents only once, select the Show Each Page Only Once check box.**

   If you don't select this option, pages that link to more than one page in your site appear more than once.

8. **If you want the table of contents to display pages in your site that don't link to other pages, select the Show Pages with No Incoming Hyperlinks check box.**

   If you mark this check box, the only access point to the page is through the table of contents because the page isn't linked to the rest of your Web site.

9. **If you want FrontPage to automatically update the table of contents as you edit pages and add new pages to your Web site, select the Recompute Table of Contents When Any Other Page Is Edited check box.**

   If you don't select this option and still want to update the table of contents, you need to recalculate your site's hyperlinks each time a page changes or you add a new page. (To recalculate hyperlinks, choose Tools⇨Recalculate Hyperlinks.)

10. **Click OK.**

    The dialog box closes, and a placeholder for the table of contents appears in the page.

To see how the actual table of contents looks, preview the page by choosing File⇨Preview in Browser (the FrontPage Preview view displays only the placeholder).

Making Sure Your Hyperlinks Work As Advertised

Broken hyperlinks are like ants at a picnic. One or two ants are mildly annoying, but if enough ants show up, they ruin the entire afternoon.

A hyperlink breaks if the destination page the link points to becomes unreachable. A link may break because the Web server on which the destination page is stored goes down or because the page's author moves or renames the page. After a visitor clicks a broken hyperlink, instead of delivering the requested page, the destination Web server delivers an error message stating that it can't find the page. Major Web-surfing bummer.

The most common cause of broken hyperlinks — renaming a page in your Web site and then forgetting to update the hyperlinks elsewhere in the Web site that lead to the page — is a moot point in FrontPage. The program automatically updates hyperlinks for you if you rename or move a page. (I describe this feat of wonder in Chapter 15.)

Certain situations are beyond FrontPage's control, however, and cause hyperlinks in your Web site to break:

 ✔ You delete a file that another page in the Web site is linked to.

 ✔ You import an existing Web site into FrontPage and leave out some files.

 ✔ You mistype a URL while creating a hyperlink to a site on the Internet.

 ✔ You create a link to a site on the Internet, and that site changes location or otherwise becomes unreachable.

Fortunately, FrontPage comes with a little marvel called the Verify Hyperlinks command. The Verify Hyperlinks command

 ✔ Finds all the broken or unchecked links in your Web site and lists them in the Broken Hyperlinks report

 ✔ Checks links to external Internet sites to make sure they work properly

 ✔ Enables you to fix individual broken links

 ✔ Updates the corrected links in selected pages or throughout the entire Web site

Verifying hyperlinks

You need to find broken hyperlinks before you can fix them. Happily, FrontPage roots out broken hyperlinks for you.

Verifying hyperlinks involves locating broken internal links (links between pages and files that reside inside the Web site), and double-checking external links to make sure they work.

To verify the hyperlinks in your Web site, follow these steps:

1. **Activate your Internet connection.**

2. **Save all open pages, if you haven't already, by choosing File⇨Save All.**

3. **Choose View⇨Reports⇨Problems⇨Hyperlinks.**

   FrontPage switches from Design view to the Hyperlinks report in the Reports view. The report displays a list of broken internal hyperlinks and as-yet-unverified external hyperlinks, as shown in Figure 5-3. Broken internal links (if any exist) are flagged with the status label Broken and a broken chain link icon, and unverified external links are flagged with the label Unknown and a question mark icon.

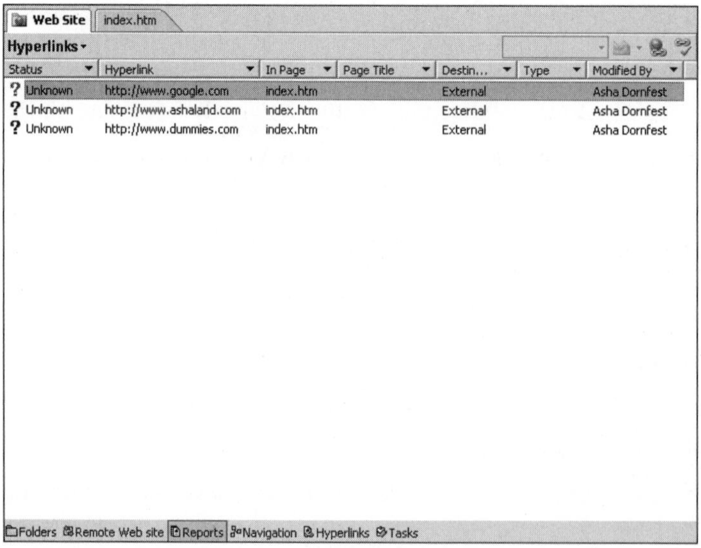

Status	Hyperlink	In Page	Page Title	Destin...	Type	Modified By
? Unknown	http://www.google.com	index.htm		External		Asha Dornfest
? Unknown	http://www.ashaland.com	index.htm		External		Asha Dornfest
? Unknown	http://www.dummies.com	index.htm		External		Asha Dornfest

Web Site | index.htm

Hyperlinks ▾

☐ Folders ⊞ Remote Web site ⊡ Reports ⅜ Navigation ⚓ Hyperlinks ⊕ Tasks

Figure 5-3:
The
Hyperlinks
report.

4. **In the top-right corner of the Hyperlinks report, click the Verifies Hyperlinks in the Current Web button.**

   The Verify Hyperlinks dialog box appears.

5. **In the dialog box, click the Start button.**

   If your Web site contains lots of external links, the verification process takes quite a while. Be sure that you have a few minutes to spare.

   After you click the Start button, FrontPage verifies each external link by contacting the destination Web server and then making sure that it can reach the page. As the verification process is going on, a progress message appears in the FrontPage status bar letting you know what's happening. As FrontPage checks each link, its status label in the report changes from a question mark to either a green check mark followed by OK (indicating valid links) or a broken chain link followed by Broken (indicating broken links). When the verification process is complete, FrontPage lists a summary of its findings in the status bar.

To stop the verification process, press the Esc key. To resume verifying hyperlinks, click the Verify Hyperlinks button again.

Fixing broken hyperlinks

If FrontPage finds any broken links, you need to fix them. To do so, follow these steps:

1. **If you haven't already, follow the steps in the preceding section, "Verifying hyperlinks."**

2. **From the Hyperlinks report, double-click the broken hyperlink you want to fix.**

   The Edit Hyperlink dialog box appears, as shown in Figure 5-4.

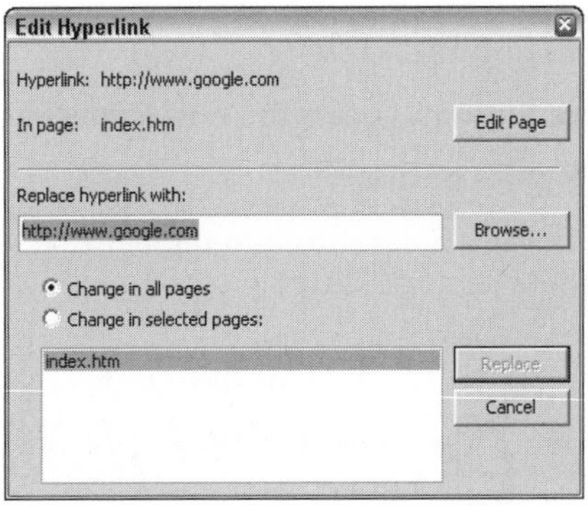

Figure 5-4:
The Edit
Hyperlink
dialog box.

3. **Decide whether you want to edit the page containing the hyperlink or update the hyperlink destination itself; then take the appropriate action.**

To edit the page containing the link, click the Edit Page button. The page opens in Design view so that you can fix the ailing link. When you switch back to the Reports view, repaired internal links disappear from the list, and the status of repaired external links change from Broken to Unknown. (FrontPage must verify the newly-edited link in order to give it a passing mark.)

To edit the link itself, in the Edit Hyperlink dialog box, type a new URL in the Replace Hyperlink With text box. If you can't recall the URL, click the Browse button to launch your Web browser. Browse to the destination, and when you switch back to FrontPage, the destination URL is visible in the text box. To change the link in selected pages (rather than throughout the entire Web site), select the Change in Selected Pages option button and then click the names of the pages you want to update in the box underneath. Click the Replace button to fix the hyperlink and close the dialog box.

4. **Continue repairing broken hyperlinks by repeating Steps 2 and 3.**

After you publish your finished site, I recommend verifying your site's hyperlinks at least every couple of weeks. Web pages move and change all the time, breaking hyperlinks in your Web site. FrontPage makes checking your links so easy — why not make it a regular habit?

Unlinking Hyperlinks

Suppose you became so intoxicated with the power of hyperlink creation that, looking at your page now, you see more links than regular text. Perhaps you overindulged. Perhaps removing a few links so that the others may shine would be wise. To obtain forgiveness for your excesses, follow these steps:

1. **Click the link you want to unlink.**

2. **Click the Insert Hyperlink button to open the Edit Hyperlink dialog box.**

3. **In the dialog box, click Remove Link.**

   The dialog box closes, and your link returns to regular text (or, if the link's a picture, returns to its original state).

Using Bookmarks to Define "Linkable" Areas inside a Page

A *bookmark* is an invisible spot inside a Web page that can be used as the destination of a link. Bookmarks enable you to control more closely where visitors end up after they click a hyperlink. A link without the benefit of a bookmark drops visitors off at the top of the destination page. When a visitor clicks a hyperlink that leads to a bookmark inside a page, the visitor jumps straight to the bookmark location.

To link to a bookmark in your page, you must first create the bookmark and then create the hyperlink that leads to the bookmark.

Creating bookmarks

A bookmark can be the current location of the cursor or any selected bit of text: a word, a phrase, or even a letter. Text defined as a bookmark looks (and acts) no different from regular text; the text is simply flagged with an invisible marker to which you can point a hyperlink.

To create a bookmark, follow these steps:

1. **In the page, select the clump of text you want to turn into a bookmark.**

   Or place the cursor in the location where you want the bookmark to sit without selecting any text.

   The bookmark eventually becomes the hyperlink destination.

2. **Choose Insert⇨Bookmark.**

   The Bookmark dialog box appears. If you selected text in Step 1, the text is visible in the Bookmark Name text box. (FrontPage wisely assumes that you want to give the bookmark the same name as the text it's made of.) Otherwise, the text box is empty.

3. **If the text box is empty (or if you want to choose a different name), in the Bookmark Name text box, type a brief name.**

   A good name describes the bookmark's function or location.

4. **Click OK.**

   The dialog box closes. If the bookmark is made of text, a dotted line appears underneath the selected text. If the bookmark is a single point, a flag icon appears at the location of the bookmark. (In real life, bookmarks are invisible. Visitors viewing your page with a browser can't distinguish bookmarks from regular text unless they sift through the page's underlying HTML code.)

5. **Click Save to save the new bookmark information.**

Linking to a bookmark

Bookmarks are like ballroom dancers: They need a partner to do their thing. Without a hyperlink, a bookmark is as lonely as a wallflower. Linking to bookmarks inside a page helps visitors find their way around long pages that otherwise require lots of scrolling and searching to navigate.

You can create a link at the top of the page to bookmarks in the interior of the same page so that visitors can jump around with swift clicks of the mouse. Likewise, you can create a link at the bottom of the page to a bookmark at the top of the page so that visitors don't have to scroll to return to the beginning of the page.

Any bookmark on any page in your Web site is an eligible candidate for a link. To forge this link, follow these steps:

1. **In the page, select the hyperlink source.**

   This step is the same as that for creating a regular link: Select the word, phrase, or picture you want to turn into a hyperlink.

2. **Click the Insert Hyperlink button to open the Insert Hyperlink dialog box.**

3. **In the dialog box's file list, click the page that contains the bookmark to which you want to link, and then click the Bookmark button.**

   Or, if the bookmark is in the same page as the hyperlink, in the dialog box's Link To area, click the Place in This Document icon.

   Depending on which item you click, either the Select Place in Document dialog box appears, or the Insert Hyperlink dialog box changes its options to display essentially the same information — the bookmarks inside the selected page.

4. **From the list of bookmarks, click the bookmark to which you want to link.**

5. **Click OK (and if the Insert Hyperlink dialog box is still open, click OK again to close it).**

   The dialog box closes, and the bookmark and hyperlink live happily ever after. (Trumpets sound.)

Dismantling bookmarks

Get rid of any bookmarks that outlive their usefulness. The procedure is quick and painless (for both you and the bookmark). If the bookmark is made up of text, right-click inside the bookmark you want to dismantle, and from the pop-up menu that appears, choose Bookmark Properties. In the Bookmark dialog box that appears, click Clear. If the bookmark is marked with a flag icon, place the cursor to the right of the flag icon and then press the Delete key.

Helping Visitors Find Their Way with Link Bars

As I was thinking of a way to explain link bars, a scene from a Saturday morning cartoon popped into my head. Bugs Bunny is lost in the desert, and while searching for an oasis, he comes upon a signpost stuck into sand. The signpost contains markers pointing every which way: "This way to Cairo," "This way to New York," "This way to Mars."

Link bars (also known as *navigation bars*) give your visitors a similar array of choices. Link bars are a collection of hyperlinks leading to the other pages inside your Web site. By placing a link bar inside each page of your site, you help your visitors find their way around. Think of link bars as signposts: "This way to the home page," "This way to the feedback form." With a single click, visitors are whisked off to the destination of their choice.

FrontPage gives you two methods for creating link bars. You can let FrontPage generate link bars based on a navigation structure you build, or you can create custom link bars containing links of your choosing. Each method has its advantages and disadvantages. Read on to find out more.

 If you want your link bar to appear in the same position inside more than one page in your Web site (a good Web design decision, in my opinion), place the link bar inside a *shared border*. I show you how to create and use shared borders later in this chapter.

Letting FrontPage generate a link bar

Wouldn't it be nice if you could map out your site — draw a flow chart illustrating how each of the site's pages relate to each other, and how a user would navigate the site — and let FrontPage create all the links between the pages based on that map? Well, you can. FrontPage can generate a link bar based on the layout of a map you create called a *navigation structure*. (The navigation structure lives in the FrontPage Navigation view, which you get to know in detail in Chapter 15.)

After you create a navigation structure, you can tell FrontPage to generate link bars based on the structure's different "levels" relative to the current page (that is, the placement in the structure of the page into which you're inserting the link bar).

Inserting a navigation structure-based link bar

FrontPage generates link bars based on the settings in the Link Bar Properties dialog box, as shown in Figure 5-5. (I show you how to access this dialog box in a moment.) The Hyperlinks to Add to Page section of the dialog box enables you to select the level of hyperlinks that appear in the link bar. Here's where the layout of the navigation structure makes a difference, because the layout determines which pages appear in each level.

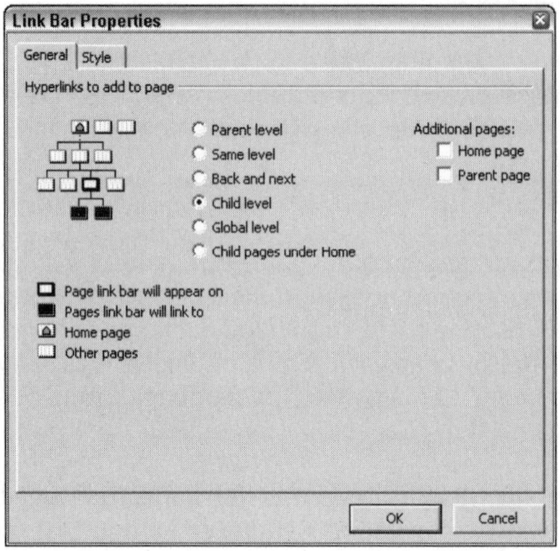

Figure 5-5:
The Link Bar Properties dialog box.

Your choices are as follows:

- ✔ **Parent Level:** This option lists hyperlinks leading to the pages in the level above the current page.

- ✔ **Same Level:** This option lists hyperlinks leading to the pages in the same level as the current page.

- ✔ **Back and Next:** In Web sites that rely on a linear, slideshow-like flow of information, this option lists hyperlinks to the previous page and the next page, both of which are on the same level as the current page.

- ✔ **Child Level:** This option lists hyperlinks leading to the pages in the level below the current page.

- ✔ **Global Level:** This option lists hyperlinks leading to pages that sit at the topmost level of the site.

- ✔ **Child Pages under Home:** This option lists hyperlinks leading to pages in the level beneath the site's entry page, regardless of the level of the current page.

You also can include links to two additional pages:

✔ **Home Page:** The home page is the site's entry page.

✔ **Parent Page:** The parent page sits in the level above the current page and contains a link to that page.

To insert a link bar based on the site's navigation structure, do the following:

1. **Using Navigation view, create a navigation structure for your site.**

   The chart doesn't need to be complete (you can add pages as you go along) but should at least reflect the site's core structure. I explain how to create a navigation structure in Chapter 15.

2. **Switch back to Design view and place the cursor where you want the link bar to appear on the page.**

   The following steps are easier if you make the Design view's Navigation Pane visible (do so by clicking the Navigation button at the bottom of the Folder List). The Navigation Pane displays the navigation structure you created in Navigation view. You'll want to refer to it when, in Step 7, you specify the link bar's contents.

3. **Choose Insert⇨Navigation.**

   The Insert Web Component dialog box appears, with the Link Bars component type selected.

4. **In the dialog box's Choose a Bar Type list box, click Bar Based On Navigation Structure, and then click Next.**

   New options appear in the dialog box, enabling you to choose how the link bar looks.

5. **In the Choose a Bar Style list box, click the illustration that reflects how you'd like the link bar to look, and then click Next.**

   Be sure to scroll down the Choose a Bar Style list box; FrontPage includes some elegant graphical possibilities. If you create a text-based link bar, you can change the text formatting using any of the FrontPage font tools (see Chapter 4 for details).

   After you click Next, new options that enable you to choose whether you want a horizontal or vertical link bar appear in the dialog box.

6. **In the Choose an Orientation box, click either the horizontal or vertical orientation illustration, and then click Finish.**

   That Finish button is a bit of a tease, as you're not actually finished. The Insert Web Component dialog box is replaced by the Link Bar Properties dialog box, which requires a few more mouse clicks.

7. **In the Hyperlinks to Add to Page section of the dialog box, choose the option(s) you want.**

   If you decide you want to change how the link bar looks, click the dialog box's Style tab, and choose new options. Otherwise. . . .

8. Click OK.

The dialog box closes, and the link bar appears in the page. Figure 5-6 illustrates one example of a navigation structure-based link bar.

Figure 5-6:
A link bar.

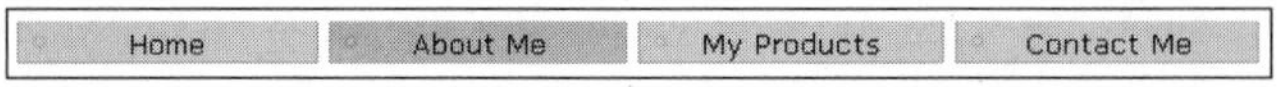

| Home | About Me | My Products | Contact Me |

If an italicized message appears in the page where the link bar buttons should be, some sort of problem exists. Chances are that you chose a link bar setting that conflicts with the page's placement in the navigation structure. For example, the page sits at the bottom level of the chart, and you specified that the link bar should contain Child level links — none of which exist. Or you may have attempted to insert a link bar into a page that hasn't yet been added to the navigation structure, and therefore FrontPage has no way to construct the link bar. The message appears only in FrontPage to alert you to a link bar problem; when you preview the page using a Web browser, you don't see a thing.

To change the link bar's settings, double-click the message to display the Link Bar Properties dialog box, choose new options, and then click OK. You may also switch to Navigation view to reshuffle the navigation structure or to add or remove link bar links. (I show you how to do so in the following section.)

Adding links to a navigation structure-based link bar

As you add new pages to your Web site, you can easily add them to the navigation structure. When you do, links to those pages automatically appear in the site's link bars. (See Chapter 15 for instructions on how to add pages to your navigation structure.)

Although the main purpose of navigation bars is to help visitors get around inside your Web site, FrontPage gives you the option to add link bar links that point to external Web sites as well. To do so, follow these steps:

1. In the main FrontPage window, click the Web Site tab.

FrontPage's site administration tools become visible.

2. At the bottom of the window, click the Navigation icon to switch to Navigation view.

3. Click anywhere inside the navigation structure, and then, in the top-right corner of Navigation view, click the Add Existing Page button.

Don't confuse the Add Existing Page button on the Navigation toolbar with the Insert Hyperlink button on the Standard toolbar. They look the same, but they do different things.

After you click the Add Existing Page button, the Insert Hyperlink dialog box appears.

4. **In the dialog box, specify the page or file to which you want to link.**

   The options in this dialog box enable you to select any page or file inside the current Web site or its subsites, or to specify a URL pointing to an external site. For details on how to use this dialog box, see the previous section in this chapter, "The Hyperlink Two-Step."

5. **Click OK.**

   The dialog box closes, and an icon corresponding to the new link appears in the navigation structure. To change the icon's placement, drag it to a new location inside the structure.

Removing links from a navigation structure-based link bar

You may eventually want to add a page to the navigation structure, but not have a link to the page appear inside the site's link bars. Here's how to exclude pages from link bars:

1. **In Navigation view, click the icon in the navigation structure that corresponds to the page that you want to exclude from link bars.**

2. **In the top-right corner of Navigation view, click the Included in Link Bars button to toggle the link bar setting.**

   The icon changes color indicating that a link to the page no longer appears in the site's link bars.

When you exclude a page from link bars, FrontPage automatically excludes that page's Child pages as well. If you want to restore those pages' positions in link bars, click their respective icons and then click the Included in Link Bars button. Note also that pages excluded from link bars can't contain FrontPage page banners (I tell you about page banners in Chapter 12).

Changing the button labels on a navigation structure-based link bar

If your link bar is made up of graphic buttons, you might find that some of the text labels are too long to fit on top of the button. To change the label text, do this:

1. **In Navigation view or the Navigation Pane of the Folder List, click the icon that corresponds to the label you want to change.**

   The icon turns blue.

2. **In the icon, click the text label.**

   The text label becomes highlighted.

3. **Type a new text label and then press Enter.**

4. **Switch back to Design view (or, if you're already in Design view, click inside the open page) and, if necessary, click the Refresh button on the Standard toolbar to display the label change.**

When you change a text label in the navigation structure, FrontPage uses the label as the page title. (If you're not sure why this matters, flip to Chapter 2 and read the section about saving a page on your computer or network.) To change the page title while leaving the navigation structure label unchanged, in the Design view's Folder List or Navigation Pane, right-click the page's icon, and choose Properties from the pop-up menu that appears. In the Properties dialog box that appears, type a new title in the Title text box, and then click OK.

Creating a custom link bar

If your site's structure isn't straightforward enough to fit within the limitations of the FrontPage navigation structure setup, you can still take advantage of link bars. You can create custom link bars that are independent of the site's navigation structure. Custom link bars require a little more initial work than navigation structure-based link bars, but they are more flexible and will save you lots of time as your site grows. You can also create several custom link bars that you can insert in different pages or sections of your Web site.

Custom link bars work only if you publish your site on a host server that has the 2002 (or later) version of FrontPage Server Extensions installed. I talk about FrontPage Server Extensions in more detail in Chapter 17.

Inserting a custom link bar

You can insert a customized link bar by following these steps:

1. **In the page, place the cursor where you want the link bar to appear.**

2. **Choose Insert⇨Navigation.**

   The Insert Web Component dialog box appears, with the Link Bars component type selected.

3. **In the dialog box's Choose a Bar Type list box, click Bar with Custom Links, and then click Next.**

   New options appear in the dialog box. These options enable you to choose how the link bar looks.

4. **In the Choose a Bar Style list box, click the illustration that reflects how you'd like the link bar to look, and then click Next.**

   After you click Next, new options that enable you to choose whether you want a horizontal or vertical link bar appear in the dialog box.

5. In the Choose an Orientation box, click either the horizontal or vertical orientation illustration, and then click Finish.

Nope, you're not really finished. The Insert Web Component dialog box closes, and the Create New Link Bar dialog box appears, prompting you to name your custom link bar.

6. In the dialog box's Name text box, type a brief name.

Depending on the setup of your Web site, you can create more than one custom link bar (say, one link bar for the site's top-level pages, and another for the site's individual sections). So choose a name that reminds you of the link bar's placement or purpose in the site.

7. Click OK.

The dialog box closes, and the Link Bar Properties dialog box appears, as shown in Figure 5-7. Note that, despite the same name, this dialog box is different than the dialog box that appears when you create a link bar based on your site's navigation structure.

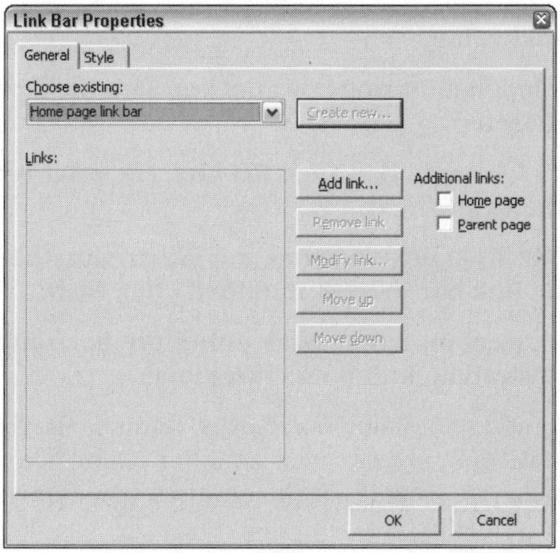

Figure 5-7:
The Link Bar Properties dialog box appears when you insert a custom link bar into your page.

8. In the dialog box, click the Add Link button.

The Add to Link Bar dialog box appears. This dialog box looks and acts very much like the Insert Hyperlink dialog box. For instructions on how to use this dialog box, refer to the section, "The Hyperlink Two-Step," earlier in this chapter.

9. In the dialog box, specify the details for the first hyperlink in the custom link bar, and then click OK.

The Add to Link Bar dialog box closes, and the Link Bar Properties dialog box comes back into view.

10. **To add another link, repeat Steps 8 and 9 as many times as is necessary to complete the link bar.**

    If you want the link bar to contain links to the home page or the current page's parent page, in the Add to Link Bar dialog box, select the corresponding check boxes.

11. **When the link bar is complete, click OK in the Link Bar Properties dialog box.**

    The dialog box closes, and a placeholder for the link bar appears in the page.

FrontPage can also generate link bars containing a linear set of back and next links. These link bars lead the visitor through links you specify sequentially (similar to a slide show). You can either create a new custom link bar with back and next links, or you can convert a link bar you created earlier.

To insert back and next links into a page, do the following:

1. **In the page, place the cursor where you want the link bar to appear.**

2. **Choose Insert➪Navigation.**

    The Insert Web Component dialog box appears, with the Link Bars component type selected.

3. **In the dialog box's Choose a Bar Type list box, click Bar with Back and Next Links, and then click Next.**

4. **In the Choose a Bar Style list box, click the illustration that reflects how you'd like the link bar to look, and then click Next.**

5. **In the Choose an Orientation box, click either the horizontal or vertical orientation illustration, and then click Finish.**

    The Insert Web Component dialog box closes. If this is the first custom link bar you're creating, the Create New Link Bar dialog box appears, prompting you to choose a name for the new link bar. Type a brief name in the dialog box's Name text box and then click OK. The dialog box closes, and the Link Bar Properties dialog box becomes visible.

    If you've created other custom link bars, the Link Bar Properties dialog box appears.

6. **If you're converting an *existing* custom link bar into a back-and-next link bar (as opposed to creating a new link bar), choose the link bar's name from the Choose Existing list box.**

7. **Add links to the new link bar, or modify the existing link bar you selected in Step 6.**

    Follow the previous set of steps in this section for detailed instructions.

8. **When the link bar is complete, click OK in the Link Bar Properties dialog box.**

    The dialog box closes, and a hyperlink with the text Next appears on the page. If you open each successive page represented in the link bar and add a back-and-next link bar to those pages (or, if you place the link bar inside a shared border, a task that's explained later in this chapter), FrontPage keeps track of the pages' sequence and inserts the appropriate links. Pretty neat.

If you don't like the words *Back* and *Next*, you can change them. To do so, choose Tools⇨Site Settings to display the Site Settings dialog box. In the dialog box, click the Navigation tab, type different labels into the appropriate text boxes, and then click OK to close the dialog box.

Editing a custom link bar

Custom link bars are easy to change. To do so, double-click the link bar on the page to display the Link Bar Properties dialog box. In the dialog box, make any changes you like:

- Change the order of the links by clicking the link names in the Links list box and then clicking the Move Up or the Move Down button.
- Change link text or destinations by clicking the link name and then clicking the Modify button.
- Add new links by clicking the Add Link button.
- Remove links by clicking the Remove Link button.

When you're done making changes, click OK to close the dialog box.

Deleting a link bar

If FrontPage link bars don't do the trick for your site, you can delete any link bar and create hyperlinks the old-fashioned way. In the Design view Folder List, click the Navigation icon to display the Navigation Pane. The Navigation Pane contains an icon for each custom link bar you've created. To delete a link bar, click its icon and then press the Delete key. The Delete Link Bar dialog box appears, explaining that, by deleting the link bar, you also remove the link bar from any other pages in which it's currently sitting. Click OK to proceed.

If you simply want to remove a link bar from a page, but you don't want to delete the link bar altogether, click the link bar on the page to select it, and then press the Delete key.

If you like the functionality of link bars but not the FrontPage link bar setup, you can create linked buttons and tabs individually. I show you how to create these interactive buttons in Chapter 12. Another option is to create a *jump list*: a drop-down menu of linked items. You find out about jump menus (and other fun effects) in Chapter 13.

Using shared borders to automatically display link bars throughout your site

Well-designed Web sites are easy to get around. Link bars help in this regard, but to be truly effective, link bars must appear in every page in the Web site — ideally in the same spot in each page. Consistently designed pages help visitors familiarize themselves with your site's layout. The more they explore, the easier finding their way becomes for them.

To help you maintain a consistent layout in your Web pages, FrontPage provides a feature called *shared borders*. Shared borders enable you to place items — link bars, page banners, copyright notices, logos, or anything else — in the margins of your pages, and to have those items automatically appear in the same position in every page in your Web site.

You can use shared borders anytime you want to include something on every page, but I find that shared borders really show their stuff when paired with link bars and page banners (you find out about page banners in Chapter 12). By placing a link bar inside a shared border, you avoid having to manually add a link bar to each page. Not only that, FrontPage automatically updates the link bar throughout the site as you change and add to the link bar or the site's navigation structure.

If you like the notion of shared content but don't want that content to sit along the borders of the page, investigate the Included Content components, which I describe along with other Web components in Chapter 12. For a more systemic approach to included content, read Chapter 16 about Dynamic Web Templates.

To add shared borders to your Web site, follow these steps:

1. **Choose Format⇨Shared Borders.**

   The Shared Borders dialog box appears, as shown in Figure 5-8.

   Note: If the Shared Borders menu item appears grayed-out, you simply need to update your Web server platform settings. To do so, choose Tools⇨Page Options to display the Page Options dialog box. In the Authoring tab, be sure the Shared Borders check box is selected, and then click OK to close the dialog box.

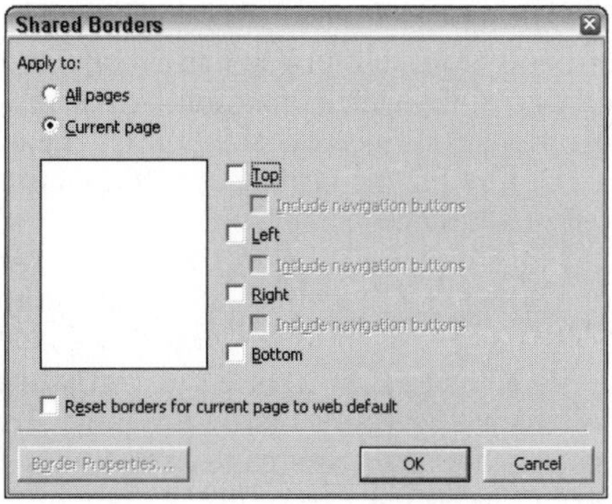

Shared Borders

Apply to:
- ○ All pages
- ● Current page

- ☐ Top
  - ☐ Include navigation buttons
- ☐ Left
  - ☐ Include navigation buttons
- ☐ Right
  - ☐ Include navigation buttons
- ☐ Bottom

☐ Reset borders for current page to web default

[Border Properties...]   [OK]   [Cancel]

Figure 5-8:
The Shared Borders dialog box.

2. **In the dialog box's Apply To section, select the All Pages option button, and then select the check boxes that correspond to the areas in your page where you want to place shared items.**

   For example, if you want a link bar to appear on the left side of every page in your Web site, click the Left check box.

   If you want FrontPage to include standard link bars in the top, left, or right border, mark the corresponding Include Navigation Buttons check boxes. I find that adding link bars by hand is easier, but if you'd rather let FrontPage pick up some of the work, by all means, give this feature a try. You can always change the link bar settings later.

3. **To give the shared border a background color or background picture, click the Border Properties button in the Shared Borders dialog box, choose options from the Border Properties dialog box, and then click OK to close the Border Properties dialog box.**

   Shared border formatting is visible only on Web sites published on host Web servers that support the 2002 (or later) version of FrontPage Server Extensions. If you publish your site on a server that doesn't support FrontPage Server Extensions or that has an older version installed, the shared border *content* will appear, but the *background formatting* will not.

4. **Click OK to close the Shared Borders dialog box.**

   The dialog box closes, and FrontPage applies the selected borders to each page in your site.

When you next open the pages in Design view, you see dotted lines demarcating the shared borders at the margins of the page. The space inside the shared border boundary acts no differently from the rest of the page, except that when you add anything to a shared border, that item appears in the same position in every page in the Web site.

When you look at the page using a Web browser, the dotted lines disappear, and only the shared border content is visible. You can change or turn off shared border settings for individual pages. For example, you may want link bars to appear in every page of your site except the home page. In that case, you can turn off the shared borders for the home page, but maintain shared borders in the rest of your site.

To change the shared border settings for an individual page, do the following:

1. **To change shared border settings in the page currently open in Design view, click the cursor anywhere inside the page. To change shared border settings in more than one page in this site, select the pages you want to edit in the Folder List while pressing the Ctrl key.**

2. **Choose Format⇨Shared Borders.**

   The Shared Borders dialog box appears.

3. **In the dialog box's Apply To section, click the Current Page option button (if you've selected more than one page, the Selected Page(s) option button appears there instead), and make whatever changes you like.**

   To return to the Web site's original shared border settings, click the Reset Borders for Current Page to Web Default check box.

4. **Click OK.**

   The dialog box closes, and FrontPage changes the border settings accordingly.

Embedding More Than One Hyperlink in a Picture

An *image map* is simply a picture that contains more than one hyperlink. Visitors activate the different hyperlinks in the image map by clicking different places inside the picture (see Figure 5-9).

The clickable areas of the picture are called *hotspots*. Hotspots work just like regular hyperlinks; they can link to an e-mail address, a downloadable file, or another location in the Web site or on the Internet. Most often, however, image maps contain links to other places inside the Web site.

FrontPage contains tools you use to "draw" hotspots on the picture of your choice. Hotspots are visible to you as you work with the image map in Front Page, but when visitors look at your page with a Web browser, hotspots are invisible. (Visitors see only the image map graphic.)

Each "button" is a clickable link

Figure 5-9:
The
"buttons"
show
visitors
where to
click to
activate a
hyperlink.

You don't want to turn just any old picture into an image map. Because hotspots are invisible to the visitor, the picture you choose should clearly indicate where to click, either with the help of a visual metaphor (the example pictured in Figure 5-9 uses buttons) or with text labels. The ideal image map picture doesn't require explanation; the clickable areas should be obvious.

Don't worry if you can't get your hands on the ideal image map graphic. Even though image map hotspots are invisible when visitors view your page with a Web browser, the pointer changes shape and the hotspot's destination address appears in the browser's status bar when a visitor hovers the pointer over a hotspot. These clues are enough to prompt most visitors to click.

After you choose your picture, open the page in which you want the image map to appear and then insert the picture into the page. (Flip ahead to Chapter 6 if you're not sure how to insert a picture.)

If you use an image map in your Web site, consider including a corresponding list of text hyperlinks somewhere else in the page. Visitors who surf the Web with their browsers' image-loading function turned off (or who use text-only browsers) cannot see regular pictures or image maps and, therefore, must rely on the text hyperlinks to move around.

Adding hotspots to a picture

After you find the right picture and insert it in your page, you're ready to draw the hotspots.

You use tools available on the Pictures toolbar to draw hotspots. You can draw rectangles, circles, and multisided shapes (polygons) around the areas you want to make clickable.

Don't confuse drawing hotspots with the graphic shapes you can create using FrontPage's drawing tools. I explain how to work with drawing tools in Chapter 6.

To draw hotspots on a picture, follow these steps:

1. **Open the page containing the image map graphic and then click the picture.**

2. **Select View⇨Toolbars⇨Pictures.**

   The Pictures toolbar appears.

3. **In the page, click the image map graphic to select it, and then, in the Pictures toolbar, click the Rectangular Hotspot, Circular Hotspot, or Polygonal Hotspot button.**

   Pick the shape that resembles the shape of the area you want to turn into a hotspot. You can always move or reshape the hotspot later, or delete the hotspot and start over.

4. **Move the pointer over the picture.**

   The pointer turns into a little pencil.

5. **Click the hotspot area and drag the cursor until the resulting hotspot surrounds the area.**

   Where to click depends on the shape you chose. Here's what to do for the different hotspot shapes:

   • **Rectangle:** Click the corner of the hotspot area and drag the rectangle until the shape surrounds the area.

   • **Circle:** Click the center of the hotspot area and drag. (The circle expands from its center point.)

   • **Polygon:** Creating a polygonal hotspot is like playing connect the dots, only you decide where the dots are: Click the first point, release the mouse button, and then move the pointer. (This action produces a line.) Stretch the line to the second point — click, stretch, click, stretch — until you enclose your hotspot area. After you've finished defining the hotspot, click the hotspot's starting point, and FrontPage closes the hotspot for you.

You can overlap hotspots. If you do so, the most recent hotspot is on top, which means this hotspot takes priority if a visitor clicks the overlapped area.

After you draw the hotspot, the hotspot border appears on top of your picture, and the Insert Hyperlink dialog box appears, enabling you to associate a hyperlink with the hotspot.

6. **Create a link for the hotspot, just as you would a regular hyperlink.**

7. **Keep creating hotspots until you define all the clickable areas inside the picture.**

   Areas not covered by a hotspot don't do anything if clicked unless you specify a *default hyperlink.* (I show you how to do this later in this chapter.)

8. **When you're finished, click anywhere outside the picture to hide the hotspot borders.**

 For a quick look at all the hotspots inside the picture, click the Highlight Hotspots button on the Pictures toolbar. The picture becomes blank, and only the hotspot borders are visible. To return to the regular display, click the Highlight Hotspots button again.

To move a hotspot, click the hotspot and then drag it to a new position.

To reshape a hotspot, click the hotspot to make its size handles visible (those little square dots along the hotspot border), and then click a handle and drag it until the hotspot looks the way you want. Size handles act differently, depending on the shape of the hotspot. Working with handles is not a precise science. Just keep clicking, dragging, and stretching until you're happy with the results.

To change a hotspot's hyperlink, click the picture to make the hotspots visible and then double-click the hotspot to open the Edit Hyperlink dialog box. Make any changes you want and then click OK to close the dialog box.

To delete a hotspot, click the hotspot and then press the Backspace or Delete key.

Drawing labeled hotspots

Hotspots are most effective when the area of the picture that visitors are supposed to click is obvious. If the clickable area isn't readily apparent, you might want to label a hotspot with descriptive text. To draw a labeled hotspot, do this:

1. **In the page, click the picture.**

   The Pictures toolbar appears. (If not, choose View⇨Toolbars⇨Pictures.)

2. **On the Pictures toolbar, click the Text button.**

   A rectangular hotspot with a flashing insertion point appears in the center of the picture.

3. **Type a descriptive text label.**

4. **Click anywhere outside the hotspot to deselect it.**

   Now you need to specify the hotspot's hyperlink.

5. **In the picture, double-click the text hotspot.**

   The Insert Hyperlink dialog box appears.

6. **Create a link for the hotspot and, when you're finished, click any-where outside the picture.**

To change the label's text, click the hotspot to select it, click inside the text label, and then type new text. You can also format the text by using any of the text tools on the Formatting toolbar or in the Font dialog box (available by choosing Format⇨Font).

Setting the default hyperlink

The final (and optional) step in creating an image map is setting the image map's *default hyperlink*. Visitors jump to the destination of the default hyperlink if they click anywhere on the image map not covered by a hotspot. If you forgo the default hyperlink, clicking an undefined area does nothing.

In general, I recommend skipping this step. Visitors expecting to click hotspots may get confused when they click outside a hotspot (which, intu-itively, should accomplish nothing) and are still sent to a different location. However, if you find it makes sense for your image map to have a default hyperlink, feel free to add one.

To set an image map's default hyperlink, follow these steps:

1. **Right-click the image map and then choose Picture Properties from the pop-up menu that appears.**

   The Picture Properties dialog box appears with the Appearance tab visible.

2. **In the dialog box, click the General tab to make the options on the tab visible.**

3. **In the Default Hyperlink area of the tab, type the default hyperlink's URL in the Location text box.**

   If you can't remember the URL, click the Browse button to display the Edit Hyperlink dialog box. I explain how to use this dialog box in the "Editing Hyperlinks" section, earlier in this chapter.

   After you specify the URL, click OK to close the Edit Hyperlink dialog box. The Picture Properties dialog box becomes visible again, with the default hyperlink's URL visible in the Location text box.

4. **Click OK to close the dialog box.**

   FrontPage applies the default hyperlink to the image map.

To test-drive the image map, preview your page and click away. (Refer to Chapter 2 if you're not sure how.)

Chapter 6

You Oughta Be in Pictures

● ●

In This Chapter

▶ Understanding how graphics affect your page

▶ Adding pictures and clip art to your page

▶ Editing the appearance and placement of pictures

▶ Deleting pictures

▶ Using thumbnails to reduce your page's download time

▶ Displaying your photographs in a photo gallery

▶ Creating a background image

▶ Working with AutoShapes and WordArt

● ●

*T*ext is important. Text is, in fact, the foundation of your Web site, the basic building block of a page, blah, blah, blah. Although that statement is essentially true, let's be honest — the Web hasn't achieved global fame because it contains a bunch of words. The pairing of information and pictures is what transforms the Web from a heap of data into a colorful adventure.

Web graphics, when used properly, create a mood and help visitors navigate your site. But, as with all Web design effects, too much of a good thing can be toxic. Cheesy clip art detracts from the site's overall image and, worse, slows its load time.

In this chapter, I let you in on tricks to keep your graphics looking good and loading fast. And, of course, I show you how to use the graphics capabilities of FrontPage.

Bitmaps and Drawn Graphics . . . They're Two Different Animals

FrontPage enables you to add two fundamentally different types of graphics to your Web pages: *bitmaps* and *drawn graphics*. I won't spend time explaining the technical differences between the two, but having a general sense of their capabilities helps you better understand your options.

Most often, when working with graphics in Web pages, you're working with *bitmaps*. Bitmaps are made up of bunches of colored dots (or *bits*). As such, these graphics can't be resized without losing quality and falling prey to *the jaggies* (the unsightly ragged edges that appear when you change a bitmap's size).

Drawn graphics (also known as *vector graphics*) are composed of lines and curves. Because these graphics are essentially the result of mathematical calculations by the computer, they can be stretched, reshaped, grouped together, colored, and generally messed with any which way without losing quality. Using FrontPage's drawing tools, you can create and manipulate shapes, lines, fancy text known as WordArt, and plenty more.

Because bitmaps and drawn graphics have such different qualities and capabilities, I talk about them separately in this chapter. Most of the chapter is devoted to bitmaps, as you'll use this type of graphic most often in your Web site. I discuss drawn graphics at the end of the chapter.

Understanding the Quirks of Web Graphics

Web graphics can bewilder the novice Web publisher. No need to worry. As long as you stick to the guidelines in this chapter, you should have a graphic-filled, stress-free Web publishing experience.

Getting to know the Web-friendly bitmap formats

The alphabet soup of bitmap graphic file formats is enough to send anyone into fits of intimidation. Good news: Web-friendly graphics come in only three flavors: GIF, JPEG, and PNG. The GIF format is the most commonly used format on the Web. The JPEG format can stuff a wide range of color into a small file size. The PNG format is the new kid on the block and surpasses both GIF and JPEG in many ways, but PNG lacks widespread browser support.

Which format do you choose? The definitive answer is . . . it depends. GIF displays a maximum of 256 colors and is therefore best suited to high-contrast, flat color pictures, such as logos and cartoons. The GIF format has a few

---

Is it pronounced GIF or JIF?

A dispute rages in the Web publishing community over the pronunciation of the acronym GIF. Is GIF pronounced with a hard *g*, as in *graphic*, or is the term pronounced *jif*, like the peanut butter brand? I say GIF with a hard *g* (after all, GIF stands for *Graphic Interchange Format*), but know-it-alls live in both camps (including the creator of the GIF format, who says *jif*). No matter how you say GIF, prepare to be corrected.

---

extra cards up its sleeve: transparency and interlacing, both of which I discuss later in the chapter. JPEG can display thousands of colors, so this format is your best choice for pictures containing subtle color changes or a wide range of color, such as photographs and complex digital art.

What about PNG? This format, developed specifically for Web use, is the wave of the future. PNG is able to display more colors than GIF, and contains more transparency options than both GIF and JPEG, to name only two of its virtues.

PNG may eventually replace GIF and JPEG as the standard image format on the Web. Unfortunately, browser support for PNG files is still taking hold. Only recent versions of advanced browsers, such as Netscape Navigator (Version 4.0 or later) and Microsoft Internet Explorer (Version 4.0 or later), display the format. Older or less sophisticated browsers are left in the dust. Therefore, until most Web surfers use PNG-compatible browsers, you're wise to stick with GIF and JPEG.

To find out more about Web graphics, take a look at `builder.cnet.com/webbuilding/0-3883-8-4892140-1.html`. And if you want to know more about PNG, check out `www.libpng.org/pub/png/pngintro.html`.

FrontPage takes the guesswork out of file formats because it automatically converts most Web-challenged formats into GIF or JPEG. I talk more about the conversion process in the "Adding a Picture to Your Page" section, later in this chapter.

Picky palettes

GIFs can display a range, or *palette,* of 256 colors. The tricky thing about color palettes, however, is that the colors are operating system specific. In other words, a particular color might look different when you view it on a PC running Windows, a PC running Linux, or a Mac. Bright colors look about the same, but pastel colors may appear surprisingly different on different platforms.

If your graphic contains a color that isn't present in your visitor's system palette, your visitor's Web browser attempts to display the color by *dithering* — that is, by mixing two other colors in a checkerboard pattern to approximate the color in the graphic. Dithered graphics, while better than nothing, lack clarity and definition.

You can reduce dithering by sticking to the *browser-safe* palette for your Web graphics (the palette is built into most graphics programs today). This palette gives you a range of 216 colors available to most of your visitors, whatever their browser or platform. If you create graphics by using these colors or apply this palette to the graphics that you convert to GIF, the dithering problem shrinks considerably.

Unfortunately, even the browser-safe palette isn't foolproof. Most people browsing the Web today enjoy millions of colors on their monitors, and yet, different browser versions still spit out color variations. Using the browser-safe palette is still your best bet, however — it will keep your graphics looking good to most of your visitors.

For more opinions about the browser-safe palette, visit `www.lynda.com/ hex.html`. On this page, graphic guru Lynda Weinman says the browser-safe palette is no longer necessary, but also gives good reasons why one might want to use it anyway. For a different viewpoint (and a more in-depth look at the state of Web color), read the technical-but-fascinating article at `hotwired.lycos.com/webmonkey/00/37/index2a.html?tw=design`.

Keeping graphics zippy

If your visitors must wait more than a few seconds for your site to appear in their browsers, your site risks falling victim to *clickitis,* a chronic condition that causes surfers to click elsewhere whenever they must wait a moment for something to download. Keeping load times brief prevents clickitis. Here are some ways to ensure that your graphics don't drag:

- ✔ **Reduce image dimensions.** Wherever possible, keep the picture file's dimensions small.

- ✔ **Limit colors.** You can shave precious seconds off the download time while maintaining your picture's quality if you use a graphics program to reduce the number of colors in your pictures.

- ✔ **Keep resolution low.** Save your graphic files at a resolution of 72 ppi (pixels per inch). This resolution, while too low for high-quality print images, works just fine for images that are displayed on a computer monitor. Anything higher and you're adding unnecessary bulk to your graphic's file size.

✔ **Repeat pictures.** As much as possible, use the same pictures throughout your site. Web browsers *cache* graphic files, which means that the browser saves a copy of the picture on the visitor's hard drive. The first time someone visits your site, the browser downloads the graphic files from the host server. After the initial download, the browser displays the cached files instead — which load almost instantly.

FrontPage displays a rough estimate of the page's download time on the right side of the status bar. If you click the time estimate, you can select a different connection speed and watch the time estimate change. Keep an eye on the download time as you add graphics to your page.

Practicing graphic restraint

Pictures are the road hogs of the Information Superhighway, but pictures make the Web such a pleasant drive. A conscientious Web publisher balances these opposing forces by using pictures judiciously and firing the bulk of the creative power into the site's text content.

The "more is better" trap is easy to fall into when adding pictures to your site. I urge you to practice restraint. Each additional picture increases the overall load time of the page and should only be added if seeing the picture is worth the wait. Use only those pictures that communicate your site's purpose and make getting around the site easier or more pleasant for your target audience.

Finally, make sure your visitors can understand your site without the pictures. Some surfers turn off their browser's image-loading option to speed up browsing sessions. (I show you how to deal with this situation in the section "Specifying alternative text," later in this chapter.)

Adding a Picture to Your Page

When you insert a picture in a Web page, FrontPage adds a reference inside the page's HTML tags that points to the location of the graphic file. The reference tells the visitor's browser to display the picture inside the page at the location of the reference. In other words, when you look at a Web page that contains pictures, you're actually looking at more than one file simultaneously: the Web page (the file that contains the text and the references to the pictures) and each individual graphic file.

Inserting a picture is similar creating a hyperlink because you simply link two different files: the Web page and the graphic file. So, like a hyperlink, a picture reference can point to a graphic file stored inside the Web site or on a remote Web server.

If the graphic files that you want to display in your Web site aren't already saved in a Web-friendly format, you're in luck: FrontPage automatically converts BMP, TIF, WMF, RAS, EPS, PCX, PCD, and TGA files to GIF or JPEG. (FrontPage converts graphics with 256 or fewer colors into GIF, and it converts graphics with more than 256 colors into JPEG.) FrontPage also knows how to insert PNGs into your pages, but because older browsers don't support PNG, I recommend sticking with GIF and JPEG for now.

If you want greater control over the conversion process, you should first open and convert your graphic file in a program specifically geared toward graphic work, such as Adobe Photoshop or Photoshop Elements, or Jasc Paint Shop Pro. By the way, you can download a fully functional trial version of Paint Shop Pro for free at www.jasc.com. If you get hooked on this program (as I think you might), turn to *Paint Shop Pro 7 For Dummies*, by David C. Kay (Wiley Publishing, Inc.) for help. If you'd like to try Photoshop Elements, download a trial version at www.adobe.com/products/tryadobe/main.jhtml#product=40.

Most graphics programs enable you to tweak any aspect of the graphic file and then save the file in the Web-friendly format of your choice.

Inserting a picture

If you have graphics already stored on your computer or network, plugging the pictures into a page is easy. Follow these steps:

1. **In Design View, open the page into which you want to insert the graphic, and then place the cursor where you want the picture to appear.**

   FrontPage only knows how to place the cursor inside a line of text or at the bottom of the page. If the cursor location doesn't exactly correspond to where you want the picture to sit inside your page, just do the best you can. I talk about other ways to position pictures later in this chapter.

2. **On the Standard toolbar, click the Insert Picture from File button.**

   The Picture dialog box appears, as shown in Figure 6-1. The dialog box displays a list of your computer's files and folders.

3. **In the dialog box's file list, navigate to the location of the picture that you want to insert, and then double-click the file's icon.**

   The dialog box closes, and the picture appears inside the page.

The next time you save the page, the Save Embedded Files dialog box appears and asks whether you want to import the inserted picture into the Web site. Click OK to import the file. See Chapter 2 for more details on how this dialog box works.

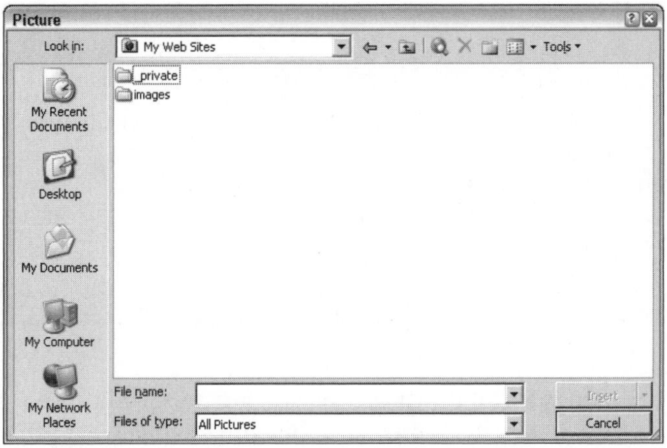

Picture

Look in:	My Web Sites

_private
images

My Recent
Documents

Desktop

My Documents

My Computer

My Network
Places

File name:
Files of type: | All Pictures

Insert
Cancel

Figure 6-1:
The Picture
dialog box.

You can copy a picture from another application and paste the picture into your page directly from the Clipboard. You can also drag a graphic file from the Folder List, your desktop, or Windows Explorer and drop the file into the page.

Using clip art

FrontPage gives you access to a bevy of colorful images that you can use to adorn your Web site. When you installed FrontPage, the program quietly slipped a bunch of clip art onto your hard drive.

To insert FrontPage clip art into a Web page, follow these steps:

1. **In the page, place the cursor where you want the clip art to appear.**

2. **Choose Insert➪Picture➪Clip Art.**

   The Clip Art task pane appears.

3. **To find clip art, in the task pane, type a key word in the Search For text box, and then click the Go button.**

   For example, if you type the word **cake**, FrontPage finds all the clips containing images of cake.

   You can narrow the search by choosing a search location from the Search In list box, or by selecting file types from the Results Should Be list box.

   After you click the Go button, the contents of the task pane change to display the results of the clip art search. FrontPage displays thumbnail images of the pieces of clip art (and, if relevant, other multimedia clips such as sounds and videos) that match your search criteria.

Gobs of graphics

Where do you find ready-made pictures to plop into your Web site? In addition to FrontPage clip art, plenty of excellent Web galleries encourage you to grab their pictures for your own personal use. Start with the Free Graphics collection at www.freegraphics.com.

Or decorate your Web site with a FrontPage theme. Themes contain nice-looking banner and button graphics and can easily spice up an entire Web site. I talk about themes in Chapter 11.

4. **If necessary, scroll down the Results box to see all the art FrontPage found for you. When you see an image you like, click the image to insert it into your page.**

   Each piece of clip art is huge. You can adjust the dimensions of an image by using the Picture Properties dialog box. I explain how in the "Setting display dimensions" section, later in this chapter.

The next time you save your page, the Save Embedded Files dialog box offers to import the clip art file into your Web site. Click OK to import the file. (For more details on how to save pages containing pictures, refer to Chapter 2.)

FrontPage's clip art search-and-retrieval system is actually a separate program called the Microsoft Clip Organizer. The Clip Organizer can do much more than display clip art based on a simple search. The program can catalog all the image and multimedia clips on your computer, organize them into related groups called *collections,* and even grab clips from the Web.

To find out more about how the Clip Organizer works, click the <u>Organize Clips</u> link in the Clip Art task pane. The Microsoft Clip Organizer dialog box appears. (If you haven't yet cataloged the contents of your computer with the Clip Organizer, the Add Clips to Organizer dialog box appears. If you'd like to run the catalog operation, click the Now button in the dialog box. Otherwise, click the Later button.) In the Microsoft Clip Organizer dialog box, choose Help⇨Clip Organizer Help to access the built-in help system.

Controlling How a Picture Is Displayed

After you insert a picture into your page, you have some control over how the picture is displayed. For example, you can specify how the picture aligns with surrounding text, change its display dimensions, and more. Read on for details.

Aligning a picture with surrounding text

New Web designers (especially those who are used to working with page layout programs such as PageMaker or Quark) are often frustrated by how difficult simply placing a picture where they want on a Web page can be.

Generally, aligning pictures with text is most accurately accomplished using a layout table, which I talk about in Chapter 9. (Positioning and layers, two other FrontPage features, are also options; I talk about both briefly in Chapter 9.) However, when you simply want to insert a picture in the same line as text, you have some control over how the picture aligns with that text. Follow these steps:

1. **In the page, double-click the picture.**

   The Picture Properties dialog box appears with the Appearance tab visible, as shown in Figure 6-2.

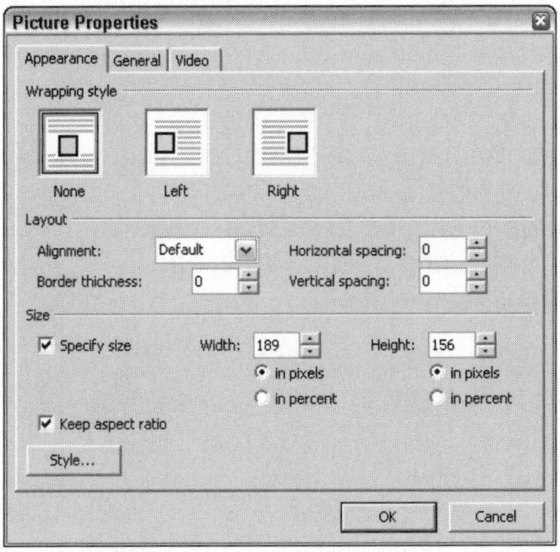

Figure 6-2:
The Appearance tab of the Picture Properties dialog box.

2. **In the dialog box's Layout area, choose an option from the Alignment list box:**

   - **Left:** Places the picture in the left margin and wraps surrounding text around the right side of the picture. (This is the default setting.)

   - **Right:** Places the picture in the right margin and wraps surrounding text around the left side of the picture. (Figure 6-3 illustrates both the Left and Right alignment options.)

   Note: In the dialog box's Wrapping Style area, clicking the Left or Right icon achieves the same thing as selecting Left or Right from the Alignment list box.

- **Top:** Aligns the top of the picture with the text.

- **Texttop:** Aligns the top of the picture with the top of the tallest text in the line.

- **Middle:** Aligns the middle of the picture with the text.

- **Absmiddle:** Aligns the middle of the picture with the middle of the tallest text in the line.

- **Baseline:** Aligns the picture with the text baseline. The *baseline* is the invisible line that the page's text sits on, something like the lines on a piece of notebook paper.

- **Bottom:** Aligns the bottom of the picture with the text.

- **Absbottom:** Aligns the picture with the bottom of the text in the line.

- **Center:** Works just like the Middle option.

3. **Click OK.**

   The dialog box closes, and the picture alignment changes accordingly.

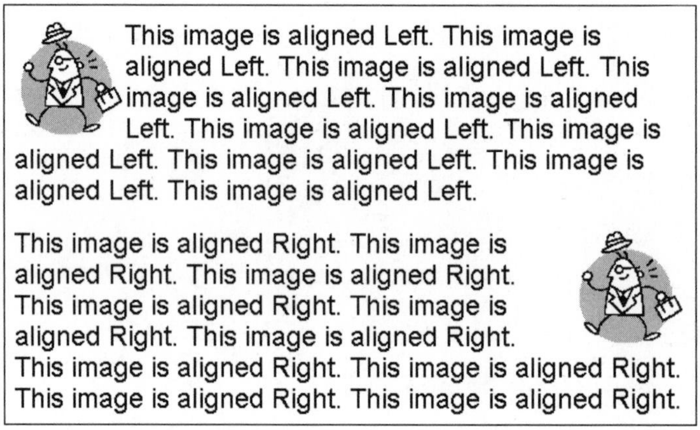

Figure 6-3:
The results
of the Left
and Right
alignment
options.

This image is aligned Left. This image is aligned Left. This image is aligned Left. This image is aligned Left. This image is aligned Left. This image is aligned Left. This image is aligned Left. This image is aligned Left. This image is aligned Left. This image is aligned Left.

This image is aligned Right. This image is aligned Right. This image is aligned Right. This image is aligned Right. This image is aligned Right. This image is aligned Right. This image is aligned Right. This image is aligned Right. This image is aligned Right. This image is aligned Right. This image is aligned Right. This image is aligned Right.

If you use the Left or Right option to align a picture, adjacent text flows, or *wraps,* around the picture. You can control the amount of text that wraps around the picture by inserting a *line break* where you want the wrapping to stop. A line break creates a new, blank line and moves all the text following the line break beneath the picture.

Pressing Shift+Enter creates a normal line break. (I discuss this type of line break in Chapter 4.) The line breaks that I describe in the following steps work specifically with left- and right-aligned pictures.

To insert a line break, follow these steps:

1. **Position the cursor on the page where you want to insert the line break.**

2. **Choose Insert⇨Break.**

   The Break dialog box appears.

3. **Select the option next to the type of line break you want.**

   The type of line break you select depends on how the picture is aligned:

   - **Clear Left Margin:** If the picture is left-aligned, choose this option to cause text after the line break to move to the first empty space in the left margin below the picture.

   - **Clear Right Margin:** If the picture is right-aligned, choose this option to cause text after the line break to move to the first empty space in the right margin below the picture.

   - **Clear Both Margins:** If the page contains several pictures — some that are left-aligned and others that are right-aligned — choose this option to cause text to shift to the first empty space where both margins are clear.

4. **Click OK to close the dialog box and insert the line break.**

Another alignment option is to use *layers*, which enable you to place a picture in any spot on the page, independent of the page's text or other content. Layers can nudge your Web site toward the cutting edge of design, but only for those visitors using state-of-the-art Web browsers. I talk about layers and other style sheet effects in Chapter 14.

Controlling the amount of space surrounding a picture

By adjusting horizontal and vertical spacing, you set the amount of space that separates a picture from its surroundings. To adjust picture spacing, follow these steps:

1. **In the page, double-click the picture.**

   The Picture Properties dialog box appears with the Appearance tab visible (refer to Figure 6-2).

2. **In the Horizontal Spacing text box, type the number of pixels of blank space that you want to insert to the left and right of the picture.**

3. **In the Vertical Spacing text box, type the number of pixels of blank space that you want to insert above and below the picture.**

4. **Click OK to close the dialog box and adjust the spacing.**

Adding (or removing) a border around a picture

Borders are useful only if the picture in question is the basis of a hyperlink. Although you can place a black border around a regular picture by using this feature, in my opinion, the border looks darn ugly.

On the other hand, borders around graphic hyperlinks can make your site easier to navigate. Graphic hyperlink borders are the same color as the page's text link colors, cueing neophyte Web surfers to click the picture to activate the link. On the *other* other hand, borders may cause visual clutter and, worse, may clash with the colors in the picture.

You can solve this design dilemma by choosing your hyperlink graphics carefully — use pictures that implicitly whisper, "Click me." For example, graphics that look like raised buttons just beg to be clicked. Even the greenest of visitors knows to click this type of picture to activate its associated hyperlink.

To give your picture a border, or to remove the border surrounding a graphic hyperlink, follow these steps:

1. **In the page, double-click the picture.**

   The Picture Properties dialog box appears with the Appearance tab visible (refer to Figure 6-2).

2. **In the dialog box's Border Thickness box, type the thickness, in pixels, of the picture border.**

   I recommend nothing thicker than 2 pixels. Anything much thicker tends to look gaudy, but experiment to see what you prefer. To remove borders from graphic hyperlinks, specify a border thickness of 0 pixels.

3. **Click OK to close the dialog box and apply the border setting.**

The best way to add a border to regular (non-hyperlinked) pictures is to open the graphic file in a graphics program and edit the file itself. I explain how to launch your graphics program from within FrontPage in the "Launching a separate graphics program" section later in the chapter.

Resampling a picture

In the "Setting display dimensions" section of this chapter, I explain how to set a picture's display dimensions, and I mention that by changing dimension settings, you don't affect the dimensions of the graphic file itself, only the size as it appears inside a Web page. Well, I'm about to go back on my word.

If you decide you prefer the new size of the picture, you can tell FrontPage to *resample* (or optimize) the picture to match its new size. Resampling doesn't perform magic, but it can smooth out the rough edges that sometimes appear when you resize a picture. Resampling

can also reduce the file size a bit. To resample a picture, click the picture and then click the Resample button on the Pictures toolbar. If the Pictures toolbar isn't visible, choose View➪ Toolbars➪Pictures.

Keep in mind that when you resample a picture, FrontPage prompts you to save the changed graphic when you next save the page. Later in this chapter, in the "Editing the Picture Itself" section, I explain how to save a changed graphic as a separate file so that you can revert back to the original if you change your mind.

Setting display dimensions

FrontPage enables you to specify the width and height of a picture as it appears when viewed with a Web browser. By doing so, you don't affect the size of the graphic file itself; you affect only the dimensions of the picture as they appear inside a Web page. It's kind of like looking at a small object through a magnifying glass; the glass makes the object look bigger, but the size of the object doesn't change.

You can use FrontPage to adjust the dimensions of your Web graphics, either in pixels or as a percentage of the browser window size.

To resize a graphic quickly, in the page, click the graphic and then drag the size handles that appear around the graphic.

For more precise control over dimensions, follow these steps:

1. **In the page, double-click the picture.**

   The Picture Properties dialog box appears with the Appearance tab visible (refer to Figure 6-2). The Width and Height text boxes already contain the picture's dimensions.

2. To change the picture's dimensions, select the Specify Size check box, and then type new numbers in the Width and Height text boxes.

You can specify a number of pixels, or you can choose a percentage of the browser window. To maintain the correct proportion, select the Keep Aspect Ratio check box.

3. Click OK to close the dialog box and adjust the picture's dimensions.

Specifying alternative text

Some Web surfers, desperate to save seconds, turn off their browsers' capability to display pictures. Instead of a graphically exciting Web site, like the example shown in Figure 6-4, the result is a no-nonsense, fast-loading, text-only site, with empty placeholders where the pictures normally sit, as shown in Figure 6-5.

Visitors who want to dispense with pretty pictures to get just the facts love this feature. But what about you? You painstakingly designed your site's graphics only to discover that some of your visitors never even see them!

Figure 6-4:
The
Dummies
Web site in
full regalia.

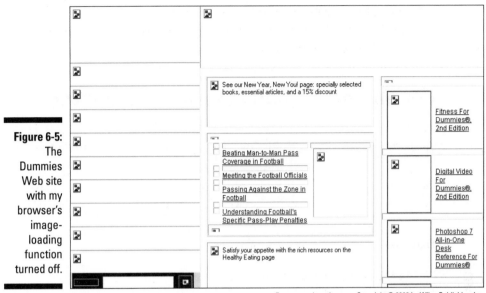

Figure 6-5: The Dummies Web site with my browser's image-loading function turned off.

This is a Web publishing reality you must accept. All you can do is specify *alternative text* (known in Web design circles as *ALT text*) for each of your pictures. ALT text appears inside the placeholder where the original graphic would have appeared if image-loading were turned on. Generally, you use ALT text to describe the graphic, giving visitors an idea of what the graphic contains and enabling visitors to decide whether the graphic is worth the load time.

ALT text comes with a bonus: Some browsers display ALT text as a caption of sorts, popping the text up in a little box when the visitor hovers the pointer over a picture.

Give every picture in your Web site meaningful ALT text. By doing so, you give visitors yet another way to enjoy your Web site (a thoughtful touch that many Web surfers appreciate).

To specify ALT text, follow these steps:

1. **In the page, double-click the picture.**

2. **In the Picture Properties dialog box that appears, click the General tab.**

3. **In the Alternative Representations section of the General tab, type a brief, descriptive blurb in the Text box.**

   You can also type a more detailed description in the Long Description text box, but keep in mind that most browsers won't know how to display this information.

4. **Click OK to close the dialog box.**

   Although nothing appears to have changed in your page, FrontPage has inserted the ALT text into your page's HTML tags.

Placing a text label on top of a picture

If a picture on your page needs a descriptive caption, or if you want to transform your favorite pictures into buttons or banners, you can easily do so by placing a bit of text on top of the picture.

The tool you use for this effect resides on the Pictures toolbar (shown in the Cheat Sheet at the front of this book). You can make this toolbar visible by choosing View➪Toolbars➪Pictures.

To create a text label, follow these steps:

1. **In the page, click the picture you want to edit.**

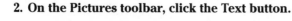

2. **On the Pictures toolbar, click the Text button.**

   After you click the Text button, an empty rectangular area with a flashing insertion point appears in the center of the picture.

3. **Type your desired text and then click anywhere outside the picture.**

   The picture is de-selected, with the new text label sitting at the center of the picture.

To reposition the text label inside the picture, click the picture. A rectangular box appears around the text label. Click inside the rectangular box and then drag the label to a new position.

You can also format the text label by using any of the text tools in the Font dialog box (available by choosing Format➪Font) and on the Formatting toolbar.

Editing the Picture Itself

FrontPage has limited image-editing capabilities that can save you the hassle of launching a separate program for little touch-ups.

When you use FrontPage to edit a graphic file, the Save Embedded Files dialog box appears the next time you save the page and prompts you to save the new, changed version of the picture. If you click OK to save the picture, you overwrite the original picture file. To be safe, consider renaming the changed picture (which prompts FrontPage to save the changed picture as a separate file) so that you can revert to the original picture if you mess up or change your mind. To do so, in the Save Embedded Files dialog box, click the Rename button, type a new filename, and then click OK to close the dialog box and save the file.

Creating a transparent GIF

The concept of a transparent GIF is more easily demonstrated than explained, so I'm going to show you one first and then tell you about the concept in a moment. Figure 6-6 shows the difference between a regular GIF and a transparent GIF. The graphic on the left is a regular GIF. See how the graphic's background color wrestles with the background color of the page? This problem disappears if you make the GIF's background color transparent, like the background of the graphic on the right. The transparent GIF blends nicely with the rest of the page.

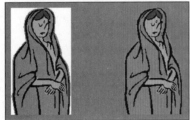

Figure 6-6:
A regular and transparent GIF side by side.

A transparent GIF has one of its colors erased (generally the background color) so that the color of the page shows through. The Pictures toolbar contains a "magic eraser" that can make regular GIFs transparent with a couple of clicks.

A GIF can have only one transparent color. Whichever color you slate for erasure disappears throughout the graphic. Unless the color you choose is unique, your GIF resembles Swiss cheese, because see-through spots appear throughout the picture. To avoid this problem, make sure that the GIF's background color does not appear anywhere else in the graphic. If you're working with ready-made graphics, you may need to alter them in a graphics program first.

To transform a regular GIF into a transparent GIF, follow these steps:

1. **Insert the GIF of your choice into your page.**

2. **In the page, click the picture.**

3. **Click the Set Transparent Color button on the Pictures toolbar that appears, and then, in the picture, move the pointer over the color you want to erase.**

   As you move the pointer over the picture, the pointer turns into a little pencil eraser with an arrow sticking out of the top.

4. **Click the mouse button.**

   The color disappears!

To change a picture's transparent color, click the Set Transparent Color button and then click a different color inside the picture. The original color reappears, and the newly chosen color becomes transparent.

To turn a transparent GIF back into a regular GIF, click the Set Transparent Color button and then click the transparent area. The old color comes back.

If you try this trick on a JPEG graphic, FrontPage prompts you to convert the picture to GIF format. (GIF and PNG are the only Web graphic formats that can be made transparent.) Proceed with care, however, because the GIF format can't accommodate as many colors as JPEG can, and your picture's quality and file size may suffer as a result.

Cropping a picture

Cropping a picture involves trimming parts of the picture away, leaving only the stuff you like. To crop a picture, do this:

1. **In the page, click the picture you want to crop.**

2. **Click the Crop button on the Pictures toolbar.**

   A set of handles and a cropping border, shown in Figure 6-7, appear inside the selected picture. The handles, which are shaped like little squares, allow you to change the shape of the cropping border (the dotted lines). Just click and drag one of the handles, and keep reshaping the cropping border until it completely surrounds the part of the picture you want to keep intact. You can also click inside the cropping border and drag the border around without reshaping it. After you crop the picture, the stuff inside the cropping border stays, and the stuff outside the border goes.

3. **After you get the cropping border right where you want it, click the Crop button again.**

   Snip! The unwanted portion of the picture goes away.

If you decide you don't like the newly cropped picture, click the Undo button on the Standard toolbar to start over.

Figure 6-7:
Cropping a
picture.

Applying a special effect to a picture

The Pictures toolbar contains a few tools that apply special visual effects to your pictures. Table 6-1 shows the buttons on the Pictures toolbar and explains what effects the buttons apply. To use any of these effects, click the picture you want to change and then click the corresponding button.

Table 6-1	Visual Effects Options on the Pictures Toolbar	
Button	*What It Is*	*What It Does*
	Rotate Left and Rotate Right	These options rotate the picture 90 degrees to the left or right.
	Flip Horizontal and Flip Vertical	These options flip the picture horizontally and vertically.
	Increase Contrast and Decrease Contrast	These options increase or decrease the picture's contrast.
	Increase Brightness and Decrease Brightness	These options increase or decrease the picture's brightness.
	Line Style	This button becomes active when you select an AutoShape or a piece of WordArt in your page. If the element that you select has any type of line in it, this button controls the line's style and thickness.

(continued)

Table 6-1 *(continued)*

Button	What It Is	What It Does
	Format Picture	This button becomes active when you select an AutoShape or piece of WordArt in your page. Click the button to open the Format dialog box for either type of graphic. This dialog box gives you a bunch of options for customizing the image.
	Color	Click this button to see four pop-up options: Grayscale, Black & White, Washout (useful when you want inactive graphic hyperlink buttons to look inactive in your page), and Automatic (which returns the graphic to its original or most recently saved self).
	Bevel	Click this button to transform a regular, flat picture into a raised button of sorts. This effect works best with square and rectangular graphics.
	Select	"Turns off" a button effect and returns the cursor to its usual pointer function.
	Rectangular Hotspot	Creates a rectangular hotspot (see Chapter 5 for details about hotspots).
	Circular Hotspot	Creates a circular hotspot (see Chapter 5 for details about hotspots).
	Polygonal Hotspot	Creates a polygonal hotspot (see Chapter 5 for details about hotspots).
	Highlight Hotspot	Highlights the hotspots inside an image map (see Chapter 5 for details about hotspots and image maps).
	Restore	If you're not happy with any of the effects, click the Restore button to return the picture to its original state. (Just be sure *not* to save the changes first; otherwise the Restore button won't work.)

Launching a separate graphics program

Want to add some finishing touches to your graphic? You can launch a separate graphics program right from within FrontPage. To do so, follow these steps:

1. **In the Folder List, right-click the graphic's icon, and from the pop-up menu that appears, choose Open With⇨Choose Program.**

   (An icon for the graphic appears in the Folder List only *after* you have saved the page containing the graphic.)

   The Open With dialog box appears.

2. **In the dialog box's list box, scroll down until you see the icon for the graphics program you want to use to edit the graphic. When you find the program's icon, click it.**

3. **Click OK.**

   The dialog box closes, and the graphic opens in the selected editing program.

When FrontPage knows which graphics program to launch, to edit an image in that program, in the page, right-click the graphic, and, from the pop-up menu that appears, choose Open With and then the name of the graphics program. The associated editing program launches with the selected graphic open and ready for a makeover.

Deleting a picture

Erasing a picture from your page hardly takes a thought. Just click the picture and press the Backspace or Delete key. That's it.

Using Thumbnails to Speed Up Your Page

Adding pictures to a Web page increases the page's load time. Because Web surfers' annoyance level rises with every second they must wait for a page to appear on-screen, you're wise to limit the number of pictures to keep the site loading fast.

But what if your site relies on pictures? Say you're building an online catalog or a Web-based art gallery. For these sites, the pictures are the main attraction. Are you (and your visitors) doomed to a slow-moving site?

Thankfully, no. Your salvation is called a *thumbnail*. A thumbnail is a tiny version of the picture that you want to display in your page. Because small pictures load faster than big pictures, thumbnails take only moments to appear on-screen. The thumbnail is hyperlinked to the full-sized picture, so if visitors want to see more detail, they can click the thumbnail. (Presumably they are willing to wait a few moments for the full-sized version to appear.) Figure 6-8 shows you how thumbnails work.

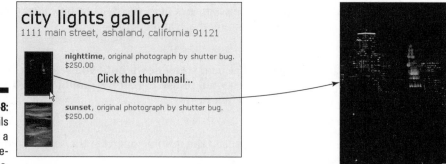

...to display the full-sized picture

Thumbnails are wonderful because visitors wait only for the pictures they really want to see. Furthermore, you can insert several thumbnails into a page and still keep the load time minimal.

Keep in mind that a page with bunches of graphics, no matter what their size, slows down the page's loading time. Keep an eye on your page's download time (FrontPage displays an estimate in the lower-left corner of the main window) and, if necessary, break hefty pages into several more sparsely filled pages.

For the FrontPage-less Web designer, thumbnails take a lot of time to produce. But for you, blessed with FrontPage as you are, thumbnails take only moments to create by following these steps:

1. **In the page, insert the picture that you want to turn into a thumbnail.**

2. **Click the picture, and then click the Auto Thumbnail button on the Pictures toolbar.**

   Note: If the Auto Thumbnail button appears dimmed, then you cannot use the selected picture as a thumbnail. Here are the no-no's: pictures that are already hyperlinked, pictures that have text labels, pictures whose original dimensions are smaller than the thumbnail, and image maps. (I introduce you to image maps in Chapter 5.)

   After you click the Auto Thumbnail button, the picture shrinks, and a colorful border appears around the picture, indicating it is now a graphic hyperlink.

To see the thumbnail in action, preview the page and click the thumbnail.

You can control the dimensions, the border thickness, and the bevel setting that FrontPage uses to create thumbnails. To access FrontPage's thumbnail settings, choose Tools⇨Page Options to display the Page Options dialog box. In the dialog box, click the Auto Thumbnail tab.

The next time you save the page, the Save Embedded Files dialog box appears, prompting you to save any thumbnail images you've created. Click OK to save the files. See Chapter 2 for more details on how this dialog box works.

Creating a Photo Gallery

Imagine sharing your travel photos with friends across the world or keeping Grandma up to date on your toddler's antics. With a FrontPage photo gallery, you can easily add a professional-looking digital photo album, like the one shown in Figure 6-9, to your Web site. The photo gallery might quickly become your favorite FrontPage goody.

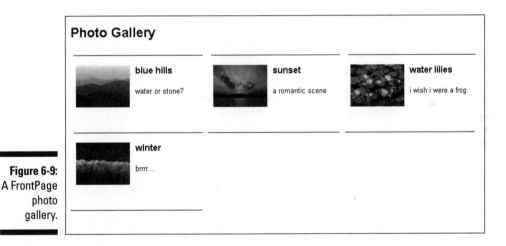

Figure 6-9:
A FrontPage
photo
gallery.

Think of photo galleries as thumbnails on caffeine. (If you're not sure what a thumbnail is, read the previous section of this chapter.) You select the photos you want to appear in your photo gallery, and FrontPage generates thumbnails, lays them out nicely (in some cases with captions and descriptive text), and links the thumbnails to the full-sized photos.

First things first: How do you get your photos onto your computer? If you use a digital camera, the process is as easy as transferring the photo files from your camera's memory card to your computer's hard drive (your camera's operating manual should explain how).

Film camera users must *scan* their photos; devices called *scanners* create a digital file from a photo print. If you happen to own a scanner, that's great. If not, you can take your photos to a well-stocked copy shop (most have scanning services), or you can send your film to a developer who scans the photos and sends you the digital files as well as the prints. (Check out www.ofoto.com.)

Digital cameras and scanners can save photo files as Web-friendly JPEGs. If your photos are saved in another graphic format, you'll need to convert them to the JPEG format to use them in your Web site. FrontPage converts files automatically, or you can convert the files by using a separate graphics program. (I talk about file conversion in the "Adding a Picture to Your Page" section, earlier in the chapter.)

After you've saved your photos as JPEGs on your hard drive or network, you're ready to begin. To create a photo gallery, follow these steps:

1. **Create a new page, or open the existing page into which you want to insert a photo gallery.**

2. **In the page, place the cursor where you want the photo gallery to appear.**

3. **Click the Web Component button on the Standard toolbar or choose Insert⇨Web Component.**

   The Insert Web Component dialog box appears.

4. **In the dialog box's Component Type list box, click Photo Gallery.**

5. **In the Choose a Photo Gallery Option list box, click the icon that corresponds to the page layout you want.**

   Don't worry — you can change your mind later.

6. **Click Finish.**

   The Insert Web Component dialog box closes and the Photo Gallery Properties dialog box appears with the Pictures tab visible, as shown in Figure 6-10. This dialog box enables you to select the photos that will appear in the photo gallery; choose design details such as the thumbnail size, caption, and descriptive text; and, if you like, select a whole new layout for the photo gallery.

7. **In the Photo Gallery Properties dialog box, click Add and choose Pictures from Files from the drop-down menu.**

   I'm assuming here that your photos are stored on your hard drive or network. If your digital camera or scanner is connected to your computer and the photos are stored in that device's memory, choose Pictures from Scanner or Cameras to grab the images directly.

   After you choose Pictures from Files, the File Open dialog box appears, enabling you to navigate your hard drive or network and select the photos that you want to appear in the photo gallery.

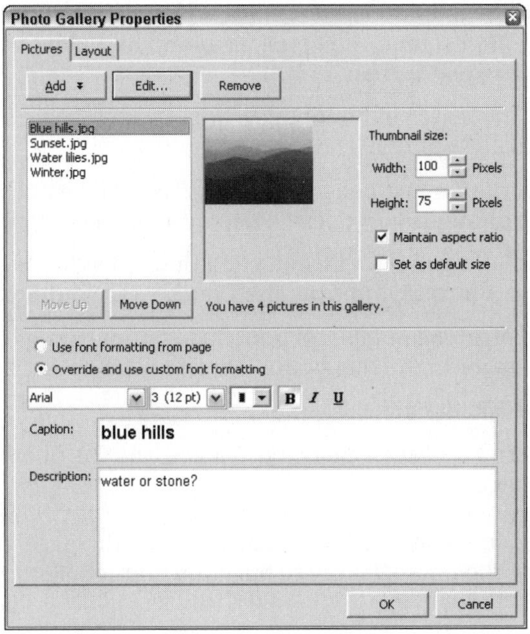

Figure 6-10:
The Photo
Gallery
Properties
dialog box.

8. **In the File Open dialog box, navigate to the location of your photo files, select them, and then click Open.**

   You can select more than one file at a time by holding down the Shift or Ctrl key while clicking file icons.

   After you click Open, the File Open dialog box closes and the Photo Gallery Properties dialog box becomes visible again. The filenames for the photos you've selected appear in the dialog box's file list, and thumbnail previews of the photos appear alongside the filenames.

   To change the size of the thumbnail image that appears in the photo gallery, change the numbers in the Width and Height boxes (be sure the Maintain Aspect Ratio option is checked or the thumbnails will appear distorted when you change their dimensions). Select the Set As Default Size option if you'd like FrontPage to use the current thumbnail dimensions in future photo galleries.

   To change the order of the photos as they appear in the photo gallery, click the photo's filename in the file list, and then click the Move Up or the Move Down button.

   You can also edit the full-sized photos. To do so, click the photo's filename in the file list, and then click the Edit button. The Edit Picture dialog box appears. This dialog box contains options that allow you to change the photo's resolution, or to rotate or crop the photo. When you're done editing the photo, click OK to close the Edit Picture dialog box and return to the Photo Gallery Properties dialog box.

9. **To add a caption and a description to each picture, click the picture's filename in the file list, and then type a caption and a description in the corresponding text boxes.**

   You can format the text in either of these boxes using the formatting options in the dialog box.

   Note: If the Description text box appears dimmed, the layout you've chosen for your photo gallery doesn't display a text description.

10. **To change the photo gallery's layout, click the dialog box's Layout tab, and then choose a new layout from the Choose a Layout box.**

    You may also control the number of photos that appear in one row by changing the number in the Number of Pictures per Row list box.

11. **When you're finished, click OK.**

    The Photo Gallery Properties dialog box closes, and the photo gallery appears in the page.

You can change the photo gallery's settings any time. In the page, double-click anywhere inside the photo gallery to open the Photo Gallery Properties dialog box.

Using Background Images

You can use a picture as the background of your page, with the page's text sitting on top. How the background image appears as viewed with a browser depends on the dimensions of the graphic file itself. The Web browser *tiles* the picture, repeating the picture over and over until it fills the browser window, which creates a consistent background for the text.

Each FrontPage theme contains a background pattern that you can use in your pages. (I show you how to work with themes in Chapter 11.) You can also download backgrounds from the Web, or you can create your own backgrounds in a graphics program.

If you decide to use a background image, choose one that harmonizes with the colors in your site. If the picture is too busy, the background may obscure the text, making the page difficult to read. Additionally, background images, like regular pictures, add time to your page's total download speed. The smaller and simpler your background image is, the faster the page loads.

To insert a background image, follow these steps:

1. **With a page open in Design View, choose Format⇨Background.**

   The Page Properties dialog box appears, with the Background tab visible.

Note: If the page uses a theme, this menu option is unavailable because all background options are determined by that theme.

2. **In the dialog box, click the Background Picture check box.**

3. **In the corresponding text box, type the graphic file's path.**

   Alternatively, click Browse to select the file from a list of files on your computer, on your local network, or in the Media Gallery.

4. **If you want the background to appear fixed, click the Make It a Watermark check box.**

   Watermarks are the same as regular backgrounds, except that watermarks appear fixed in place if viewed with a Web browser — when a visitor scrolls around the screen, the text appears to float above the fixed background. (With regular background images, the background and text move together when a visitor scrolls around the page.) As of this writing, Microsoft Internet Explorer is the only browser that can display watermarks.

5. **Click OK to close the dialog box.**

   The background image appears in your page.

If the background image is stored in a location other than in the currently open Web site, then the Save Embedded Files dialog box offers to import the graphic file to your Web site the next time you save the page. Click OK to import the file.

You can choose a solid color as your page background instead of a picture. Solid background colors load instantly and are often easier to coordinate with the color scheme of the page. To specify a background color, choose Format➪Background to display the Page Properties dialog box. Choose a color from the Background list box (or choose More Colors to pick a color from the More Colors dialog box), and then click OK.

Working with Drawn Graphics

If you've read the earlier parts of this chapter, forget everything you just read. *Drawn graphics* differ from bitmap graphics in more ways than they are similar, and, as such, are subject to a different set of rules.

Drawn graphics, such as lines, shapes, and bits of fancy text, are more flexible than bitmaps. Whereas you can edit bitmaps only in minimal ways, you can manipulate a drawn graphic however you like. You can change its shape, color, size, or orientation. You can apply special effects, such as shadows and a 3-D appearance. You can group drawn graphics together and then make changes to the group as a unit.

The big drawback to using drawn graphics is browser compatibility. FrontPage creates drawn graphics using VML (short for *Vector Markup Language*), a Microsoft technology that can render vector graphics (the technical term for drawn graphics). Because VML is not an accepted standard on the Web, the only browser able to display VML graphics is Microsoft Internet Explorer (version 5 and higher). Although FrontPage compensates for browser differences by creating GIF equivalents of VML graphics, the graphics aren't always consistent across different browser platforms and versions. Therefore, your safest bet is to use drawn graphics in an IE-only intranet setting. If you decide to use drawn graphics for a general-purpose Web site, be sure to preview the page using several browsers.

Awesome AutoShapes

No need to hunt around the Web for clip art when you simply want to draw a shape in your page. AutoShapes are commonly used presentation shapes, such as lines, arrows, basic geometric shapes, flowcharts, callouts, and banners.

Inserting AutoShapes into your page

You can draw your own shapes, or you can plop ready-made AutoShapes into your page with a few quick clicks. To do so, follow these steps:

1. **Click anywhere inside the page, and then choose Insert➪ Picture➪AutoShapes.**

   The AutoShape and Drawing toolbars appear inside the FrontPage window.

2. **From the AutoShapes toolbar, click the button that corresponds to the type of AutoShape you want, and from the drop-down menu that appears, choose the AutoShape you want (refer to Figure 6-11).**

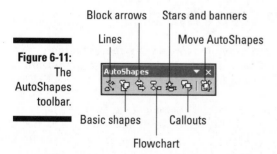

Figure 6-11: The AutoShapes toolbar.

You can float any of the AutoShape menus to make them visible all the time. To do so, move your cursor over the solid line at the top of the menu, and when it changes color, click and drag the menu to another place on your screen.

After you select your AutoShape, the cursor changes from a pointer into a drawing crosshatch.

3. **Move the cursor to the location in the page where you want the AutoShape to appear, and then click and drag to draw the AutoShape. When you're happy with what you see, release the mouse button.**

The AutoShape appears in your page. If you drew the AutoShape over existing text or content in the page, the AutoShape sits on top of that content.

Changing how AutoShapes look

If you're not satisfied with your AutoShape's attributes, you can change them easily enough. Here are tips for making changes to AutoShapes.

All the buttons I mention in this section are on the Drawing toolbar, which, most likely, is sitting at the bottom of the FrontPage window. If you can't see the entire Drawing toolbar, the Pictures toolbar may be hogging too much space at the bottom of the FrontPage window; hide the Pictures toolbar by choosing View➪Toolbars➪Pictures, and the Drawing toolbar will appear in its entirety.

- ✔ **Moving:** Click and drag the AutoShape to a new location on the page. To move the AutoShape just a tiny bit, click the AutoShape; choose Draw➪Nudge; and then choose Up, Down, Left, or Right.

- ✔ **Placing the AutoShape on top of or below other content on the page:** Click the AutoShape; choose Draw➪Order; and then choose Bring to Front, Send to Back, Bring Forward, or Send Backward.

- ✔ **Changing the dimensions:** Click the AutoShape to display its size handles. Click and drag any of the size handles until the shape is the size you want. Some AutoShapes have a yellow handle that modifies the AutoShape's shape as well.

- ✔ **Rotating:** Click the AutoShape to display its size handles. Click and drag the green handle to rotate the AutoShape freely. Alternatively, you can choose Draw➪Rotate or Flip and then choose Rotate Left, Rotate Right, Flip Horizontal, or Flip Vertical.

- ✔ **Changing the fill color:** Click the AutoShape, and then click the Fill Color button. To display a menu of color options, click the arrow next to the Fill Color button, and choose the fill color you want.

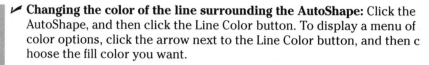 ✔ **Changing the color of the line surrounding the AutoShape:** Click the AutoShape, and then click the Line Color button. To display a menu of color options, click the arrow next to the Line Color button, and then c hoose the fill color you want.

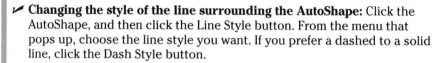 ✔ **Changing the style of the line surrounding the AutoShape:** Click the AutoShape, and then click the Line Style button. From the menu that pops up, choose the line style you want. If you prefer a dashed to a solid line, click the Dash Style button.

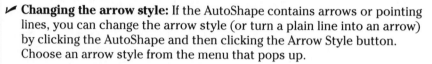 ✔ **Changing the arrow style:** If the AutoShape contains arrows or pointing lines, you can change the arrow style (or turn a plain line into an arrow) by clicking the AutoShape and then clicking the Arrow Style button. Choose an arrow style from the menu that pops up.

 ✔ **Adding a shadow or 3-D effect:** Click the AutoShape and then click the Shadow Style or 3-D Style button. From the menu that pops up, choose the style you want.

✔ **Placing text on top of an AutoShape:** Move the cursor over the AutoShape until the cursor looks like an I-Beam, click, and start typing. You can format the text — change its color and size, for example. Some AutoShapes don't accept text placement, in which case you need to place a text box on top of the AutoShape.

 ✔ **Creating a text box:** Click the Text Box button, and then move the cursor to the place in the page where you want the text box to appear. Click, and then, while holding down the mouse button, drag the cursor down diagonally to create a box. After you release the mouse button, a blinking insertion point appears inside the box. Type your desired text (you can format the text using any of FrontPage's text tools). To change the formatting of the box, double-click the box to show the Format Text Box dialog box. In this dialog box, you find options for changing the box's size, color, line color, margins, and more.

✔ **Applying any effect to more than one AutoShape:** While holding down the Shift key, click the AutoShapes to select them, and then click the corresponding Drawing toolbar button. If you want to group the AutoShapes together to turn them into a single unit, you can select the AutoShapes and choose Draw⇨Group.

✔ **Aligning AutoShapes or distributing the space between them evenly:** Select the AutoShapes you want to align or distribute; choose Draw⇨Align or Distribute; and then choose Align Left, Align Center, Align Right, Align Top, Align Middle, Align Bottom, Distribute Horizontally, or Distribute Vertically.

 For even more control over an AutoShape's attributes, double-click the AutoShape to display the Format AutoShape dialog box. This dialog box contains all the options that I describe in the previous list, plus a few more. Don't be afraid to experiment. The trusty Undo button is always within reach.

Working with WordArt

At times, plain old text just doesn't cut it, especially if you're creating a page heading or banner. These times call for WordArt, the Microsoft Office feature that lets you choose from a gallery of flashy effects you can apply to text. Figure 6-12 shows you just one of the effects you can create using WordArt.

Figure 6-12:
WordArt
at work.

To insert WordArt into your page, do the following:

1. **In the page, place the cursor where you want the WordArt to appear, and then choose Insert⇨Picture⇨WordArt. Or click the Insert WordArt button on the Drawing toolbar.**

   The WordArt Gallery dialog box appears.

2. **In the dialog box, double-click the graphic that most closely approximates how you want the text to look (you can more finely tune the graphic's appearance in a moment).**

   The WordArt Gallery dialog box closes, and the Edit WordArt Text dialog box appears with the WordArt text highlighted.

3. **Type your desired WordArt text.**

   You can also change the text's font, size, and attributes using the options in the Edit WordArt Text dialog box.

4. **When you like what you see, click OK.**

   The Edit WordArt Text dialog box closes, and the WordArt appears on your page.

As with AutoShapes, you can change the shape of and rotate the WordArt by clicking and dragging its size handles. WordArt is placed in line with text and other page content by default. You can change WordArt positioning by using the settings in the Format WordArt dialog box.

After you insert WordArt into your page, the WordArt toolbar appears, offering even more options for changing how the WordArt looks. Have fun experimenting with the buttons on this toolbar. For finer control, right-click the WordArt and then, from the pop-up menu that appears, choose Format WordArt to display the Format WordArt dialog box. This dialog box contains options for changing the WordArt's attributes.

Chapter 7

Arranging Information Inside Grid Tables

In This Chapter

- Creating a grid table
- Building a table around existing text
- Inserting text, pictures, or even another table into a table
- Changing how a table looks
- Modifying cells, columns, and rows

Put away that hacksaw and hammer! True, after you finish this chapter, you can build a table — but not the kind at which you play cards with your buddies. No, in this chapter, I introduce you to the wonders of the *grid table*. Grid tables cordon off individual bits of data into little boxes called *cells,* which are arranged in horizontal *rows* and vertical *columns.* Figure 7-1 illustrates a typical grid table.

Flavor of the Day

Monday	Butter Brickle
Tuesday	Mint Chip
Wednesday	Bubble Gum
Thursday	Strawberry
Friday	Chocolate Explosion

Figure 7-1: A grid table.

REMEMBER

In Chapter 9, you become familiar with the *layout table,* which is structurally identical to a grid table, but is used for a different purpose. Although you will likely use layout tables more often than grid tables, familiarizing yourself with how grid tables work makes using layout tables much easier.

Creating a Grid Table

FrontPage 2003 offers no less than four methods for creating a table. In this section, I detail what I consider to be the two easiest methods.

Using the Insert Table button

The Insert Table button suits people who want fast results. Two clicks of the mouse, and you have a perfectly good table. Try this:

1. **Place the cursor in the page where you want the table to appear.**

   If the cursor location doesn't exactly correspond to where you want the table to sit inside your page, just do the best you can; you can more precisely position the table later by using alignment options (described later in this chapter) or positioning (described in Chapter 9).

2. **On the Standard toolbar, click the Insert Table button.**

   A grid of white boxes representing table rows and columns appears underneath the button.

3. **Click and drag your pointer on the grid until the number of highlighted boxes equals the number of rows and columns you want your table to contain (see Figure 7-2).**

   As you highlight boxes, the table dimensions appear at the bottom of the grid. If you drag past the last box in a column or row, the grid expands.

   If you don't know exactly how many rows or columns you need, just pick something close. You can always add or delete rows and columns later.

4. **Release the mouse button.**

   A new, empty table appears in your page.

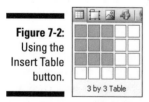

Figure 7-2:
Using the
Insert Table
button.

3 by 3 Table

Scrunching existing text into a grid table

If you're more comfortable with your trusty word processor than you are with FrontPage, you can convert text separated with tabs, commas, or any other character into a table. To do so, follow these steps:

1. **In the page, insert the text you want to appear inside the table.**

   Separate each line of text you want to appear in its own row by placing the text inside its own paragraph. Section each row into "columns" by separating the text with tabs, commas, or some other character. Don't worry if the spacing is uneven — everything lines up nicely when you convert the text into a table.

2. **Highlight the text and then choose Table⇨Convert⇨Text to Table.**

   The Convert Text to Table dialog box appears.

3. **Select the option next to the text separator you want FrontPage to recognize when it creates columns.**

   If the text separator in your page isn't a tab or comma, select the Other option and then, in the accompanying text box, type the text separator character.

4. **Click OK.**

   The dialog box closes, and a table materializes around the selected text.

FrontPage can also convert Microsoft Word tables and Excel or Lotus 1-2-3 worksheets into Web page tables. Just cut and paste portions of a Word, Excel, or Lotus 1-2-3 file into an open page in FrontPage.

Inserting Stuff into a Table

You can insert anything into a table cell that you can into a regular page: text, pictures, and even other tables. Just click inside a cell and proceed as usual. By default, cell height and width stretch to accommodate whatever you place inside.

Text entered into a cell *wraps* as you type, which means that, when the text reaches a cell boundary, the word being typed jumps down to a new line. You create new paragraphs in a cell by pressing Enter and create line breaks by pressing Shift+Enter.

If you're ready to type text in another cell, press Tab until the cursor ends up in the destination cell and then type away. If you press the Tab key when the cursor is sitting in the last cell in the bottom row of the table, a new table row appears, and the cursor jumps to the first cell in that new row so that you can continue to add to the table. To move the cursor backward through a table, press Shift+Tab.

To effortlessly fill a row or column with the same contents as the first cell of that row or column, insert something into the first cell in the row/column, select the row/column, and then click the Fill Down or Fill Right button on the Tables toolbar. (If you're having trouble selecting a row or column, I share the secret later in this chapter, in the "Selecting table parts" section.) If the Tables toolbar isn't visible, choose View⇨Toolbars⇨Tables.

Table Tinkering

After you plug stuff into your table, you can tinker with the table's layout until the thing looks the way you want.

Changing table height and width

You have two options for controlling the dimensions of your table: You can give the table *absolute measurements* (a fixed size) or *proportional measurements* (the particulars of which are based on the size of the visitor's browser window).

You may be tempted to opt for absolute measurements so that you can retain control over the table size. Consider, however, the unfortunate visitor who must view your page inside a small or low-resolution monitor. That visitor may need to scroll all over the place to see the table in its entirety and may curse the inconsiderate person who created such a table.

By using proportional measurements, you enable the visitor's browser window to determine the dimensions of the table. You give up precise control, but your visitor gets to see the entire table inside the browser window, no matter what the monitor or window size.

Which option is best? The choice depends on how you intend to use your table. If the table's overall structure is more important than the precise placement of its contents, use proportional measurements. If you require control, use absolute measurements.

Another option is to forgo specifying the table's height and width altogether. If you do this, the table stretches to accommodate the dimensions of whatever sits inside the table's cells, and no more.

A good middle ground is to specify the dimensions of each column instead of the dimensions of the table as a whole. In this way, you can give some columns an absolute width and others a proportional width, creating a more flexible table. In the "Changing cell, row, and column dimensions" section, later in this chapter, I show you how to change column dimensions.

To eyeball your table's absolute dimensions, click one of the outer table borders and drag the border to the desired size.

If you want to fine-tune your table's absolute dimensions, follow these steps:

1. **Display the Table Properties dialog box by right-clicking the table and choosing Table Properties from the pop-up menu that appears.**

2. **In the Table Properties dialog box (see Figure 7-3), select the Specify Width check box, and in the corresponding text box, type the width of the table.**

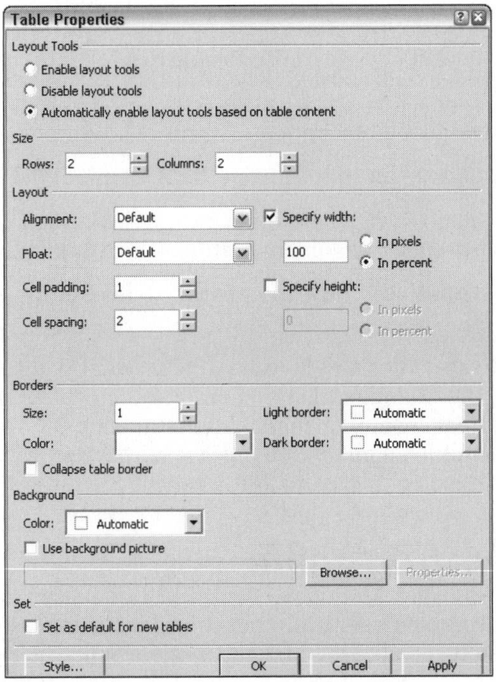

Figure 7-3:
The Table
Properties
dialog box.

Table Properties

Layout Tools
- ○ Enable layout tools
- ○ Disable layout tools
- ● Automatically enable layout tools based on table content

Size
Rows: 2   Columns: 2

Layout
Alignment: Default   ☑ Specify width:
Float: Default   100   ○ In pixels ● In percent
Cell padding: 1   ☐ Specify height:
Cell spacing: 2   0   ○ In pixels ○ In percent

Borders
Size: 1   Light border: ☐ Automatic
Color: Dark border: ☐ Automatic
☐ Collapse table border

Background
Color: ☐ Automatic
☐ Use background picture
Browse...   Properties...

Set
☐ Set as default for new tables

Style...   OK   Cancel   Apply

To specify a proportional width, type the width of the table as a percentage of the width of the browser window. For example, if you type **50**, FrontPage sets the width of the table at 50 percent, or half the width of the browser window. To specify an absolute width, type the table width in pixels. To turn off table width specifications, de-select the Specify Width check box.

3. **Select the option that corresponds to the measurement you specified in Step 2.**

   If you specified a proportional width, select the In Percent option. If you specified an absolute width, select the In Pixels option.

4. **If you want to specify a table height, select the Specify Height check box; in the corresponding text box, type the table's height in pixels or as a percentage value, and then select the corresponding option.**

5. **Click OK to close the dialog box and change the table size.**

Aligning a table on the page

You can left-align, right-align, or center a table on the page. Just follow these steps:

1. **Right-click the table and choose Table Properties from the pop-up menu that appears.**

   The Table Properties dialog box appears.

2. **In the dialog box, choose an option from the Alignment list box.**

   Your choices are Default, Left, Right, and Center. The Default option uses the visitor's default browser alignment setting, which is left-aligned.

3. **Click the Apply button to see how the change looks before you close the dialog box.**

   If you like what you see, click OK. If you don't like what you see, choose a new option from the Alignment list box or click Cancel to close the dialog box without making any changes. After you click OK, the dialog box closes, and the table alignment changes accordingly.

Creating a floating table

No levitation occurs during this operation, but the effect is impressive just the same. Similar to a picture, adjacent text can wrap around the right or left side of a table. This effect is referred to as *floating*. Figure 7-4 shows an example of a floating table.

Figure 7-4:
A floating
table.

To make your table float, do the following:

1. **Display the Table Properties dialog box by right-clicking the table and choosing Table Properties from the pop-up menu that appears.**

2. **In the dialog box, choose an option from the Float list box.**

   The Default setting creates no floating effect. The Left setting causes the table to float over to the left margin, with adjacent text wrapping around its right side. The Right setting causes the table to float over to the right margin, with adjacent text wrapping around its left side.

3. **Click OK to close the dialog box and change the table's floating setting.**

Older browsers aren't able to display floating tables; the table appears left-aligned with no text wrapping.

Inserting blank space inside or between table cells

Adding space between the contents of table cells and the cell borders is called *cell padding*. Padded cells open up a table by placing white space around the contents of each cell. Figures 7-5 and 7-6 illustrate the difference a little padding makes.

Figure 7-5:
A table
with no cell
padding.

Monday	Butter Brickle
Tuesday	Mint Chip
Wednesday	Bubble Gum
Thursday	Strawberry
Friday	Chocolate Explosion

Monday	Butter Brickle
Tuesday	Mint Chip
Wednesday	Bubble Gum
Thursday	Strawberry
Friday	Chocolate Explosion

Cell spacing determines how much space exists between cells and also affects the appearance of table and cell borders. Figures 7-7 and 7-8 illustrate how changes in cell spacing affect a table.

Monday	Butter Brickle
Tuesday	Mint Chip
Wednesday	Bubble Gum
Thursday	Strawberry
Friday	Chocolate Explosion

Monday	Butter Brickle
Tuesday	Mint Chip
Wednesday	Bubble Gum
Thursday	Strawberry
Friday	Chocolate Explosion

To change cell padding or spacing, follow these steps:

1. **Display the Table Properties dialog box by right-clicking the table and choosing Table Properties from the pop-up menu that appears.**

2. **To enlarge the table cells, in the dialog box's Cell Padding text box, type the desired amount of white space (in pixels) that you want to separate cell contents from cell borders. To add space between the cells, in the dialog box's Cell Spacing text box, type the desired amount of space (in pixels) separating table cells.**

3. **Click OK to close the dialog box and change the cell padding and/or spacing settings.**

Changing the borders

In FrontPage, tables are born with 1-pixel-thick, white and gray, beveled borders. Within certain limitations, you can change how the borders look.

Tables have two types of borders: those surrounding individual cells and those surrounding the entire table. Cell borders can be a maximum of 1 pixel thick. Table borders can be of any thickness. To change a table's border setting, follow these steps:

1. **Display the Table Properties dialog box by right-clicking the table and choosing Table Properties from the pop-up menu that appears.**

2. **In the dialog box's Size text box, type the desired border thickness in pixels.**

   The number you type refers to the thickness of the border surrounding the table; the borders inside the table remain at 1 pixel. If you want to make table and cell borders invisible, type **0** in the Size text box.

3. **To change border color, from the Color list box, choose the color you like.**

   Alternatively, you can choose colors from the Light Border and Dark Border list boxes to simulate the shadows in a raised table. However you choose to color your borders, *be sure* to thoroughly preview your table, as different browsers display table color differently.

4. **To "thin" borders, select the Collapse Table Border check box.**

   This setting turns borders into thin lines. FrontPage creates this effect by applying Cascading Style Sheets (CSS) commands to the table, which means that the effect doesn't show up in older browsers that don't recognize CSS. Also, the table looks different in different browsers (even those that *do* know how to deal with CSS). Be sure to preview your table in several browsers for an accurate idea of what your visitors will see on the Web.

5. **Click OK to close the dialog box and change the border setting.**

If you turn off your table's borders, the solid border lines shown in Design view are replaced with dotted lines. These lines appear only in FrontPage — when viewed with a Web browser, the borders are invisible.

You can also control which table borders appear by experimenting with the Borders button on the Formatting toolbar. To do so, select the part of the table you want to affect (or select the entire table), and then click the arrow next to the Borders button to display a menu of options. Choose the option you want and see how your table changes.

Another option is to use the Table⇨AutoFormat command. To do so, click anywhere inside the table, and then click the Table AutoFormat button on the Tables toolbar. Using the Table AutoFormat dialog box that appears, you can slap attractive sets of colors, border styles, and alignment options onto your table. When you like what you see, click OK to close the dialog box and apply the format.

Keep in mind that FrontPage creates these effects using Cascading Style Sheets. Although the CSS coding that FrontPage adds to your page's HTML is perfectly valid, browsers display the effects inconsistently. At the risk of sounding like a broken record . . . preview, preview, preview.

Changing the background

You can apply a solid background color or a background image to a table (or selected cells, columns, or rows), just as you can to an entire page. (I show you how to change your page's background in the "Using Background Images" section of Chapter 6.)

To add a background color or image to a table, follow these steps:

1. **Select the cells, columns, or rows you wish to change (if you're not sure how, read the "Selecting table parts" section of this chapter). To change the background settings for the entire table, right-click the table and choose Table Properties from the pop-up menu that appears.**

   If, instead, you're changing the background of selected cells, choose Cell Properties from the pop-up menu. Depending on your choice, the Table Properties or Cell Properties dialog box appears.

2. **To change the background color, in the Background section of the dialog box, choose a color from the Color list box.**

3. **To use a background image, select the Use Background Picture check box, and in the accompanying text box, type the location of the background image.**

   If you don't remember the file's location, click the Browse button to display the Select Background Picture dialog box. After you select the file, the dialog box closes, and the picture's location appears in the text box of the Table Properties (or Cell Properties) dialog box.

4. **Click OK to close the dialog box and apply the background setting.**

Older browsers, such as Internet Explorer (version 3.0 or greater) or Netscape Navigator (version 4.0 or greater), are able to display table background color and images.

Fiddling with Cells, Columns, and Rows

In addition to tinkering with the table as a whole, you can fiddle with the layout, format, and structure of individual table cells, rows, and columns.

Many of the operations in this section take advantage of buttons on the Tables toolbar, as shown in Figure 7-9. To make the Tables toolbar visible, choose View➪Toolbars➪Tables.

Figure 7-9:
The Tables
toolbar.

Selecting table parts

Selecting table parts. . . . It sounds like something you do at a hardware store. I'm not about to discuss buying lumber or wood screws; I talk about how to highlight, or select, different parts of your table in order to format those parts in some way.

Here's how you select the following table parts:

- ✓ **Cells:** To select a cell, click inside the cell and then choose Table➪ Select➪Cell. To select more than one cell, select the first cell and then press and hold down the Shift key as you click other cells.

- ✓ **Columns:** To select a column, click inside the column and then choose Table➪Select➪Column. Or, pass the cursor over the table until the cursor hovers just above a column. The cursor turns into a stubby down-pointing arrow. Click once to select the column. To select more than one column, select the first column and then drag until you high- light the area you want.

- ✓ **Rows:** To select a row, choose Table➪Select➪Row or pass the cursor over the left side of the table until the cursor hovers just to the left of a row. The cursor turns into a stubby arrow pointing to the right. Click once to select the row. To select more than one row, select the first row and then drag until you highlight the area you want.

- ✓ **Entire table:** Choose Table➪Select➪Table.

Adding new columns, rows, and cells

Here's how to add a new column to your table:

1. **Place the cursor anywhere inside the column to the right of where you want the new column to appear.**

2. **Click the Insert Columns button on the Tables toolbar.**

   A new column appears to the left of the selected column.

Adding new rows involves a similar procedure. To add a new row to an existing table, follow these steps:

1. **Place the cursor anywhere inside the row that is beneath where you want the new row to appear.**

2. **Click the Insert Rows button on the Tables toolbar.**

   A new row appears above the selected row.

If you want to add a single cell rather than an entire row or column, you can do that, too. Just follow these steps:

1. **Click inside the cell to the right of where you want the new cell to appear.**

2. **Choose Table➪Insert➪Cell.**

   A new cell appears.

When you insert a single cell, the cell dislocates the other cells in the row, creating a somewhat lopsided table. Not a problem if that's the effect you're looking for. However, if you want to add a cell to a table and, at the same time, maintain the table's grid-like structure, consider splitting an existing cell into two. I show you how to do this in the "Merging and splitting cells" section, later in this chapter.

Deleting columns, rows, and cells

Want to shave a cell, row, or column off your table? No problem. Just follow these steps:

1. **Select the cell(s), row(s), or column(s) you want to consign to oblivion.**

2. Click the Delete Cells button on the Tables toolbar.

The selected cells, rows, or columns and their contents disappear. (Had you pressed the Delete key instead, only the cell contents would have disappeared; the cells would have remained in place.)

Aligning cell contents

You can control the vertical (up and down) and horizontal (left and right) alignment of the stuff inside table cells. By selecting several cells, a row or column, or even the entire table, you can apply alignment controls to a group of cells in one fell swoop.

Button	What It Is	Found On	What It Does
	Align Top, Center Vertically, Align Bottom	Tables toolbar	Changes the vertical alignment of selected cells, rows, or columns.
	Align Left, Center, Align Right	Formatting toolbar	Changes the horizontal alignment of selected cells, rows, or columns.

The Cell Properties dialog box contains an extra vertical alignment option that lines cell contents up along the baseline (the invisible line on top of which text sits) and an extra horizontal alignment option that justifies cell contents. To access the Cell Properties dialog box, right-click the selected cells and choose Cell Properties from the pop-up menu that appears.

Tables and tribulations

FrontPage contains a bug (or is this quirk actually a feature?) that makes it possible to set the width of table columns to a number not equal to the total width of the table. For example, if you set the width of a two-column table to 100 pixels, you can also set the width of the table's columns to a number totaling more or less than 100.

FrontPage's display also gets confused if you set different widths for individual table cells (as opposed to entire columns of cells), especially if the table is complex. The solution is to keep your tables relatively simple. At the very least, preview your page in a Web browser (preferably more than one model) to see how your table looks to your visitors.

Changing cell, row, and column dimensions

Controlling the dimensions of table cells (and by extension, columns and rows) is similar to working with table dimensions, because you can set an absolute size in pixels or a proportional size based on the size of the entire table. If you want to use absolute measurements, the easiest way to adjust the dimensions of cells, rows, and columns is to click a border and drag it to a new position.

To use proportional measurements to adjust the height and/or width of a cell, column, or row (or for more control over the absolute dimensions), follow these steps:

1. **Select the cells, columns, or rows you want to format.**

2. **Right-click the selection and choose Cell Properties from the pop-up menu that appears.**

    The Cell Properties dialog box appears, as shown in Figure 7-10.

3. **In the dialog box's Specify Width text box, type the desired width.**

    (If the text box appears dimmed, be sure the Specify Width check box is selected.)

    If you are specifying a proportional width, type the width of the cell or column as a percentage of the width of the table. For example, if you type **50**, FrontPage sets the width of the cell or column at 50 percent, or half the width of table.

    If you are specifying an absolute width, type the width in pixels.

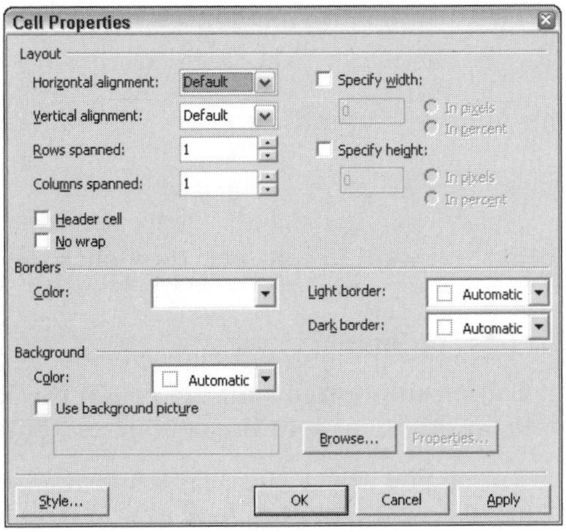

Cell Properties

Layout

Horizontal alignment: Default

Vertical alignment: Default

Rows spanned: 1

Columns spanned: 1

☐ Header cell
☐ No wrap

☐ Specify width:
0 ○ In pixels ○ In percent

☐ Specify height:
0 ○ In pixels ○ In percent

Borders

Color: Light border: ☐ Automatic
 Dark border: ☐ Automatic

Background

Color: ☐ Automatic
☐ Use background picture

Browse... Properties...

Style... OK Cancel Apply

Figure 7-10:
The Cell
Properties
dialog box.

To turn off width specifications, click to de-select the Specify Width check box. (If you do this, the size of the selected area is determined by the size of its contents.)

4. Select the option that corresponds to the measurement you specified in Step 3.

If you are specifying a proportional width, select the In Percent option. If you are specifying an absolute width, select the In Pixels option.

5. Select the Specify Height check box; in the corresponding text box, type the desired height in pixels or as a percentage value and then select the corresponding option.

To turn off height specifications, deselect the Specify Height check box.

6. Click OK to close the dialog box and change the dimension settings.

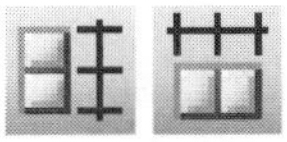

To distribute the rows and/or columns equally in the table, select the row or column and then click the Distribute Rows Evenly or the Distribute Columns Evenly button.

To adjust the dimensions of columns and rows to fit their contents precisely, click inside the table and then click the AutoFit To Contents button.

Merging and splitting cells

When you merge cells, you remove the borders between the cells, creating one big, combined cell. Splitting cells divides one cell into two or more cells that are arranged in rows or columns.

To merge cells, select the cells you want to merge and then click the Merge Cells button.

 Or click the Eraser button and swipe over the borders you want to erase.

To split cells, follow these steps:

1. **Select the cell (or cells) you want to split and then click the Split Cells button.**

    The Split Cells dialog box appears.

2. **Select the Split into Columns option to split the cell(s) vertically, or select the Split into Rows option to split the cell(s) horizontally.**

   Depending on which option you select, the diagram next to the options shows a representation of how the cell will look after it is split.

3. **In the Number of Columns text box (or Number of Rows text box, depending on your selection in Step 2), type the number of cells into which you want to divide the selected cell(s).**

4. **Click OK to close the dialog box and split the selected cells.**

Merging cells is different than using the Table AutoFormat command to render the border between cells invisible. When you merge cells, you actually transform more than one cell into a single cell (merging the cell contents as well). When you use the Table AutoFormat command, some of the cell borders become invisible, but the cells themselves remain distinct. I describe the Table AutoFormat command in detail earlier in this chapter, in the "Changing the borders" section.

Deleting a Table

Building the perfect table takes some work, but deleting a table is effortless. You can either preserve the table's contents by converting the contents to regular paragraphs, or you can erase the table and its contents completely.

To convert the contents of a table into regular paragraphs, click inside the table and then choose Table⇨Convert⇨Table to Text.

To *really* delete a table, select the table by choosing Table⇨Select⇨Table, and then press the Backspace or Delete key.

Chapter 8

Forms Aren't Only for the IRS

. . . .

In This Chapter

▶ Understanding how forms work

▶ Creating a form

▶ Working with different types of form fields

▶ Saving form results

▶ Adding a confirmation page to your site

. . . .

*W*hat's the first thing that pops into your mind when I say *forms?* Bureaucracy-perpetuating pieces of paper? Multipage monstrosities in triplicate? Well, put those thoughts aside for a moment, because I'm going to introduce you to the wonders of the *interactive form.* Interactive forms transform your Web site from a showpiece into a workhorse. Here are a few things you can do with forms:

✔ Survey your visitors and ask for their opinions.

✔ Enable visitors to search the contents of your site for keywords.

✔ Host a discussion group in which visitors post their thoughts on a continuously updated Web page.

✔ Promote community by providing a guest book that visitors "sign" by submitting a form.

All this, and you don't even need to hire an accountant.

How Do Forms Work?

Before you build a form, understanding the basics of how forms work can help. If this stuff seems a little tricky, don't worry. FrontPage 2003 takes care of the hard part. All you need to do is decide how you want to use forms in your Web site.

Like paper forms, interactive forms collect different types of information. Web site visitors fill in *fields,* either by typing information or selecting an item from a list. After visitors complete the form, they click a button to submit the information. The form shown in Figure 8-1 illustrates how this process works.

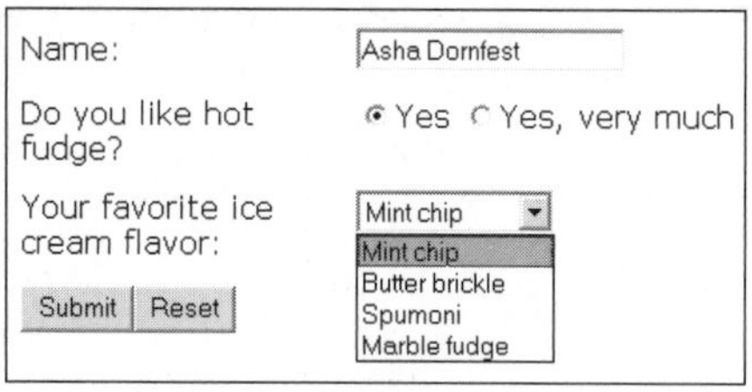

Figure 8-1:
A typical
Web page
form.

The information submitted from forms is organized into a list of *field names* (also known as *variable names*) and *field values.* The *field name* is a unique identifying descriptor assigned to each field in your form. The field name is invisible to your visitors; it exists inside the form's HTML and is visible only to the person (or computer) receiving the information submitted from the form. The pieces of text that you see in Figure 8-1 — Name, Your favorite ice cream flavor, and so on — are not field names; they are bits of regular text sitting inside the page, prompting the visitor to fill in the accompanying field.

The *field value* is the information that the visitor submits. Depending on the type of field, the value is either the stuff the visitor types or an item that the visitor chooses from a list you define. (In Figure 8-1, for example, the value of the third field is Mint Chip.)

What happens to that information after a visitor submits the completed form depends on the type of form handler assigned to the form. A *form handler* is a program that resides on the host Web server. This program receives the form data and then does something with it. Depending on the type of form handler, the program may, for example, save the data (also known as the *form results*) in a text file, format the results as a Web page, or even send the information back to the site administrator in an e-mail message.

Creating a Form

After that rah-rah introduction, no doubt you're pumped up and ready for some serious form creation. FrontPage is happy to oblige with three different methods: You can use a prefab form page template, you can tag along with the Form Page Wizard, or you can build your own form.

Using a form page template

FrontPage contains the following templates for forms that often show up in Web sites:

- ✔ **Feedback Form:** This template creates a simple form that visitors use to send comments, questions, or suggestions.

- ✔ **Guest Book:** This template also collects comments, but it saves the submissions in a public Web page that other visitors can read.

- ✔ **User Registration:** The User Registration template creates a registration page that enables you to track or restrict who visits the Web site. With a registration system in place, visitors can choose their own access user names and passwords, and you decide what level of access these visitors have to your site. (With regular permissions, which I discuss in Chapter 17, you choose the user names and passwords for your site's visitors.) FrontPage registration systems have fairly specific server requirements; for details, refer to the FrontPage Help system by choosing Help➪Microsoft FrontPage Help.

To create a form using a template, follow these steps:

1. **Choose File➪New.**

   The New task pane appears.

2. **In the New Page section of the task pane, click the More Page Templates link.**

   The Page Templates dialog box appears.

3. **In the dialog box's list of templates, double-click the template you want to use.**

   The dialog box closes, and a new page based on the template you chose appears in Design view.

Inside pages created by using form templates, the form consists of all the stuff inside the space surrounded by dotted lines, also known as the *form area*. The colorful comments at the top of the page give you hints about how to customize the form. The rest of what appears on-screen is a regular old Web page. Treat the entire page (including text inside the form area) just as you would any Web page: Format the text, insert graphics — whatever you want. These templates are pretty basic, so you'll most likely want to dress them up.

Using the Form Page Wizard

The Form Page Wizard possesses magical powers — at least, that's what I thought when I discovered how easy this wizard makes creating a form. The wizard walks you through the entire process of creating a form, including choosing form fields, suggesting questions to prompt visitors for different types of information, setting up the layout of the page, choosing a form handler, and deciding how to format form results.

Unless you have a Web form or two under your belt, you may not understand some of the Form Page Wizard's options at first glance. For that reason, before you activate the wizard, you might want to skim the rest of this chapter to familiarize yourself with forms. The form-creation process makes more sense after you do so, and you'll realize just how ingenious the Form Page Wizard really is.

To create a form with the help of the Form Page Wizard, follow these steps:

1. **Choose File⇨New.**

   The New task pane appears.

2. **In the New Page section of the task pane, click More Page Templates.**

   The Page Templates dialog box appears.

3. **In the dialog box's list of templates, double-click Form Page Wizard.**

   The dialog box closes, and the Form Page Wizard launches. The wizard's initial dialog box explains what the wizard is about to do. As with all wizards, click Next to advance to the next screen or Back to return to a previous screen. You can also click Cancel at any time to close the wizard.

4. **In the Form Page Wizard dialog box, click Next.**

   The next dialog box appears. Here, you decide what kind of information to include in your form.

5. **Click the Add button.**

   In the Select the Type of Input to Collect for This Question list box, the wizard lists several categories of information commonly collected with forms, as shown in Figure 8-2. Scroll down the list to see all your options.

6. **In the list box, click the first category of information you want your form to contain.**

   A description of the category appears inside the Description area. The text question that prompts visitors to fill in the field appears in the Edit the Prompt for This Question text box.

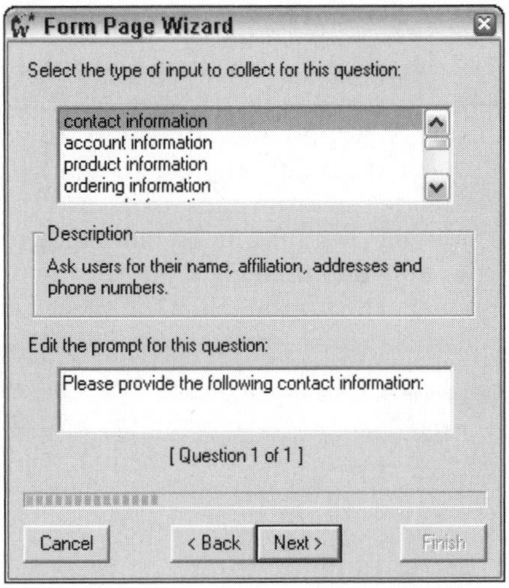

Figure 8-2:
The Form
Page
Wizard
helps you
decide what
kind of
information
to collect.

7. **If you like, change the wording of the text question in the Edit the Prompt for This Question box, and then click Next.**

The dialog box that appears next depends on the category you selected in Step 6. In this dialog box, you choose the specific types of information that you want the form to collect (see Figure 8-3). If some options don't seem to make sense to you yet, keep this book close at hand as you work and skim the rest of this chapter to clear things up.

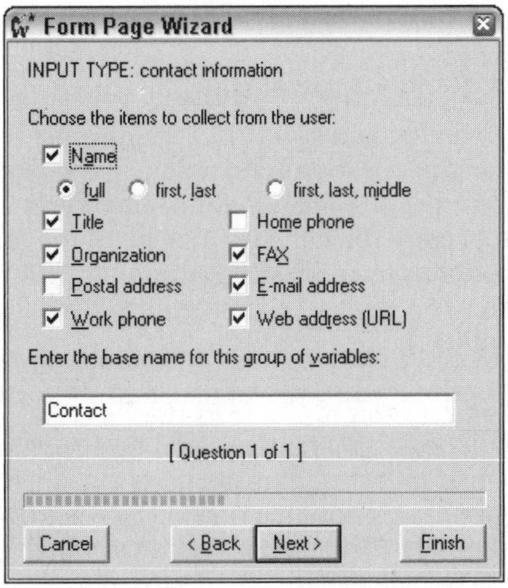

Figure 8-3:
Specify the
information
you want
the form to
contain.

8. After you choose the items you want the form to contain, click Next.

You return to the section of the wizard in which you add more questions to the form (see Figure 8-4). The question you chose in the previous steps appears inside the list box. To add more questions to your form, click the Add button and repeat Steps 6 through 8. To change the order in which questions appear inside the form, click an item in the list and then click the Move Up or Move Down button. To modify or remove any item in your form, select the item and then click the Modify or Remove button. To erase everything and start again, click the Clear List button.

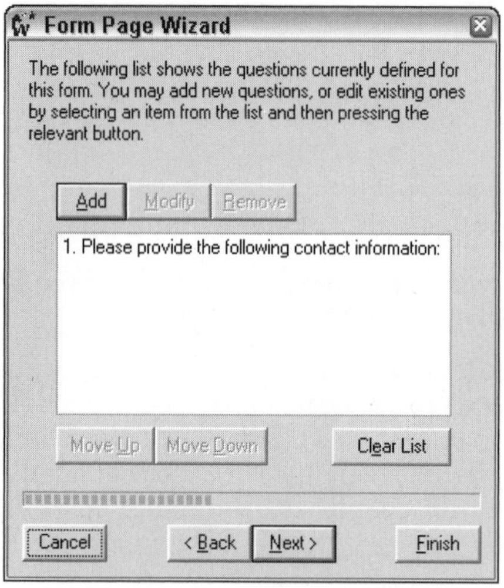

Figure 8-4:
Adding
questions to
your form.

9. When you finish adding questions, click Next.

The Presentation Options dialog box appears. Here, you decide how you want FrontPage to arrange the questions and fields on the page: as a series of paragraphs or as a list of items. (Refer to Chapter 4 for a description of each type of list.) You can also include in the form page a Table of Contents that contains links to each section of the form. Finally, you can tell the wizard to use a table to align the form fields. (Chapters 7 and 9 tell you all about tables.)

10. Select the presentation options you want to use, and then click Next.

The Output Options dialog box appears. Here, you decide what happens to the information contained in form submissions. (I explain each output option — plus a couple of options not included in the wizard — later in this chapter.) You also choose a filename for the file in which the information submitted from forms will eventually be stored.

11. Choose an output option and then click Next to advance to the final dialog box of the Form Page Wizard.

12. Click Finish to create the form page.

The wizard disappears after it generates a new page containing a form based on your specifications.

Adding a form to an existing page

A form is nothing more than a particular type of HTML that sits inside a page. You can, therefore, add a form to any Web page. To do so, you can rely on the assistance of the Form Page Wizard, or you can create a form from scratch.

 If you want the help of the Form Page Wizard but want to add the resulting form to an existing page, follow the steps in the preceding section to create a new form, and then copy and paste the form (including the form area) into an existing page.

To build your own form, follow the directions in the next section of this chapter.

Working with Form Fields

If the FrontPage form templates and Form Page Wizard don't create the kind of form you want, you can easily build your own form by adding individual form fields to a page.

Form fields are the collection plates into which visitors drop bits of information. The kinds of fields you include in your form depend on the kinds of information you want to gather. Do you want visitors to select from a predefined list of choices? Would you rather let them fill in whatever information they like? The answers to these questions determine the types of fields you should use in your form.

To create your own form, you add one or more fields to a page and then customize the fields so that they look and act the way that you want them to. By *customize,* I mean that you assign the field a *name* — in some cases, a *value* — and you adjust how the field looks. (I explain what field names and values are earlier in this chapter.) You can also create data entry rules for certain fields that restrict the kind of information visitors can enter there.

The first time you add a form field to a page, FrontPage sets aside a space for the form (indicated by a box surrounded by dotted lines) and inserts Submit and Reset buttons. (Visitors click these buttons to submit completed forms and to clear form contents; I talk more about how these buttons work later in this chapter.) You add fields to the form by inserting one or more fields inside the form area. You can add as many fields as you like to your form. You can cut, copy, and paste fields. You can also drag and drop fields to different locations.

To add fields to your page, you use the Insert⇨Form command. You can build a field-laden form more quickly by *floating* the Insert⇨Form menu — that is, transforming the menu into a toolbar. To do so, choose Insert⇨Form, and then move your pointer over the thin stripe at the top of the menu that appears. When the stripe appears highlighted, click and drag the menu elsewhere inside the FrontPage window.

When you add fields to a form, you must insert the fields *inside* the form area. If you insert a form field outside the form area, FrontPage thinks that you want to create a second form and creates a new form area, complete with its own Submit and Reset buttons. These two forms will then work independently of each other. Although technically one Web page can contain multiple forms, I assume that your intention is to create a single form.

As you create your form, be sure to preview the page to get a more accurate picture of how the page will look after it's published. If you're not sure how to preview a page, refer to Chapter 2.

Form design tips

Here are a few tricks to make your homegrown forms easy for visitors to fill out:

✔ **Place helpful descriptors next to each field.** If, for example, you include a field in your form for the visitor's e-mail address, use the text descriptor E-mail address (username@domain.com) to make it absolutely clear what information you want.

✔ **Help visitors provide you with the correct information.** If your form contains mandatory fields or fields that require information to be entered in a certain way, include a note that demonstrates the correct format or at least that reads *This field is required.*

✔ **Use a layout table to keep the form's layout neat and tidy.** Insert the first form field in the page. Inside the form area, create a two-column layout table, and then drag and drop the field into the top-right table cell. Next,

place text descriptors in the left column and more form fields in the right column. (Chapter 9 explains how to build a layout table.)

✔ **Pay attention to the order of the fields.** Most Web browsers enable visitors to use the Tab key to advance to the next field. You, therefore, should arrange fields in sequential order.

✔ **Use default text in text box fields (also known as the field's initial value) to save visitors' time and effort.** For example, if your form asks the visitor's country of origin and most of your visitors are American, use *USA* as the field's default text.

✔ **Consider rewarding your visitors for taking the time to fill out the form.** Enter them in a drawing (with their permission) or give them access to free downloadable goodies.

Finally, I've held off on explaining two types of form fields in this section: the list form and the list field. These fields are specific to a site that's published on a Web server that supports SharePoint Team Services. I talk briefly about SharePoint in Chapter 17.

Text boxes

Text boxes are plain-vanilla fields into which visitors type a single line of text. Use a text box when you want to collect small bits of information, such as a name or an e-mail address. Figure 8-5 shows a filled-in text box as it appears in a Web browser.

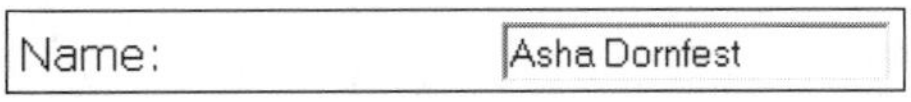

Figure 8-5:
A text
box field.

Name: |Asha Dornfest

Creating a text box

To add a text box to your page, follow these steps:

1. **Place the cursor in the page where you want the field to appear (for a new form, anywhere in the page, or to add a field to an existing form, inside the form area), and then choose Insert⇨Form⇨Textbox.**

   A text box appears on your page.

2. **In the page, double-click the text box.**

   The Text Box Properties dialog box appears.

3. **In the dialog box's Name text box, type the field name.**

   Choose a one-word, generic name that describes the information that the text box collects. If, for example, you're creating a text box to collect a visitor's e-mail address, type **E-mail** or **E-mail_address**.

   Always keep your field names restricted to one word. (You can use the underscore character to cheat a bit, as I did in the preceding example.) Some Web servers aren't able to process forms with longer field names. The name you choose does not need to match the text descriptor you insert in the page to identify the field to visitors.

4. **If you want the text box field to appear with default text inside (instead of empty), type the text in the Initial Value text box.**

5. **In the Width in Characters text box, type the visible width of the text box field.**

The number you type affects the visible size of the text box, not the amount of text a visitor can type in the text box. To limit the amount of text a visitor can type into a text box, use a validation option, as described in the following section.

If you prefer to adjust the width of a text box by hand, skip this step. Instead, after you're finished defining the text box's properties, click the text box in the page and then drag the field's size handles until you're satisfied with its new width.

6. Optionally, type a number in the Tab Order text box.

The *tab order* is the order in which the cursor advances to the next field when a visitor presses the Tab key. By default, the tab order is sequential; the visitor fills out the first form field and then presses Tab to advance to the next field in the form. By entering a number in the Tab Order text box, you can control the sequence in which the cursor moves. For example, type **1** in the Tab Order text box if you want the current field to be the first field in which the cursor appears, even if that field isn't the first field on the page.

As of this writing, only Internet Explorer (version 4.0 or later) can display changes in tab order. In other browsers, the tab order is sequential, starting with the first field in the form.

7. Specify whether the text box is a password field.

Password fields are no different from regular text boxes except that, when viewed with a browser, text that someone types into a password field appears on-screen as dots or asterisks. These characters prevent nosy passersby from seeing the characters that you type.

Including a password field in your form *does not* automatically add password protection to your Web site. I show you how to work with passwords in Chapter 17.

8. To restrict the type of information visitors can enter into the text box, click the Validate button.

The following section explains how to use validation options. If you don't want to restrict the information visitors can enter, skip this step.

9. Click OK.

The dialog box closes, and any default text you specified appears inside the text box. If you changed the width of the text box, it stretches or shrinks accordingly.

Validating information entered into a text box

FrontPage enables you to make certain form fields mandatory. Unless visitors complete these fields, they can't submit the form. You can also control the format of information that visitors type into text boxes. This control is especially helpful if you want to standardize the format of form results.

Before you use FrontPage validation features, you must first specify how you want FrontPage to create the data rules. See the section, "Setting Up FrontPage Form Validation," later in this chapter, for details.

After you click the Validate button in the Text Box Properties dialog box, the Text Box Validation dialog box appears, as shown in Figure 8-6.

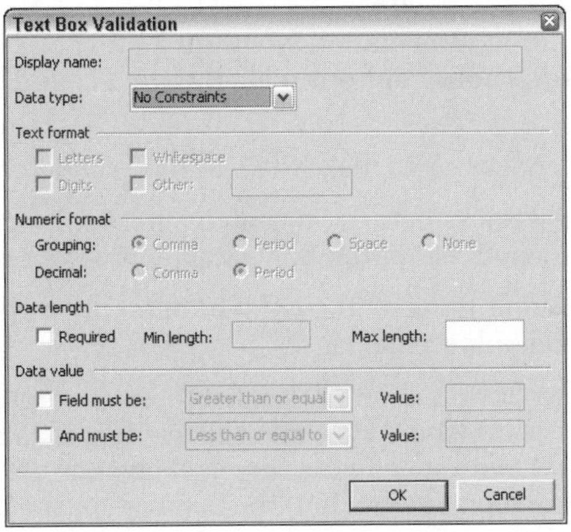

Figure 8-6:
The Text
Box
Validation
dialog box.

To validate information entered into text boxes, follow these steps:

1. **To restrict the type of data that can be entered into the text box, choose an option from the Data Type list box.**

   Choose one of the following options: No Constraints (no restrictions on data type), Text (letters, characters, or numerals), Integer (whole numbers only), or Number (all numbers, both whole and decimal).

2. **Depending on the option you chose in Step 1, choose an option from either the Text Format or the Numeric Format area of the dialog box.**

   If you chose the Text data type, choose from the following options in the Text Format area of the dialog box:

   • **Letters:** Creates a text box that can contain only alphabetic characters.

   • **Digits:** Creates a text box that can contain only numeric characters.

   • **Whitespace:** Creates a text box that can contain white space (such as spaces, tabs, and line breaks).

   • **Other:** If you want to allow other types of characters (such as commas or hyphens, for example), select the Other check box and type the characters in the corresponding text box.

If you chose the Integer or Number data type, choose from the following options in the Numeric Format area of the dialog box:

- **Grouping:** Enables you to control how visitors punctuate numbers greater than or equal to 1,000: with a comma (1,000), with a period (1.000), or with no punctuation (1000).

- **Decimal:** Enables you to choose which punctuation character visitors can use as a decimal point: a period or a comma.

3. **To control the amount of information typed into a text box or to make a text box mandatory, choose options from the Data Length area of the dialog box.**

   Select the Required check box to make the text box mandatory.

   Type a number of characters in the Min Length and Max Length text boxes to control the length of information entered into the text box.

4. **To place restrictive conditions on the content of text box data, choose options from the Data Value area.**

   If you choose the Text or No Constraints data type, these options compare the information that visitors type into the text box against the order of the alphabet. If you specify that the field must be greater than *E*, for example, all information entered into the text box must start with the letter *F* or any other letter later in the alphabet (such as *H, Q,* or *Z* — but not *A, C,* or even *E*). I can't imagine why anyone would use this option, but there it is.

   If you choose the Integer or Number data type, these options make a numerical order comparison. If you specify that the field must be less than or equal to 10, for example, a visitor may type *10* or any lesser number in the text box.

5. **Click OK to close the dialog box.**

If a visitor enters information that doesn't stick to the validation rules, a *validation warning message* appears. The warning message identifies the offending field to the visitor by using the field name you entered in the Name text box in the Text Box Properties dialog box. If the field name you used wouldn't make sense to a visitor (say, the field collects phone numbers and you chose field name phon_num), you can specify a friendlier display name (such as Phone Number) for the purposes of the validation warning. To do so, type the display name text in the Display Name text box, which is at the top of the Text Box Validation dialog box (refer to Figure 8-6).

Text areas

Text areas are just like text boxes, except that this type of field holds more than one line of text. Text areas are ideal for verbose visitors who want to send lots of comments.

To create a text area, follow these steps:

1. **Place the cursor in the page where you want the field to appear (for a new form, anywhere in the page, or to add a field to an existing form, inside the form area) and then choose Insert⇨Form⇨Text Area.**

   A text area field appears on the page.

2. **In the page, double-click the field.**

   The TextArea Box Properties dialog box appears.

3. **In the Name text box, type the text area's field name.**

   The name you choose does not need to match the text descriptor that you insert in the page to identify the field to visitors.

4. **If you want the text area to appear with default text inside, type that text in the Initial Value text box.**

5. **In the Width in Characters text box, type the visible width of the text area.**

6. **In the Number of Lines text box, type the number of lines of text that the text area can hold.**

   Effectively, this option controls the field's height. You can also adjust the height and width by hand (after you finish defining the field's properties) by clicking the text area and dragging the size handles until the field is the size you want.

7. **Optionally, type a number in the Tab Order text box.**

   You can find out more about the tab order in Step 6 in the section, "Creating a text box," earlier in this chapter.

8. **To restrict the type of information that visitors can type into the text area, click the Validate button.**

   Before you use FrontPage validation features, you must first specify how you want FrontPage to create the data rules. See the section, "Setting Up FrontPage Form Validation," later in this chapter, for details.

   Refer to the preceding section, "Validating information entered into a text box," for details on how to use validation options. If you don't want to restrict this information, skip this step.

9. Click OK.

The dialog box closes, and any default text you specified appears inside the text area. If you changed the size of the text area, it stretches or shrinks accordingly.

Check boxes

Check boxes are like teenagers: They're independent but still prefer to hang around in groups. (Figure 8-7 shows an example of what a group of check boxes looks like in a Web browser.) Use check boxes if you want visitors to select as many items as they want from a predefined list. You can include one check box or many in your form.

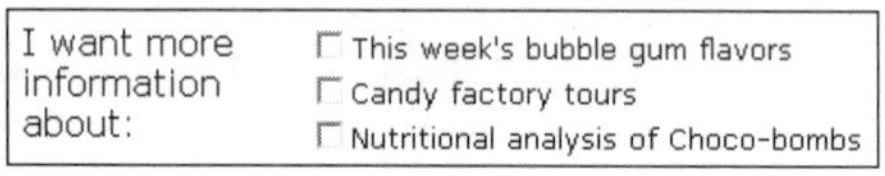

Figure 8-7:
A gang
of check
boxes.

I want more information about:

☐ This week's bubble gum flavors
☐ Candy factory tours
☐ Nutritional analysis of Choco-bombs

To insert a check box, follow these steps:

1. Place the cursor in the page where you want the field to appear. (For a new form, place the cursor anywhere in the page; to add a field to an existing form, place the cursor inside the form area.) Then choose Insert⇨Form⇨Checkbox.

A check box appears on your page.

2. In the page, double-click the check box.

The Check Box Properties dialog box appears.

3. In the Name text box, type the check box's field name.

The name you choose does not need to match the text descriptor that you insert in the page to identify the field to visitors. You should, however, stick to one word for the field name.

4. In the Value text box, type a word or two that describes what the selected check box means.

For example, suppose you're using a check box to enable visitors to request more information about a particular product. Using the first check box in Figure 8-7 as an example, flavors is a good name choice, and more info is a good value choice, because if visitors select that check box, their choice means "I want more information about bubble gum flavors."

5. **If you want the check box to appear checked initially, select the Checked option.**

6. **If you want to specify a tab order, type a number in the Tab Order text box.**

   You can find out more about the tab order in Step 6 in the section, "Creating a text box," earlier in this chapter.

7. **Click OK to close the Check Box Properties dialog box.**

To add more check boxes, repeat the preceding steps until you have all the check boxes you want.

Option buttons

If check boxes are independent teens, *option buttons* are a giddy high school clique. Option buttons are never seen alone and base their identity solely on the others in the group.

Use a group of option buttons to present visitors with a list of choices from which only one option may be selected. Figure 8-8 shows an example of what a group of option buttons looks like in a Web browser.

Figure 8-8:
A gathering
of option
buttons.

To create an option button group, follow these steps:

1. **Place the cursor in the page where you want the field to appear (for a new form, anywhere in the page, or to add a field to an existing form, inside the form area) and then choose Insert⇨Form⇨Option Button.**

   A single option button appears on your page.

2. **In the page, double-click the option button.**

   The Option Button Properties dialog box appears.

3. **In the Group Name text box, type a name that applies to the entire group (even though you've created only one option button so far).**

   In the example shown in Figure 8-8, the Group Name is LikeFudge.

The group name you choose does not need to match the text descriptor that you insert in the page to identify the list of option buttons to visitors.

4. In the Value text box, type the value for the individual option button.

In the example shown in Figure 8-8, the value for the first option button is Yes.

5. If you want the option button to appear deselected initially, click the Not Selected option button.

By default, the first option button in a group appears selected.

6. If you want to specify a tab order, type a number in the Tab Order text box.

You can find out more about the tab order in Step 6 in the section, "Creating a text box," earlier in this chapter.

7. If you want to require visitors to choose one of the items in the list of option buttons, click the Validate button.

Before you use FrontPage validation features, you must first specify how you want FrontPage to create the data rules. See the section, "Setting Up FrontPage Form Validation," later in this chapter, for details.

(In this case, validation applies only to an option button group in which none of the option buttons appears initially selected.) In the Option Button Validation dialog box that appears, select the Data Required check box. If you want the validation warning message to identify the option button group by a name other than the group name that you specified in Step 3, type a display name in the Display Name text box. (The "Validating information entered into a text box" section, earlier in the chapter, explains the purpose of the display name.) Click OK to close the Option Button Validation dialog box.

8. Click OK to close the Option Button Properties dialog box.

Now you must create at least one more option button to complete the group. To do so, follow these steps:

1. Place the cursor inside the form area (ideally, near the first option button field) and then choose Insert⇨Form⇨Option Button.

A second option button appears on the page, to the right of the first one.

2. In the page, double-click the second option button.

The Option Button Properties dialog box appears. The Group Name is the same as for the first option button. (I told you they stick together.) All you need to do is give the second option button a unique value. In the example shown in Figure 8-8, the value for the second option button is Very Much.

3. **Choose the option button's initial state.**

   If you want the second option button to appear initially selected, click the Selected option. (By default, the first option button in a group appears selected. If you choose this option, the first option button in the group appears initially empty.) If you want the second option button to appear empty, click the Not Selected option.

4. **If you want to specify a tab order, type a number in the Tab Order text box.**

5. **Click OK to close the Option Button Properties dialog box.**

Validation options apply to the entire option button group, so whatever you specify for the first option button applies to all the option buttons in that particular group.

Drop-down boxes

Drop-down boxes are so named because, after you click the field, a list of choices "drops down." Figure 8-9 shows how a drop-down box works when viewed with a Web browser.

Figure 8-9: A drop-down box.	Your favorite ice cream flavor: [Mint chip ▾]
	Mint chip
	Butter brickle
	Spumoni
	Marble fudge

Like option button groups, drop-down boxes let visitors choose from a predefined group of options. In some cases, drop-down boxes have some advantages over option button groups, such as the following:

- ✔ Drop-down boxes save space on your page by popping open only after a visitor clicks the down arrow next to the option.

- ✔ You can set up a drop-down box to accept more than one choice at a time.

To create a drop-down box, follow these steps:

1. **Place the cursor in the page where you want the field to appear (for a new form, anywhere in the page, or to add a field to an existing form, inside the form area) and then choose Insert⇨Form⇨Drop-Down Box.**

   A drop-down box field appears on your page.

2. **In the page, double-click the drop-down box.**

   The Drop-Down Box Properties dialog box appears, as shown in Figure 8-10.

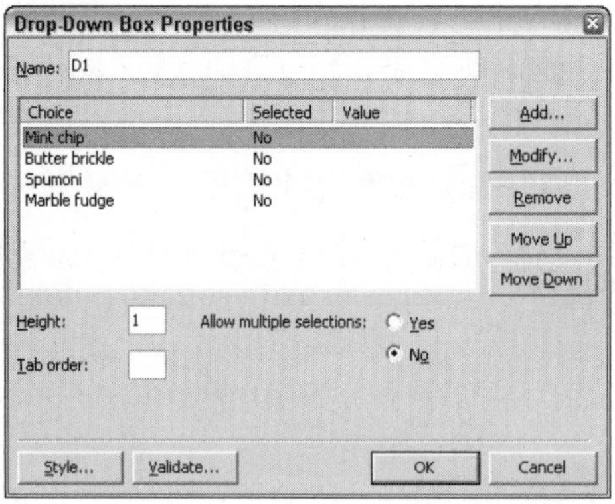

Figure 8-10:
The Drop-Down Box Properties dialog box.

3. **In the Name text box, type the field name.**

   In the example in Figure 8-10, the name is `Favorite_flavor`.

   The name you choose does not need to match the text descriptor you insert in the page to identify the field to visitors.

4. **To add menu choices, click the Add button.**

   The Add Choice dialog box appears, as shown in Figure 8-11.

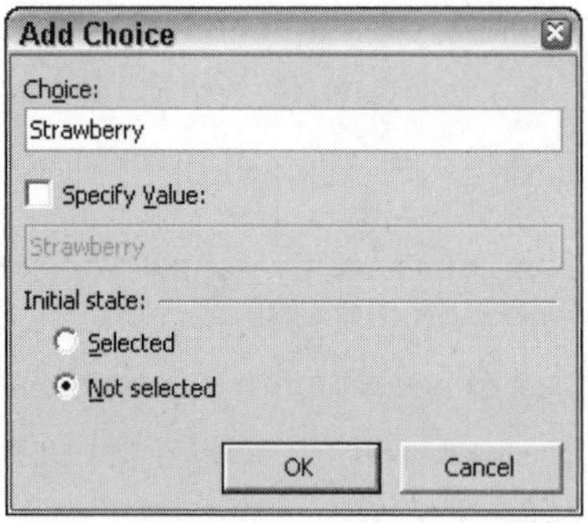

Figure 8-11:
The Add Choice dialog box.

5. **In the Choice text box, type the text that you want to appear in the drop-down box.**

   In the example shown in Figure 8-10, the choices are Mint Chip, Spumoni, and so on.

6. **If you want the choice's value to be something other than the information you type in the Choice text box, select the Specify Value check box and then type the value in the accompanying text box.**

   For example, you add a choice of Chocolate/Fudge to the drop-down box, but when you transfer the form results into a database, the database program is unable to process the / character. By selecting the Specify Value check box in the Add Choice dialog box, you can instead specify a value of Chocolate_Fudge. That way, visitors select an item from the drop-down box that reads Chocolate/Fudge, but the database receives the value Chocolate_Fudge.

7. **If you want the choice to appear initially selected, click the Selected option.**

8. **Click OK to close the Add Choice dialog box.**

9. **Repeat Steps 4 through 8 to add more menu choices until the drop-down box is complete.**

   You can rearrange, modify, or remove menu items by selecting the item in the list and then clicking the Move Up, Move Down, Modify, or Remove button (in the Drop-Down Box Properties dialog box).

10. **In the Height text box (refer to Figure 8-10), type the number of menu choices that are visible before a visitor clicks the drop-down box and causes it to "drop down."**

    You can also manually adjust the height and width of a drop-down box (after you're finished defining the field's properties) by clicking the drop-down box in your page and dragging its size handles.

11. **To enable visitors to select more than one item from the list, select the Yes option in the Allow Multiple Selections area of the dialog box.**

    When visitors view the form with a Web browser, they select more than one option by pressing and holding the Ctrl key or the Apple Command key (⌘) as they click their selections.

12. **If you want to specify a tab order, type a number in the Tab Order text box.**

    You can find out more about the tab order in Step 6 in the section, "Creating a text box," earlier in this chapter.

13. **If you want to restrict choices in the drop-down box or make choosing an item mandatory, click the Validate button.**

    The Drop-Down Box Validation dialog box appears.

    Before you use FrontPage validation features, you must first specify how you want FrontPage to create the data rules. See the next section, "Setting Up FrontPage Form Validation," for details.

    To require that visitors choose an item from the list, select the Data Required check box. (In the case of multiple-selection lists, you can specify a minimum and maximum number of choices.) To disallow the first list choice as a valid selection (if, for example, the first item on your list reads *Choose one*), select the Disallow First Item check box. Click OK to close the Drop-Down Box Validation dialog box.

14. **Click OK to close the Drop-Down Box Properties dialog box.**

    The first menu choice becomes visible in the drop-down box in your page. (If you specified that more than one menu choice is initially visible, the drop-down box expands to display the specified number of choices.)

Group boxes make your forms friendlier

You build a long form. It contains many fields. Your users have visions of final exams, tax day, and associated unpleasantness.

Don't like where this image is heading? Take it from me, neither do your visitors. When you include a form in your site, you must give your visitors every reason to fill it out. A surefire way to scare away your respondents is to load your form with lots of time-consuming fields.

Group boxes can ease the sting of a long form by creating visual groupings of related form fields. Group boxes are empty, captioned rectangles into which you can insert form fields. Group boxes don't *do* anything per se, but, if your form must contain lots of fields, group boxes do visually divide your form into palatable chunks of information. For example, imagine users must fill in a lengthy form in order to register for your site. Instead of bombarding your visitors with 30 empty fields, you can group related details (such as contact information, interests, and referral information) inside group boxes to break the form into more manageable pieces.

See if your form can benefit with the addition of a group box or two. Adding group boxes is easy; just follow these steps:

1. **Click anywhere inside the form area and then choose Insert⇨Form⇨Group Box.**

    A group box appears inside your form.

2. **Insert the fields of your choice inside the group box, or drag existing fields into the group box.**

    You can do anything inside the group box that you can do inside the form area — add descriptive text, format text, align the form fields using a layout table, and more.

3. **To change the group box caption, select the caption and type new text.**

4. **To change the caption alignment, right-click inside the group box and choose Group Box Properties from the pop-up menu that appears.**

    The Group Box Properties dialog box appears.

5. **Choose an option from the Align list box and then click OK to close the dialog box.**

You can nest group boxes (place group boxes within group boxes), you can format the caption text, and you can format the box itself by accessing Cascading Style Sheets (CSS) commands using the Style button in the Group Box Properties dialog box. (See Chapter 14 for more about the capabilities of a CSS.) Note that group boxes look different in different browsers (and may not appear at all in older browsers).

Setting Up FrontPage Form Validation

Note: You only need to read this section if you set up validation rules for any of your form fields.

If you use FrontPage form validation, FrontPage takes down all the data-entry requirements you specify as a set of rules. You can tell FrontPage to store these data rules in one of two locations: either as a script that sits inside the HTML of your Web page, or as a script stored on the host Web server. Why do you care? Because if you choose the wrong method, a few of your visitors may be able to slip past your data rules, making their presence a moot point. Here's why.

By default, FrontPage stores the data rules as a script inside the Web page. The advantage to this method is the speed at which the browser is able to check the information. If a visitor enters information that doesn't conform to a data rule, a pesky dialog box pops up right away prompting the visitor to change the entry. Unfortunately, this approach comes with a big downside: If a visitor using an older browser fills in the form, the validation doesn't work because the browser doesn't know how to process the script and so simply ignores the data rules.

The other option is to tell FrontPage to store the data rules on the host server. If you choose this method, after a visitor fills in the form and clicks the Submit button, the form handler checks the submission against the data rules. If everything checks out, the server sends back a response letting the visitor know all is well. If not, the visitor gets an error message and is returned to the form to try again. This method is clunkier for visitors, but it ensures that all visitors, regardless of browser choice, must comply with the form's data rules. The only requirement is that you publish your Web site on a host Web server that has FrontPage Server Extensions installed (I talk more about FrontPage Server Extensions in Chapter 17).

To choose the method or scripting language that FrontPage uses to create data rules, follow these steps:

1. **Choose Tools⇨Site Settings.**

   The Site Settings dialog box appears.

2. **At the top of the dialog box, click the Advanced tab.**

3. **From the Client list box, choose the appropriate option.**

   To store data rules inside the Web page, choose JavaScript or VBScript. (Only Internet Explorer 3.0 or later understands VBScript, whereas recent versions of both Internet Explorer and Netscape Navigator understand JavaScript.)

   To store the data rules on the host Web server, choose <None>.

4. **Click OK to close the dialog box.**

   The Microsoft FrontPage dialog box appears, prompting you to recalculate the Web site.

5. **Click Yes.**

   The dialog box closes, and FrontPage recalculates the site. You can now set up data rules for your form.

Specifying What Happens to Form Results

All the real action occurs *after* a visitor submits the form. What happens to the form results is up to you; you decide how and where the information eventually ends up. The FrontPage Server Extensions come with a brilliant built-in form handler that can format the information visitors submit and then dump the information into a text file, a Web page, or an e-mail message. If, for some reason, the FrontPage form handler doesn't fit the bill, you can use FrontPage to hitch your form to a custom form-handling script.

Adding Submit and Reset buttons

When you first insert a form field into a page, the field appears along with two hangers-on: the *Submit button* and the *Reset button.* The Submit button is the linchpin of the entire operation. After visitors click this powerful button, their browsers activate the form handler program, which takes over from there, processing the form results.

If a standard gray Submit button is too boring for your taste, you can replace it with a *picture field.* Rather than a staid button, you can insert a snazzy picture. Clicking the picture submits the form results, just as a Submit button would.

The Reset button is another handy form tool. After visitors click the Reset button, their browsers clear all the information they entered into the form so that they can start over fresh. Alas, Reset buttons cannot be replaced by picture fields and are fated to look like plain gray rectangles.

FrontPage automatically places a Submit button and a Reset button inside every form you create. In case you accidentally delete the buttons, the following sections give instructions for manually inserting the buttons (as well as a picture field).

Inserting a Submit or Reset button

To insert a Submit button or a Reset button, follow these steps:

1. **Place the cursor inside your form and then choose Insert⇨Form⇨ Push Button.**

   A push button field (with the label *Button*) appears on your page.

2. **In the page, double-click the push button field.**

   The Push Button Properties dialog box appears.

3. **In the Name text box, type** Submit **or** Reset, **depending on the kind of button you're creating.**

4. **If you want the text on top of the button to read something other than the word Button, type new text in the Value/Label text box.**

   How about something vivid? A Submit button could read *Come to Mama!* and a Reset button could read *I changed my mind.*

5. **In the Button Type area, select the Submit or Reset option.**

6. **If you want to specify a tab order, type a number in the Tab Order text box.**

   You can find out more about the tab order in Step 6 in the section, "Creating a text box," earlier in this chapter.

7. **Click OK to close the Push Button Properties dialog box.**

Another push button field type sits quietly inside the Push Button Properties dialog box: the Normal push button. You can program this type of button to do just about anything. You can, for example, include a button in your Web page that plays a sound clip or opens a new Web page when a visitor clicks the button.

For such a feature to work, however, you need to write an associated script (a mini-program that gets embedded into the page's HTML code) using a client-side scripting language such as JavaScript. Intrigued? Check out *JavaScript For Dummies,* 3rd Edition, by Emily A. Vander Veer (Wiley Publishing, Inc.) to find out more.

What about the Advanced Button option, which you can find by choosing Insert⇨Form⇨Advanced Button? This option creates a push button field that looks and acts similarly to the Normal push button described earlier. Unfortunately, many browsers don't recognize the HTML tag required to create an advanced button, so I don't recommend using this feature.

Take my file, please

With the *file upload field,* visitors can send you much more than just their feedback. They can actually upload files (real, honest-to-goodness files, such as Web pages, Microsoft Word documents, or any other type of file) to a special folder in your Web site.

Say you're working on an online family tree. Instead of managing a bunch of unwieldy e-mail attachments, your relatives can instead upload their files and photos to a common folder in your Web site. All the files are in one place, nice and tidy.

Adding a file upload field to your form isn't difficult, but does require a few extra steps. File upload fields also have specific browser and server requirements. I'll leave you in the capable hands of article #299763 in the Microsoft Knowledge Base, which explains, step-by-step, how to proceed. See `support.microsoft.com/default.aspx?scid=kb;en-us;299763` for details.

Inserting a picture field

To use a picture field in place of a Submit button, follow these steps:

1. **Choose Insert➪Form➪Picture.**

   The Picture dialog box appears, because you can use any graphic file as the basis for a picture field.

2. **Insert the picture of your choice into your page.**

3. **In the page, double-click the picture field.**

   The Picture Properties dialog box appears with the Form Field tab visible.

4. **In the Name text box, type a field name (such as** Submit**).**

5. **Click OK to close the dialog box.**

Designating where form results go

The Submit button is useless unless you specify where and in what manner to send the form results. In the following sections, I describe the ways in which you can save the information submitted from your form.

The built-in FrontPage form handler described in the next few sections works only if the host Web server on which you publish your site supports FrontPage Server Extensions. If your host Web server doesn't support FrontPage Server Extensions, jump ahead to the section called, "Sending form results to a custom form-handling script." If you're not sure what FrontPage Server Extensions are, see Chapter 17.

Saving form results as a file in your Web site

By default, FrontPage saves form results in a text file stored in your Web site. The first time a visitor submits a form, FrontPage creates the file and stores the information inside that file. From then on, each time a new visitor submits a form, FrontPage appends the new form results to the file (old submissions don't disappear).

After visitors submit the form, they are greeted by a *confirmation page* (a page that tells them that the form was successfully submitted) or a *validation failure page* (a page that appears if data they entered into the form didn't obey a server-based data rule), in which case they must return to the form and enter new information.

To control how FrontPage saves form results in a file, follow these steps:

1. **Right-click inside the form area and choose Form Properties from the pop-up menu that appears.**

   The Form Properties dialog box appears (see Figure 8-12).

   In this dialog box, the Where to Store Results area contains options that let you choose where you want form results to go.

2. **Leave the contents of the File Name text box alone.**

   By default, FrontPage saves form results in a text file (the filename extension CSV denotes *comma-separated value*). In Step 4, you can choose a different file format for the results page, such as a plain text file or a comma-delimited text file (which makes form results easy to import into a database).

   By default, FrontPage saves form results inside the _private folder. Documents stored in the _private folder remain hidden from Web browsers and from the Web Search component (a Web component that you find out about in Chapter 12).

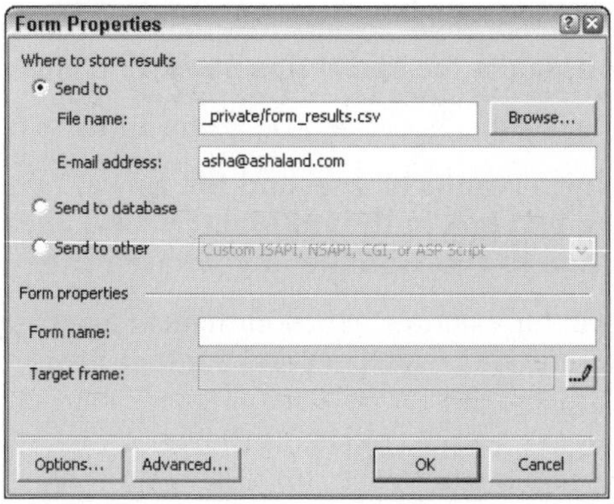

Figure 8-12:
The Form Properties dialog box.

3. In the dialog box, click the Options button.

The Saving Results dialog box appears, with the File Results tab visible (see Figure 8-13). This dialog box enables you to customize the results page.

4. In the File Format list box, choose your desired page format.

You can save the results file as an HTML file (that is, as a Web page), an XML file, or as a text file. You can format HTML files as definition lists, bulleted lists, numbered lists, or formatted text. You can save text files as formatted plain text (a nicely laid-out list of field names and values) or as a file with commas, tabs, or spaces separating names and values. (The latter format is handy if you want to import the data into a database or spreadsheet later.)

5. If you want the field names as well as the field values to appear in the results file, select the Include Field Names check box.

6. If you want the most recent form results to appear at the bottom of the file instead of the top, select the Latest Results at End check box.

Note: If the results file is a new file, this check box appears dimmed.

7. If you want to save form results in a second file as well, type the file path in the File Name text box in the Optional Second File area, or click the Browse button to choose a file in your Web site.

This option is handy if, for example, you want FrontPage to generate one file for importing info into a spreadsheet and another file for your own private viewing.

8. **At the top of the dialog box, click the Confirmation Page tab.**

   The Confirmation Page tab becomes visible. (I cover the E-mail Results tab in the next section.)

   This tab enables you to specify custom confirmation and validation failure pages. (You discover how to create confirmation pages later in this chapter.) If you leave this section empty, FrontPage automatically creates generic pages (and you can skip ahead to Step 11).

9. **In the URL of Confirmation Page text box, type the location of the confirmation page (or click the Browse button to choose a page in your Web site).**

10. **In the URL of Validation Failure Page text box, type the validation failure page location (or click the Browse button to choose a page in your Web site).**

    Note: This text box is available only if your form uses server-based data validation rules.

11. **At the top of the dialog box, click the Saved Fields tab.**

    If you want only the results of certain form fields to appear in the results page, you can say so in this tab. You can also save additional information in the results file.

12. **In the Form Fields to Save text box, delete the names of the fields for which you don't want results saved.**

13. **In the Date and Time area, choose options from the Date Format and Time Format list boxes.**

    By doing so, you tell FrontPage to affix a date and/or time stamp to each form submission.

14. **In the Additional Information to Save area, select the check boxes next to the other types of information that you want the results file to contain.**

    FrontPage can track the visitor's network user name, the name of the computer from which the form was submitted, and the type of Web browser the visitor was using at the time.

15. **Click OK to close the Saving Results dialog box.**

16. **Click OK to close the Form Properties dialog box.**

Keep in mind that FrontPage creates and saves the results file you just specified on the host server on which you publish your Web site, *not* on your local computer's hard drive.

Sending form results to an e-mail address

Sometimes, keeping track of form results as they arrive in your e-mail inbox is easier and more fun than checking a separate results page. FrontPage makes routing form results directly to yourself (or anyone else) as e-mail messages easy.

Before you proceed, check with your ISP or system administrator to be sure that the host Web server on which you will eventually publish your site is set up to handle e-mail form submissions.

You can set up your form to send results via e-mail by following these steps:

1. **Right-click inside the form area and choose Form Properties from the pop-up menu that appears.**

    The Form Properties dialog box appears.

2. **In the E-mail Address text box, type the e-mail address of the person who will receive form results.**

    Presumably that person is you. If so, type your e-mail address here. (It should look like this: username@domain.com.)

    If both the File Name and the E-mail Address text boxes are filled in, FrontPage saves form results in the specified file *and* sends individual submissions via e-mail.

3. **In the dialog box, click the Options button.**

    The Saving Results dialog box appears.

4. **At the top of the dialog box, click the E-mail Results tab.**

    The E-mail Results tab appears. These options enable you to customize the particulars of the e-mail message format.

5. **In the E-Mail Format list box, choose the desired e-mail format.**

    The default value is formatted text, but you can choose other document formats as well.

6. **If you want the field names as well as the field values to appear in the e-mail message, select the Include Field Names check box.**

7. **In the Subject Line text box, type the text that you want to appear in the Subject line of the e-mail message.**

    You might want to choose something descriptive, such as *Web Site Visitor Fan Mail.*

If you select the Form Field Name check box, you can specify a field name here instead of static text. That way, visitors can specify what appears in the subject line of the e-mail message by filling out the corresponding form field inside the Web page. For example, say you add a text field to your form and name the field *Subject.* In this step, you would select the Form Field Name check box and type **Subject** in the Subject Line text box.

8. **In the Reply-to Line text box, specify the information that you want to appear in the reply-to line of the e-mail message.**

   Here's where using a form field name really makes sense, especially if you use your form to collect visitor feedback. For example, you can tell FrontPage to replace the reply-to line in the form results e-mail message with the contents of a form field that collects visitors' e-mail addresses. Then, when you receive a form result message, you simply reply to that message, and it goes directly to the person who sent you the feedback (assuming that person entered her e-mail address correctly in the appropriate field).

9. **Click OK to close the Saving Results dialog box.**
10. **Click OK to close the Form Properties dialog box.**

After you click OK, you might see the very intimidating dialog box pictured in Figure 8-14.

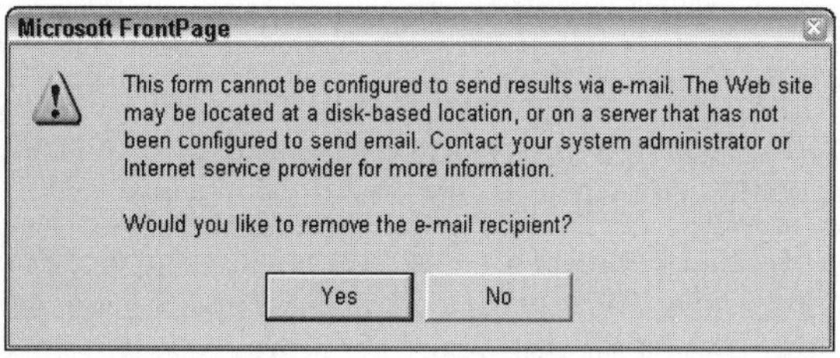
Microsoft FrontPage
This form cannot be configured to send results via e-mail. The Web site may be located at a disk-based location, or on a server that has not been configured to send email. Contact your system administrator or Internet service provider for more information.
Would you like to remove the e-mail recipient?
Yes
No

Figure 8-14: This dialog box may appear when you set up your form to submit results to an e-mail address.

Don't be alarmed. The dialog box shown in Figure 8-14 pops up because FrontPage noticed that you're creating a form that requires certain conditions on the host Web server to be able to work (namely, that the Web server has FrontPage Server Extensions installed, and that the Web server knows how to process form results as e-mail messages). If you haven't already, check with your ISP or system administrator to be sure that the host Web server can handle e-mail form submissions. If the answer is yes, you can ignore this dialog box (click No to close the dialog box and proceed on your merry way).

If the answer is no, you're out of luck; click Yes to close the dialog box and remove the e-mail recipient from your form.

Sending form results to a custom form-handling script

If your host Web server doesn't support FrontPage Server Extensions or if you need special data-processing capabilities that the FrontPage form handler can't accommodate, you can process form results by using a custom *form-handling script.* A custom script does the same job as the form handler included with FrontPage Server Extensions: It receives and processes form data and then outputs the results. The script's internal programming determines how form results are formatted and where they are sent.

Chances are good that your ISP or system administrator has a form-handling script already in place on the Web server. (After all, folks were submitting Web forms long before FrontPage was born!) Speak to your ISP or administrator to discover the script's capabilities and find out where the script is located on the server (that is, the script's URL).

To write a custom form-handling script, you need programming experience or a programmer friend who owes you a big favor.

To use a custom script as your form handler, follow these steps:

1. **Right-click inside the form area and choose Form Properties from the pop-up menu that appears.**

   The Form Properties dialog box appears.

2. **Select the Send to Other option.**

   The corresponding list box comes into view, with the Custom ISAPI, NSAPI, CGI, or ASP Script options visible.

   If you must know, ISAPI stands for Internet Server Application Programming Interface, NSAPI stands for Netscape Server Application Programming Interface, CGI stands for Common Gateway Interface, and ASP stands for Active Server Pages.

3. **In the dialog box, click the Options button.**

   The Options for Custom Form Handler dialog box appears.

4. **In the Action text box, type the URL of the form handler.**

   If you don't know the URL, ask your ISP or system administrator.

5. **If it's not already visible, choose POST from the Method list box.**

6. **Leave the Encoding Type text box alone.**

7. **Click OK to close the Options for Custom Form Handler dialog box.**

8. **Click OK to close the Form Properties dialog box.**

Creating a Confirmation Page

A *confirmation page* is a Web page that appears after visitors submit a form. This page lets visitors know that the form submission was successful and (depending on how you set up the page) confirms the information that visitors entered in the form. A confirmation page is a nice way to reassure visitors that the information they just sent didn't float off into the ether after they clicked the Submit button.

For all forms except those submitted to custom scripts, FrontPage automatically generates plain-Jane confirmation pages. If you want your confirmation page to blend in nicely with the rest of your site's design, you can create your own page. (If you submit your form to a custom script, the script's programming determines whether it can work in conjunction with a confirmation page. Your ISP or system administrator can fill you in on the script's capabilities.)

The confirmation page can be as simple as a polite acknowledgment and a hyperlink back to the Web site's home page ("Thank you for filling out our survey. Return to the Acme home page."). Alternatively, the page can display some or all of the information that visitors entered into the form, so that the visitors can note the information for future reference. How does the confirmation page know to display visitors' form entries? Because you can insert little jewels called confirmation fields into the confirmation page.

Confirmation fields are simple references to the existing fields in your form. If used as part of a Web page, confirmation fields display the information that the visitor typed into the corresponding form fields.

FrontPage comes with a canned confirmation page template, but chances are the generic confirmation page the template creates won't fit into your site's design very well. So instead of using the template, create your own confirmation page.

You can add confirmation fields to any page in your Web site and then use that page as your form's confirmation page. To do so, follow these steps:

1. **Create or open the Web page that you want to use as your confirmation page.**

2. **Place the cursor at the point in the page where you want the first confirmation field to appear.**

 3. **Click the Web Component button on the Standard toolbar.**

   The Insert Web Page Component dialog box appears.

4. **In the dialog box's Component Type list box, choose Advanced Controls.**

5. **In the Choose a Control list box, double-click Confirmation Field.**

    The Confirmation Field Properties dialog box appears.

6. **In the Name of Form Field to Confirm text box, type the name of the field that you want to confirm.**

    Pay attention to uppercase and lowercase letters while typing the field name; if the field names don't match exactly, the confirmation fields won't work.

7. **Click OK to close the dialog box.**

    The confirmation field appears in the page.

8. **On the Standard toolbar, click the Save button to save the page.**

After you create a custom confirmation page, you must specify its URL when you choose the form's handler. Refer to the section, "Designating where form results go," earlier in this chapter, for details.

Making Sure Your Form Works

After you finish your form, you may as well check to see whether the darn thing works. Unfortunately, if you preview the page in a Web browser, fill out your form fields, and then click the Submit button, FrontPage dings you with an error message.

Because forms require a form handler to be able to work, you must go a step beyond simply previewing the page: You must call upon the services of a Web server. To do so, you must publish your Web site and then preview and test the "live" version of the form. (For directions on how to publish your site, see Chapter 17.)

Part III
Pump Up Your Web Site!

The 5th Wave   By Rich Tennant

"I have to say I'm really impressed with the interactivity on this car wash Web site."

In this part . . .

After you build a sturdy, attractive Web site, you may feel the urge to add on to it. Perhaps you want to embellish your Web site with a graphical theme or enable visitors to search your site for keywords. You may even be ready to dabble in a little HTML. Read on for details!

Chapter 9

Layout Tables: The Secret of Professional Page Design

In This Chapter

▶ Discovering how layout tables can improve page design

▶ Creating and working with layout tables and layout cells

▶ Embellishing layout tables with color, shadows, and corner effects

▶ Deleting a layout table

*I*f you've already read Chapter 7, you know that tables are useful for arranging data into orderly groups of columns and rows. Handy, utilitarian, functional. Certainly not glamorous or exciting. And yet, would you believe that these same tables are the secret behind some of the best-designed pages on the Web?

That's right. Grid tables, with their borders turned off, are called (in FrontPage lingo) *layout tables.* Layout tables create a framework into which you place chunks of text, pictures, and even other tables. The result is a layout similar to what you can achieve by using a desktop-publishing program. Layout tables are a boon for designers who feel constrained by the traditional one-paragraph-after-another Web page layout.

FrontPage 2003 gives you a powerful set of layout table tools to use in your site. In this chapter, I show you how to put these tools to work.

Creating a Layout Table

The layout table's job is to act as a container for all the stuff inside a Web page (the text, pictures, and other elements collectively known as *content*). By changing the table's layout and dimensions, you change how content is arranged inside the page. For example, if you want to create a two-column layout for your Web page, create a two-column table, and then insert the text and pictures into the table's columns (see Figures 9-1 and 9-2). By fiddling with the table's specifics, such as column width, alignment, and more, you gain even finer control over your page's layout.

Figure 9-1: I use tables to create columns of text and pictures in my Web site.

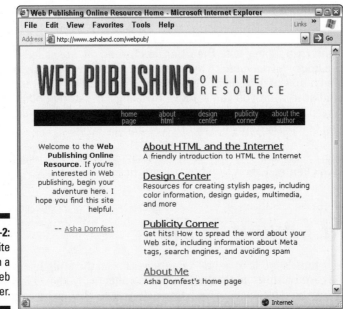

Figure 9-2: How my site looks in a Web browser.

Puttering with positioning

Layout tables take on the Web design challenge admirably, even though the creators of HTML never intended tables to be used as layout tools. *Positioning,* on the other hand, was created specifically with Web page layout in mind. Positioning, an effect created using Cascading Style Sheets, enables you to place elements in your page with more precision than is possible with a layout table.

Unfortunately, whereas most browsers are able to display tables, only (relatively) advanced Web browsers are able to display positioned elements. What's more, these browsers sometimes display positioned elements inconsistently. Although it pains me to say this because I am a big fan of Cascading Style Sheets, I recommend sticking with layout tables until more consistent browser support for CSS positioning takes hold.

That doesn't mean you shouldn't find out more about this fascinating technology, because it's poised to overtake tables eventually. The Web brims with articles about CSS positioning. See The BrainJar.com CSS positioning tutorial at `www.brainjar.com/css/positioning/` and "Positioning with CSS Level 2" at `builder.cnet.com/webbuilding/pages/Authoring/CSS/ss07.html` (both articles are geared toward the HTML-literate, but they're still helpful even if you don't know HTML). If you'd like to experiment with FrontPage positioning tools, play with the Format⇨Position and the Format⇨Layers commands (the FrontPage Help system explains how these features work; press F1 for help).

Check out the Web for more information about how to use tables as layout tools. A good place to start is the Page Layout section of the excellent Web Style Guide at `www.webstyleguide.com/page/layout.html` (be sure to bookmark this site so you can read the whole thing when you have more time . . . great stuff).

The easiest way to work with a layout table is to use it as the starting point for a new, empty page, and then to insert content into the layout table. It's certainly possible to add a layout table to an existing page, but the operation requires some cutting and pasting to get the content already sitting in the page into the new layout table. No matter. In the long run, structuring all your pages with layout tables helps give your site polish and consistency.

While on the HTML level, layout tables and regular (or "grid") tables are technically the same, FrontPage treats these two table varieties as fundamentally different animals. Therefore, creating and working with layout tables involves using a distinct set of tools.

Layout table tools live inside the Layout Tables and Cells task pane, shown in Figure 9-3. When you create a new, blank Web page, this task pane pops open automatically. If it doesn't, or if you want to display the task pane while working with an existing page, choose View⇨Task Pane (or press Ctrl+F1). Then click the task pane's title to reveal a drop-down list, and choose Layout Tables and Cells.

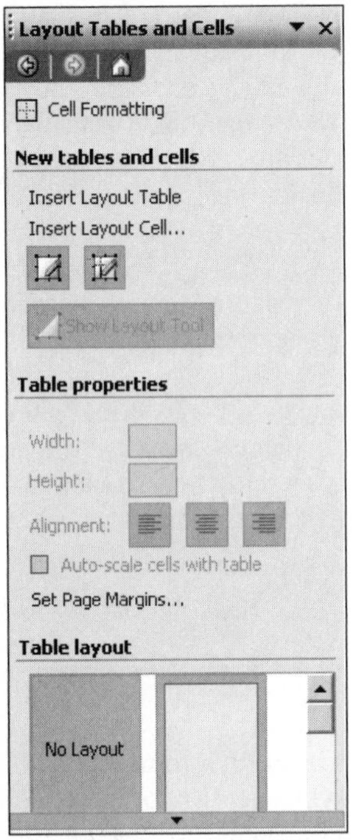

Figure 9-3:
The Layout Tables and Cells task pane.

Using a "canned" table layout

The easiest way to add a layout table to your page is to choose one of the layouts FrontPage provides. To do so, place the cursor in your page where you want the layout table to appear. In the Table Layout box of the Layout Tables and Cells task pane, scroll until you see a format you like, and then click it. Just like that, a layout table appears inside your page (see Figure 9-4). (If none of the layouts looks exactly like what you want, just pick the closest approximation — you can change the table setup later.)

REMEMBER

By default, the Layout Tables and Cells task pane appears each time you create a new, empty Web page, prompting you to choose a layout table right away.

The table's green outside border displays pixel measurements for each row and column in the table. If you click on one of the blue interior borders inside the table, measurements for the selected cell appear. (By the way, these borders are only visible in Design view. When you see the table in a Web browser or in Preview view, the borders are invisible.)

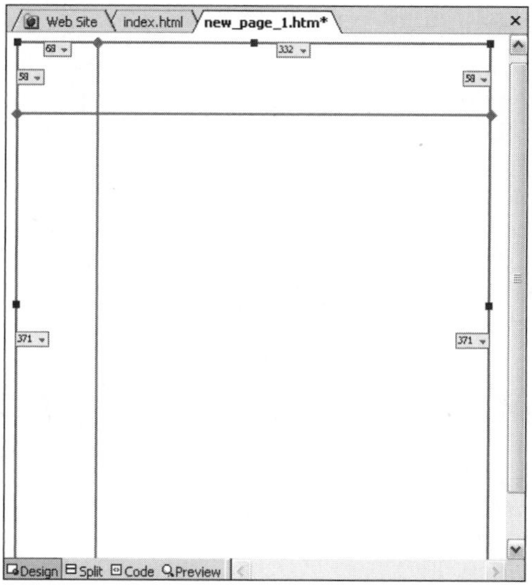

Figure 9-4:
An empty
layout table.

Drawing a layout table from scratch

After you're familiar with how layout tables work, you may find it easier to draw your own. FrontPage gives you two methods for creating new layout tables; here's my take on the easiest method:

1. **Place the cursor in the page where you want the layout table to appear, and then, in the Layout Tables and Cells task pane, click Insert Layout Table.**

   An empty 450 pixel-by-450 pixel layout table appears inside the page.

   You may find it easier to draw your table with FrontPage rulers and grids visible; to show rulers and/or grids, choose View⇨Ruler and Grid⇨Show Ruler or View⇨Ruler and Grid⇨Show Grid.

2. **To add cells to the table, in the Layout Tables and Cells task pane, click the Draw Layout Cell button.**

   After you click this button and move your cursor over the layout table, the cursor turns into a little drawing tool.

3. **Click inside the layout table, and, while holding down the mouse button, drag the cursor diagonally to draw a rectangle the size and shape of your desired cell.**

   To create a simple row or column, click on one of the green table borders and then drag the cursor to the opposite corner of the table. Or click anywhere inside the table and draw a rectangle that's any size or shape.

4. **Release the mouse button to create the cell.**

   The layout cell you drew appears inside the table, surrounded by a blue border. Depending on how you drew the cell, other "placeholder" cells may appear inside the table to fill out the table's structure.

You can fill a layout table with as many layout cells as you like (within reason, of course). Drawing layout table cells takes a bit of practice, so don't be afraid to press Ctrl+Z to undo your changes if you don't like the results. You can always try again, or you can tweak the exact measurements of the cells later.

Turning a grid table into a layout table

If you're more comfortable using the grid table tools to build tables, no problem. You can easily transform filled grid tables into layout tables. To do so, follow these steps:

1. **Create the grid table and insert the content of your choice (see Chapter 7 for step-by-step instructions).**

   If you're working with an existing table, skip this step.

2. **Right-click the table, and from the pop-up menu that appears, choose Table Properties.**

   The Table Properties dialog box appears.

3. **In the dialog box, select the Enable Layout Tools option.**

4. **If you haven't already, turn off table borders by entering 0 in the Size text box.**

5. **Click OK.**

   The Table Properties dialog box closes.

Although the table looks no different than before its transformation, FrontPage now considers the table a layout table (you can tell, because when you pass your cursor over the table, its outer border turns green, and its inner borders turn blue). This is a Good Thing, because you can now use FrontPage layout table tools to play with how the table looks, and these tools give you more visual formatting options than do grid table tools.

Filling Layout Tables with Content

You can insert anything into a layout table that you can into a regular page. Just click inside a cell and proceed as usual. By default, cell height and width stretch to accommodate whatever you place inside. Also, if it isn't already, any cell you fill with content turns into a layout cell, which means that you can later use FrontPage's layout cell formatting tools to change how the cell looks.

Text entered into a cell *wraps* as you type, which means that, when the text reaches a cell boundary, the word being typed jumps down to a new line. You create new paragraphs in a cell by pressing Enter and create line breaks by pressing Shift+Enter.

If you're ready to type text in another cell, click inside that cell (unlike with grid tables, pressing the Tab key doesn't advance the cursor to the next cell).

If you add a layout table to a page that already contains text, pictures, and other content, simply cut and paste the content into the appropriate places in the table.

Keep in mind that you don't have to fill *every* cell in your layout table. Because the table is ultimately invisible to your visitors, you can use entire rows and columns as spacers between rows and/or columns filled with content. Keep playing around and adjusting until everything looks just the way you want, and preview often.

Fiddling with the Size and Shape of Layout Tables

After you've got a layout table sitting comfortably in your page, you can change any aspect of its structure.

Changing a layout table's width, height, and alignment on the page

Web site visitors love pages designed using layout tables. No one wants to scroll all over a page to read it, and with your pages' content tucked inside layout tables, you can adjust the tables' dimensions to keep everything visible within the width of a browser window.

To change a layout table's dimensions and/or alignment, follow these steps:

1. **If it's not already showing, display the Layout Tables and Cells task pane by choosing View⇨Task Pane (or pressing Ctrl+F1). Then click the task pane's title to reveal a drop-down list, and choose Layout Tables and Cells.**

2. **In Design view, click anywhere inside the layout table.**

3. **To change the table's width, in the task pane's Width text box, enter a number of pixels or a percentage figure followed by the percent sign (%).**

   If you specify a percentage, FrontPage automatically adjusts the width of the table based on the size of the browser window. For example, if you enter **50%** in the Width text box, the width of the table remains at half the width of the browser window.

   If you want to specify an absolute pixel measurement, but you're not sure how wide or tall to make your layout table, FrontPage can give you some ballpark numbers. Click the Page Size box in the lower-right corner of the FrontPage window (the box contains two numbers separated by an *x*). The menu that appears shows you, in pixels (width x height), the amount of page space you have inside common browser window sizes at different monitor resolutions.

   For example, the default browser window size on a monitor that's able to display 640 x 480 pixels is 536 x 196 pixels. In other words, if you want to design your pages so that they look good when viewed at that resolution, your layout tables should be no wider than, say, 500 pixels (they can be taller, however, as visitors are more willing to scroll up and down than they are to scroll side to side).

   The FrontPage Ruler and Grid may make it easier for you to eyeball the dimensions of your table. To turn on the ruler and/or grid, choose View⇨Ruler and Grid⇨Show Ruler, and/or View⇨Ruler and Grid⇨Show Grid.

4. **To set or change the table's height, in the task pane's Height text box, enter a number of pixels.**

   By default, the layout table's height equals the height of the page, which will ultimately be determined by the size of the table's contents. You can generally leave the table height as it is, unless you specifically want to control the table height.

5. **To change the dimensions of the cells inside the table to maintain the table's proportion, select the Auto-scale Cells with Table check box.**

   If this check box is unmarked, when you change the width or height of the layout table, FrontPage automatically adds new "placeholder" cells to the table to maintain the existing cells' original dimensions while increasing the dimensions of the table.

6. To change the table's alignment on the page, in the task pane, click the Align Left, Align Center, or Align Right button.

By default, layout tables are left-aligned.

Changing row and column widths and heights

While setting a layout table's overall dimensions is perfectly valid, you gain more control when you change a table's dimensions by changing the dimensions of the individual rows and columns inside the table.

For example, you can precisely set the width of each column to line up with a background image (sites that have a band of color running along the left margin use this trick, as I did in my Web site; see Figure 9-5).

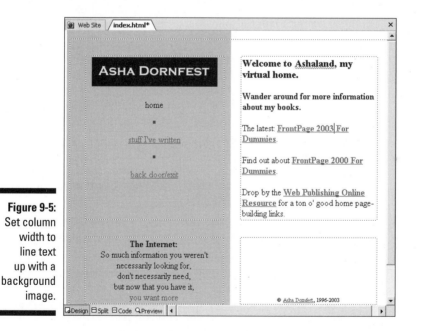

Figure 9-5:
Set column
width to
line text
up with a
background
image.

FrontPage also gives you the option of using a well-worn Web designer's trick to keep layout tables looking good in older browsers: the *spacer image*. Older Web browsers treat empty table cells differently; some browsers pay attention to the cells' height and width measurements, while others "collapse" empty cells, effectively ignoring their dimension settings unless the cells contain something. By inserting an invisible GIF image (a 1-pixel dot that has been made transparent) into empty table cells, and then "propping open" the cells by adjusting the width and height of the image, your table's dimensions stay true, even in older browsers. A hack, to be sure, but it works.

Here's how to change the dimensions of individual columns and rows in your layout table:

1. **In Design view, move your cursor over the layout table's outer border until it turns green, and then click on the outer border.**

   The table's row and column pixel dimensions become visible. Column widths are visible in little boxes along the table's top and bottom borders, and row heights are visible in little boxes along the left and right borders.

2. **To change a column's width, click the down arrow inside the column's width box, and choose an option from the menu that appears:**

   • **Change Column Width:** Choose this option to change the column's width (in pixels). In the Column Properties dialog box that appears, enter a number of pixels in the Column Width text box, and then click OK to close the dialog box.

   • **Make Column Autostretch:** Choose this option to cause the column to automatically stretch to fill the available space in the browser window. This option is most often used in the farthest right column in layout tables, so that the column's contents can stretch as a visitor widens or narrows the browser window.

   • **Use Column Spacer Image:** Choose this option to insert an invisible spacer image (a transparent 1-pixel GIF) into the column to maintain the column's width in older browsers. This option is generally used in empty columns that exist only to add space between two columns filled with content.

3. **To change a row's height, click the down arrow inside the row's height box, and choose an option from the menu that appears.**

   (The options in this menu work just like the options for column width, which I describe in Step 2.)

You can also change the dimensions of individual layout cells by right-clicking the layout cell you want to change, and then choosing Cell Formatting from the pop-up menu that appears (not Cell Properties, as you would with a traditional grid table). The Cell Formatting task pane becomes visible. In the Layout Cell Properties section of the task pane, enter pixel values in the Width and Height text boxes.

Adding and deleting rows and columns

To add a new row or column to your layout table, follow these steps:

1. **Place the cursor inside the layout table next to where you want the new row or column to appear.**

2. **Choose Table⇨Insert⇨Rows or Columns.**

   The Insert Rows or Columns dialog box appears.

3. **Select the Rows or Columns option button (depending upon what you want to create).**

4. **In the Number of Rows/Columns box, enter the number of rows or columns you want to create.**

5. **In the Location section of the dialog box, select the option corresponding to where you want the new row(s) or column(s) to appear.**

   Your choices are Above Selection or Below Selection (for rows), or Left of Selection or Right of Selection (for columns).

6. **Click OK.**

   The dialog box closes, and the new row(s) or column(s) appear.

To delete a row or column, click inside the row or column you want to delete and then choose Table⇨Select⇨Row (or Table⇨Select⇨Column). Then press the Delete key. Gone!

Changing How Layout Cells Look

Here's where layout tables get even more interesting. You have lots of options for changing the alignment, spacing, and visual details for each layout cell in your layout table. You can add borders, corners, shadows, headers, and footers to your layout cells. Mmmmm, nice.

The tools you use in this section are sitting inside the Cell Formatting task pane (see Figure 9-6). To make this task pane visible, press Ctrl+F1. Click the title bar of the task pane that appears and choose Cell Formatting from the drop-down list. Or, if the Layout Tables and Cells task pane is already visible, in the task pane, click the Cell Formatting link. Or right-click anywhere inside a layout table and choose Cell Formatting from the pop-up menu that appears.

The options in this section apply to individual layout cells, so if you want to apply affects to more than one cell at a time, you will need to click inside subsequent cells and repeat the steps.

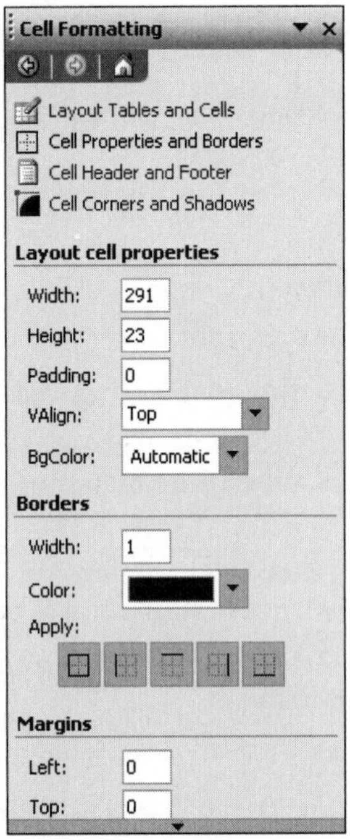

Figure 9-6:
The Cell
Formatting
task pane.

Also, these options only apply to *layout cells;* that is, cells whose inner borders turn blue when you pass your cursor over them.

Aligning and spacing cell contents

You have more alignment and spacing options for layout tables than you have for grid tables. The main difference is the ability to add *margins* to your layout cells.

Margins, like another table spacing feature, *padding,* enable you to insert blank space between the contents of the cell and the cell's borders. Whereas padding simply adds blank space around the cell contents, margins can be changed individually (that is, you can control the left, right, top, and bottom margins independently).

Furthermore, padding adds space without affecting the cell's background color. Margins effectively add a "moat" of white space to the inside of the cell, moving cell contents and erasing background color in the margin area.

Figure 9-7 illustrates the difference between padding and margins. The left cell has 20 pixels of padding, and the right cell has margins 20 pixels wide (left, right, top, and bottom).

Figure 9-7:
Padding
versus
margins.

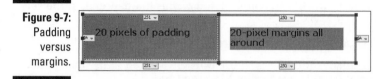

You can change the alignment and spacing inside a layout cell as follows:

1. **Click inside the layout cell you want to format.**

2. **If it's not already visible, display the Cell Formatting task pane.**

   I explain how in the section, "Changing How Layout Cells Look."

3. **Open the Cell Properties and Borders section of the task pane by clicking the Cell Properties and Borders link inside the task pane.**

4. **To add padding to the cell, enter a number of pixels in the Padding text box.**

5. **To change the alignment of the cell contents, select an option from the VAlign drop-down list.**

   Your options are Top, Middle, and Bottom.

   If you want to change the horizontal alignment, as with grid tables, you can click the Align Left, Center, Align Right, or Justify buttons in the Formatting toolbar.

6. **To change the cell's margins, enter a number of pixels into Left, Top, Right, and/or Bottom text boxes.**

Adding background and border color

You can add background color to a cell. You can also add borders to each or all sides of a cell. Here's how:

1. **Click inside the layout cell you want to format.**

2. **If it's not already visible, display the Cell Formatting task pane.**

   I explain how in the section, "Changing How Layout Cells Look."

3. **Open the Cell Properties and Borders section of the task pane by clicking the Cell Properties and Borders link inside the task pane.**

4. **To add a background color to a cell, select a color from the BgColor drop-down list.**

   I explain how to work with color-related menus in Chapter 4, in the section, "Changing text color."

5. **To add a border, choose a color from the Color drop-down list.**

6. **To change border thickness, in the Borders section of the task pane, enter a number of pixels in the Width text box.**

7. **To choose where you want to apply borders to the selected cell, click one of the buttons in the Apply area (refer to Figure 9-8).**

   You can choose to apply border settings to all cell borders, or only to the left, right, top, or bottom border.

To add a background image to a layout cell, right-click the cell and choose Cell Properties from the pop-up menu that appears. In the Background section of the Cell Properties dialog box that appears, select the Use Background Picture check box, and then click the Browse button to choose a picture file from a file list.

You can also apply border settings to the cell's header or footer. I explain how to add a header or footer to a layout cell in the next section of this chapter.

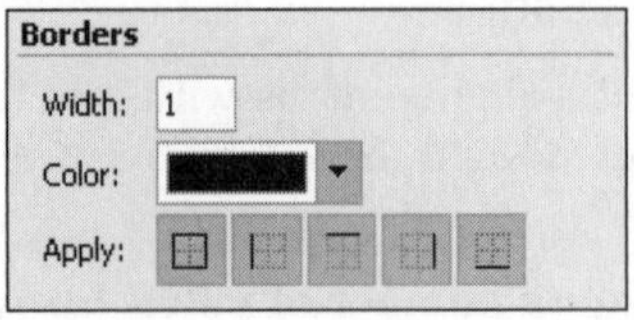

Figure 9-8:
Layout cell
border
options.

Borders
Width: 1
Color:
Apply:

Adding a header or a footer

Here's a slick effect: You can add a thin stripe to the top or bottom of your cell, into which you can either enter a bit of text or leave blank just for the colorful contrast. Figure 9-9 shows an example of a layout cell that contains a header — it's the dark stripe at the top of the cell.

Figure 9-9:
This layout
cell con-
tains a
header.

Header text
Body text

To add a header and/or a footer, do this:

1. **Click inside the layout cell you want to format.**

2. **If it's not already visible, display the Cell Formatting task pane.**

   I explain how in the section, "Changing How Layout Cells Look."

3. **Open the Cell Header and Footer section of the task pane by clicking the Cell Header and Footer link inside the task pane.**

4. **To add a header and/or footer, select the Show Header and/or Show Footer check box.**

   A header/footer appears inside the cell. You can click inside the header or footer and type some text, or you can leave it alone.

5. **To change the height of the header or footer, enter a number of pixels into the corresponding Height text box.**

6. **To add blank space between the header/footer text and the edges of the header/footer, enter a number of pixels in the corresponding Padding text box.**

7. **To change header/footer color, choose an option from the corresponding BgColor list box.**

8. **To change the alignment of header/footer text, choose an option from the corresponding VAlign list box.**

   Your options are Top, Middle, and Bottom.

   If you want to change the horizontal alignment of header/footer text, you can click the Align Left, Center, Align Right, or Justify buttons in the Formatting toolbar.

9. **To add a border to the header/footer, enter a number of pixels in the corresponding Border Width text box, and choose a color from the corresponding Border Color drop-down list.**

Adding corners

You can streamline your layout cells with rounded corners, as shown in
Figure 9-10.

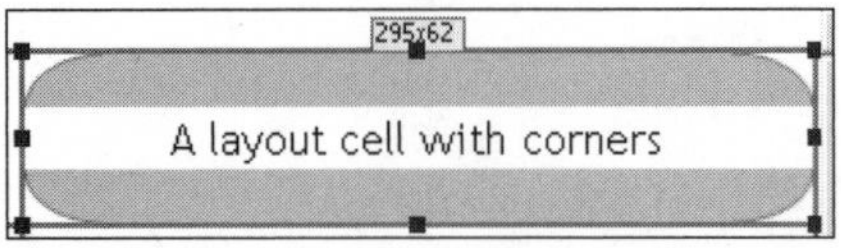

Figure 9-10:
This lay-
out cell
contains
corners.

295x62

A layout cell with corners

To add corners, follow these steps:

1. **Click inside the layout cell you want to format.**

2. **If it's not already visible, display the Cell Formatting task pane.**

   I explain how in the section, "Changing How Layout Cells Look."

3. **Open the Cell Corners and Shadows section of the task pane by clicking the Cell Corners and Shadows link inside the task pane.**

   In the steps that follow, I assume that you want to create corners using
   FrontPage's default image, which is a basic stripe with rounded edges.
   FrontPage gives you the option of using a custom image of your choice
   in place of the stripe, but I find the effect doesn't work nearly as well.
   Feel free to experiment; you may hit upon a look you like.

4. **Choose a corner color from the Color drop-down list.**

   The corner effect only appears after you apply the corners to the layout
   cell in Step 7, so, for now, choosing a corner color appears to have no
   effect. Have faith — the color will appear soon enough.

5. **Choose a corner border color from the Border Color drop-down list.**

6. **Set the corner's curve by entering pixel values in the Width and
   Height text boxes.**

7. **To cause the corner(s) to appear inside the layout cell, click one of the
   buttons in the Apply area (see Figure 9-11).**

   The corner(s) appear inside the layout cell.

You can change the corners' settings by changing any of the corners' attributes, and then clicking one of the Apply buttons again.

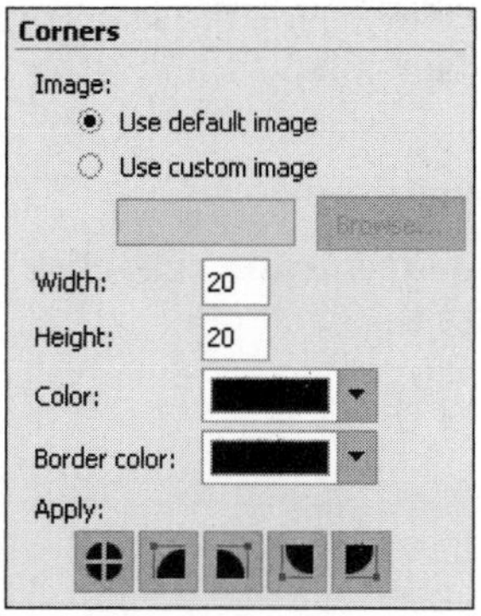

Figure 9-11:
Applying
corners.

Adding shadows

If you're looking for more subtle embellishment than corners provide, consider adding shadows to your layout cells (see Figure 9-12, which illustrates the use of shadows and borders together). Shadows appear "behind" selected layout cells, causing them to "pop off" the page.

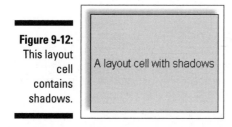

Figure 9-12:
This layout
cell
contains
shadows.

A layout cell with shadows

To add shadows, follow these steps:

1. **Click inside the layout cell you want to format.**

2. **If it's not already visible, display the Cell Formatting task pane.**

   I explain how in the section, "Changing How Layout Cells Look."

3. **Open the Cell Corners and Shadows section of the task pane by clicking the Cell Corners and Shadows link inside the task pane.**

4. **In the Shadows section of the task pane, choose a shadow width by entering a pixel value in the Width text box.**

5. **To control how "strong" the shadow appears, enter a percentage value in the Softness text box.**

The higher the percentage value you enter here, the fainter the shadow appears. For example, enter 90 for a faint shadow, and 10 for a strong, dark shadow.

6. Choose a shadow color from the Color drop-down list.

7. To cause the shadow to appear inside the layout cell, click one of the buttons in the Apply area (see Figure 9-13).

The shadow appears inside the layout cell.

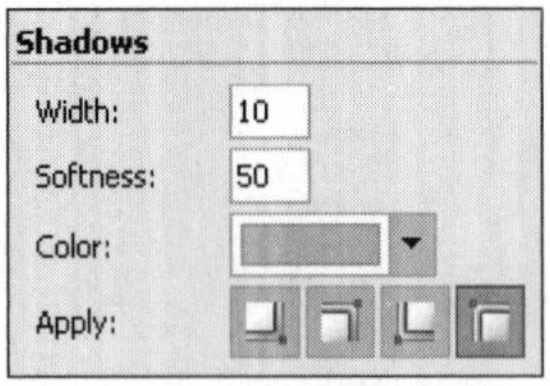

Figure 9-13:
Applying
shadows.

You can change the shadow's settings by changing any of the shadow's attributes, and then clicking one of the Apply buttons again.

Deleting a Layout Table

If you change your mind about using a layout table in your page (which I hope you won't), you can easily delete the table. Unfortunately, all the table's content goes, too.

To preserve the table's content, you must first cut all of the table's content and paste it elsewhere in the page, outside of the table. Oy, what a pain.

To delete the layout table, choose Table➪Select➪Layout Table, and then press the Backspace or Delete key.

Chapter 10

Creating a Flexible Site Layout with Frames

· ·

· ·

*O*f all the design effects to arrive on the Web publishing scene, few have caused a bigger stir than frames. Frames don't just make something happen on a page — frames change the way visitors experience the Web site as a whole.

In this chapter, I show you how to create a framed Web site. I also show you how to insert an inline frame into a Web site that doesn't contain frames.

What Are Frames and Why Would You Want to Use Them?

Frames are dividers that separate the Web browser window into sections. Each section contains a separate Web page, enabling you to display more than one page at the same time, as shown in Figure 10-1.

In this example, the browser window contains three frames, each of which displays a separate page. The top frame contains a banner-like heading, the left frame contains a list of navigational hyperlinks, and the frame on the right contains the site's main content.

welcome to my home page! you can find out all about me here.

[home] [about me] [my hobbies] [contact]

Figure 10-1:
A typical framed Web site.

Sure, frames look slick. Looks are the least of it, however, when compared to frames' navigational power. Behold — in the site shown in Figure 10-1, when you click a hyperlink in the left frame, the link's destination page appears in the right frame. In this way, you can use frames to keep certain elements visible all the time (as the decorative heading and navigational links in Figure 10-1 are visible at all times), while the rest of the site's content changes based on where the visitor wants to go.

Inline frames (also known as *floating frames*) work differently than regular frames. Whereas regular frames change the fundamental structure of the Web site, inline frames can be inserted into a Web site that doesn't contain frames. Inline frames are scrollable boxes that can display the contents of another page — for example, the scrollable box shown in Figure 10-2. I explain how to create inline frames at the end of the chapter.

You should know that not all Web browsers can display frames, regular or inline. Netscape Navigator (version 2.0 or later) and Microsoft Internet Explorer (version 3.0 or later) are frames-capable, but older or frames-challenged browsers can't even display an approximation of a framed site; the visitor sees only a blank page. The good news is that most Web surfers use a frames-capable browser. For those who don't, FrontPage sidesteps the problem by creating an alternative for browsers that can't display frames. (I discuss this alternative later in this chapter, in the section, "Creating an Alternative for Browsers That Don't 'Do' Frames.")

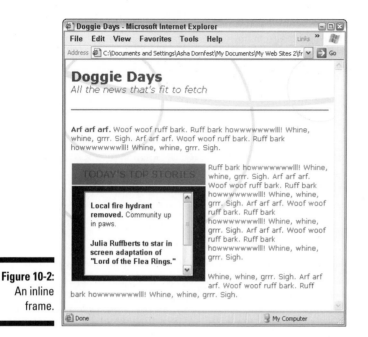

Creating a Framed Web Site: The Game Plan

Creating a framed site involves the following three basic steps:

- ✔ Creating the frames page
- ✔ Filling the frames with content pages (and, if necessary, modifying the pages to work inside the frames)
- ✔ Adjusting the overall layout and properties of each individual frame

A *frames page* is a special type of Web page that defines the size, placement, and properties of the site's frames. A frames page can display as many frames as you want, in whatever layout you want.

After you create a frames page, you fill the frames with *content pages.* Content pages are regular old Web pages that appear inside each frame as a visitor views the frames page with a Web browser. (The frames page itself is transparent, except for the placement of each frame.) *Initial pages* are the first content pages that appear as a visitor views the frames page with a Web browser.

You can either use an existing Web page as a frame's initial page, or fill the frame with a new, blank page. Finally, you adjust the layout and properties of the individual frames so that the site functions the way you want.

After you finish creating the framed site, you save and preview the whole package by using the FrontPage Preview view or a frames-capable browser. By previewing your site, you can see how the site's hyperlinks and frames work together, and you can be sure that the links work correctly.

Ah, but I get ahead of myself. The best place to begin is at the beginning . . . with the frames page.

Creating the Frames Page

The hardest part about creating a framed Web site can be deciding on the layout of the frames in the first place. FrontPage anticipates this problem by providing templates for popular frames page layouts. After you create the frames page by using a template, you can modify the page's layout by adding, deleting, or resizing the page's frames.

To create a new frames page, follow these steps:

1. **With your Web site open in FrontPage, choose File⇨New.**

   The New task pane appears.

2. **In the New Page section of the task pane, click the More Page Templates link.**

   The Page Templates dialog box appears.

3. **In the dialog box, click the Frames Pages tab to display FrontPage's frames page templates, as shown in Figure 10-3.**

4. **In the template list, click one of the template icons.**

   A description of the frames page template appears in the Description area, and a mini-preview of the frames page layout appears in the Preview area.

5. **After you find a template that resembles the frame layout you want, click OK.**

   If no template looks exactly the way you want, choose the closest approximation — you can adjust the layout later.

   The Page Templates dialog box closes, and a new frames page appears in Design view, as shown in Figure 10-4. (I selected the Header, Footer and Contents template for this example.)

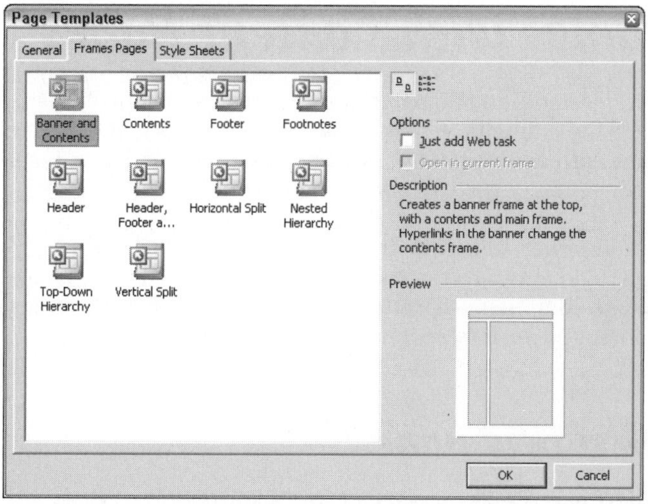

Figure 10-3:
FrontPage
provides
plenty of
templates
for frames
pages.

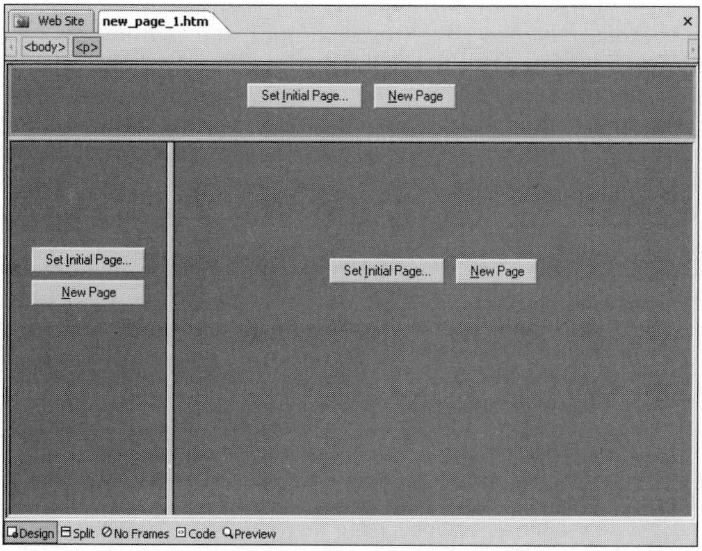

Figure 10-4:
A new,
empty
frames
page, as it
appears in
Design
view.

In addition to the frames page, a new option appears at the bottom of the
FrontPage window: No Frames. You use the No Frames view to create a message for those of your visitors whose browsers can't display frames. (I
explain how to do this later in this chapter, in the "Creating an Alternative for
Browsers That Don't 'Do' Frames" section.)

Now you need to fill the frames page with content pages.

Filling Frames with Content Pages

As with frames around fine paintings, the frames in your Web site exist only to enhance the contents. A new frames page is empty, and you need to fill each frame with an *initial page.* You can either create a new, blank page or choose one of the pages already sitting in your Web site.

If you would rather adjust the frames page layout *before* working with content pages, skip ahead to the section, "Tweaking the Frames Page." After you've made your changes, return to this section for instructions on how to insert content pages into each frame.

Using a new page

To fill a frame with a new page, click the New Page button in one of the frames. A new, empty page appears inside the frame.

To add stuff to the new page (text, graphics, and anything else you would add to a regular Web page), click inside the page and proceed as usual. If the page is sitting inside a narrow frame and you feel cramped, right-click the page and choose Open Page in New Window from the pop-up menu that appears. FrontPage pops open a new, full-sized window so that you can have a little elbow room while adding content to the page. After you've finished working on that page, close the window to see how the page looks inside its frame.

Opening a content page in a new window also enables you to view that page's HTML by clicking Code or Split at the bottom of the newly-opened window. If you switch to Code or Split view while the frames page occupies the Design view window, you see the HTML for the frames page, but *not* for any of the contents pages filling the frames.

Using an existing page

To fill the frame with an existing page, follow these steps:

1. **In one of the frames, click the Set Initial Page button.**

   The Insert Hyperlink dialog box appears.

   The appearance of the Insert Hyperlink dialog box makes sense because, on the HTML level, you're actually creating a special type of hyperlink between the frames page and the content page.

2. **In the dialog box, select the page you want to use as the frame's initial page.**

If the initial page you want to use is stored elsewhere on the World Wide Web, type the page's URL in the Address text box.

3. Click OK.

The dialog box closes, and the page appears inside the frame.

To edit the page, click inside the page and proceed as usual. To display the page in a full-sized window, right-click the page and choose Open Page in New Window from the pop-up menu that appears.

Tweaking the Frames Page

The FrontPage frames page templates represent popular frame layouts in use on the Web today. That's great if you're the type who likes tried-and-true. The rest of you are probably itching to rearrange the frames page. In this section, I show you how.

Adding new frames

Adding new frames to a frames page involves splitting existing frames. Just as splitting a table cell divides the cell in two, splitting a frame divides the frame in two. (Refer to Chapter 7 for information about grid tables.)

A word to the wise: More is not better when it comes to frames. Framed sites containing four or more frames can be difficult to navigate and visually overwhelming. I'm not stating an indisputable fact here; I simply encourage you to value simplicity and design your site with your visitors in mind.

To split a frame, you hold down the Ctrl key, click a frame border (including the outer borders), drag the border to a new position, and then release the mouse button. As soon as you release the mouse button, a new, empty frame appears. If you don't like what you see, click the Undo button (or press Ctrl+Z) and try again.

If you create a frames page you'd like to use for future Web sites, save the page as a template. (I explain how to do this in Chapter 2.)

Deleting frames

If the frames page looks too convoluted, delete a frame or two. By deleting a frame, you don't delete the content page inside; you simply remove the frame from the frames page. The content page remains untouched. To delete a frame, click inside the frame and then choose Frames⇨Delete Frame.

Changing frame properties

In addition to changing the overall layout of the frames page, you can change the following details:

- ✔ Frame name
- ✔ Presence of scrollbars
- ✔ Frame size
- ✔ Amount of space separating frame content from frame borders
- ✔ Presence of frame borders
- ✔ Amount of space between frame borders

To change any or all of these properties, follow these steps:

1. **Right-click inside the frame you want to edit and choose Frame Properties from the pop-up menu that appears.**

   The Frame Properties dialog box appears (see Figure 10-5).

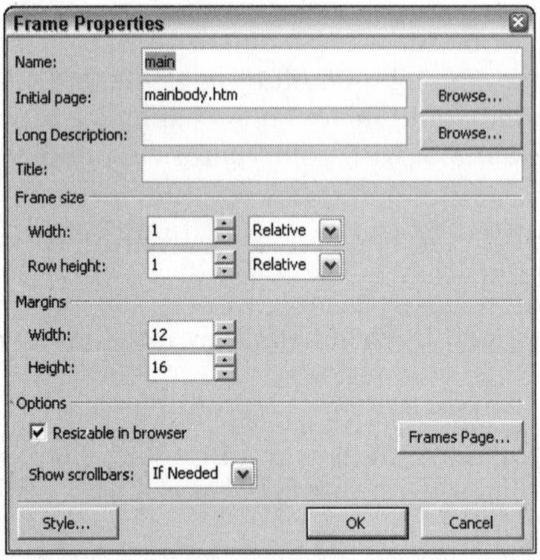

Figure 10-5:
The Frame
Properties
dialog box.

Note: The following steps describe how to change every frame property. Choose only those steps that apply to the property or properties that you want to adjust.

2. **In the Name text box, type a frame name that makes sense to you.**

   The frame's name acts as an identifying label. The name isn't visible to visitors, so choose something that makes sense to you. For example, If the frame will contain a table of contents page, you could type the name **TOC**. Or, if you prefer to identify the frame by its position, choose something like **Left** or **Top**.

3. **To change the initial page, type a new page filename, path, or URL in the Initial Page text box or click the Browse button to select the page you want from a file list.**

4. **In the Title text box, enter a title for the frames page.**

   In a framed site, the title of the frames page is the only title visible as a visitor views the site with a Web browser. The titles of the individual content pages don't appear. Make sure you choose a descriptive title for the frames page.

   If you like, you can also enter a more detailed site description in the Long Description text box, but keep in mind that most browsers are unable to display this information.

5. **In the Width and Row Height boxes, type dimension measurements.**

   As with table dimensions, you can specify a frame's size as an absolute pixel value or a relative percentage based on the size of the browser window. (Refer to Chapter 7 for information about how table dimensions work.)

   You can choose Relative if you want the browser to set the frame's dimensions relative to the other frames in the page. For example, if the frames page contains two frames, and the width of the first frame is set to 100 pixels, and the width of the second frame is set to Relative, the second frame expands to fill the rest of the browser window, whatever the window's size.

6. **In the Width and Height boxes, type the number of pixels with which you want to separate the content page text from the frame borders.**

   The effect works in a similar way to cell padding inside a table. (See Chapter 7 for details.)

7. **If you want to lock the position of the frame so that visitors can't resize the frame when they view the site in a browser, de-select the Resizable in Browser check box.**

   If this check box is selected, when visitors view the framed site with a Web browser, they can adjust the position of frame borders to work with the size of their monitors. By doing so, they don't affect the frames page, just how the framed site appears on their screens. If this check box is de-selected, the frame position is locked in place.

8. **In the Show Scrollbars list box, choose an option that describes when you want scrollbars to appear inside the frame.**

   You have the following options:

   - **If Needed:** If the visitor's browser window is too small to display the entire contents of a frame, scrollbars appear so that the visitor may move around inside the frame.

   - **Always:** Scrollbars are visible at all times, even when they aren't necessary.

   - **Never:** Scrollbars never appear, no matter what.

9. **Click the Frames Page button.**

   The Page Properties dialog box appears, with the Frames tab visible. When you change the settings inside this tab, the changes apply to the entire frames page.

10. **In the Frame Spacing box, type the frame border width (in pixels).**

    This option works similarly to cell spacing in tables. By changing this setting, you change the appearance of the frame borders. (Refer to Chapter 7 for more information about cell spacing in tables.)

11. **To make frame borders invisible, de-select the Show Borders check box.**

12. **Click OK.**

    The Page Properties dialog box closes, and the Frame Properties dialog box becomes visible again.

13. **Click OK to close the Frame Properties dialog box.**

    The dialog box closes, and the selected frame's settings change accordingly.

Changing the target frame

Each frames page template assigns a target frame to the content page sitting inside each frame. The *target frame* is the frame in which hyperlink destination pages appear. In Figure 10-1, for example, after a visitor clicks a navigational link inside the left frame, the corresponding page appears in the right frame. The right frame, therefore, is the target frame for the links in the left frame.

Each frame page template contains default target frame settings. (To determine a frame's default target frame, in Design view, click a hyperlink inside the frame while holding down the Ctrl key. The frame in which the destination page appears is that frame's default target frame.) In the following sections, I show you how to change the target frame's settings.

Common target frame options

You can use the following four target frame options (available in the Target Frame dialog box) to create different effects:

✔ **Same Frame:** This setting causes the hyperlink destination page to open inside the same frame in which the hyperlink source page is located, replacing the source page.

✔ **Whole Page:** This setting causes the hyperlink destination page to replace the frames page in the browser window.

✔ **New Window:** This setting causes the hyperlink destination page to open inside a new (unframed) Web browser window.

✔ **Parent Frame:** If you want to get fancy, you can use a second frames page as the content page for one or more frames in your site. The result is a *nested frames page:* A secondary level of frames appears inside one of the frames in the top-level (or parent) frames page. When you choose the Parent target frame setting, links in the secondary frames page load inside the parent frame. If you use nested frames, be sure to keep the site simple enough to navigate easily.

Changing the target frame for all the hyperlinks in a page

To change the target frame for all the hyperlinks in a page (also referred to as changing the *default target frame*), follow these steps:

1. **Right-click inside the frame containing the page whose target frame you want to change, and choose Page Properties from the pop-up menu that appears.**

   The Page Properties dialog box appears, with the General tab visible. The Default Target Frame text box contains the name of the current target frame. (If the text box is empty, hyperlink destination pages appear inside the same frame.)

2. **In the dialog box, click the Change Target Frame button.**

   The Target Frame dialog box appears, as shown in Figure 10-6.

3. **In the Current Frames Page section of the dialog box, click the frame you want to target, or, in the Common Targets area, click the name of the target you want to use.**

   The frame name appears in the Target Setting text box.

   I describe what each common target option does in the nearby sidebar, "Common target frame options."

4. **Click OK to close the dialog box.**

   The Page Properties dialog box becomes visible again.

5. **Click OK to close the Page Properties dialog box.**

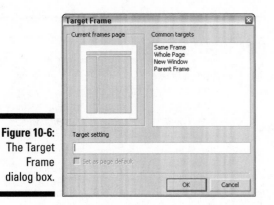

Figure 10-6:
The Target
Frame
dialog box.

These directions also apply to the target frames for form results and for image map hotspots. If you're not sure what an image map or a hotspot is, see Chapter 5. If you're not familiar with forms, take a look at Chapter 8.

To change the target frame for image map hotspots, right-click the image map, and from the pop-up menu that appears, choose Picture Properties. In the Picture Properties dialog box that appears, click the General tab, and then click the Change Target button. From there, follow the preceding steps.

To change the target frame for form results, right-click the form, and from the pop-up menu that appears, choose Form Properties. In the Form Properties dialog box that appears, click the Change Target button, and then follow the preceding steps.

Changing the target frame for a single hyperlink

If you want to change the target frame setting for only a single hyperlink (leaving the other links in the page using the default target frame setting), follow these steps:

1. **In the content page, create a new hyperlink or click an existing hyperlink, and then click the Insert Hyperlink button on the Standard toolbar.**

   The Insert Hyperlink or Edit Hyperlink dialog box appears. (Refer to Chapter 5 if you're not sure how to create a new hyperlink.)

2. **In the dialog box, click the Target Frame button to choose a frame from the Target Frame dialog box.**

   Refer to the steps in the preceding section, "Changing the target frame for all the hyperlinks in a page," for instructions on how to use the Target Frame dialog box.

3. **Click OK to close the dialog box.**

Frames forethought

If you want to give visitors the choice of viewing your site with or without frames, you must place a hyperlink that points to the frames page in another page in your site. Or you can specify the frames page as the site's home page so that the frames page is the first thing visitors see when visiting your site. (To do this, in the Folder List, right-click the icon for the frames page and choose Set as Home Page from the pop-up menu that appears. FrontPage takes care of updating hyperlinks and renaming your old home page so it won't be overwritten.) Because FrontPage knows how to set up a No Frames alternative for browsers that can't handle frames, you're in the clear. Almost.

You need to make sure that visitors who are viewing the site without frames can still get around. For example, say you place all your navigational hyperlinks inside a frame (similar to the layout of the framed site in Figure 10-1). Fine design for the framed layout, but how would the site work without the frames? If you use a copy of the main body page as the No Frames message, how would visitors get around the site when that page contains no navigational links?

You can make sure your visitors can navigate your site by reproducing in the main body page all the links found in the navigational page (many designers include a small-scale set of text links at the bottom of the page, as shown in Figure 10-1). Or you can create a separate set of pages for browsers that can't display frames. *Or* you can create a No Frames message that requires visitors to use a frames-capable browser to view your site and provides links to the download sites of these browsers. Whatever you decide, test, test, and test again to be sure that your site is accessible to *all* your visitors.

Creating an Alternative for Browsers That Don't "Do" Frames

The majority of your visitors surf the Web by using frames-capable browsers, but a few people use browsers that can't display frames. How do you accommodate such visitors? With a *No Frames message.*

When visitors with frames-impaired browsers attempt to view the frames page, they see the No Frames message instead. The No Frames message looks and acts like a separate Web page — it can contain text, graphics, hyperlinks, and so on — but, in reality, the message is a chunk of HTML sitting inside the frames page.

To create a No Frames message, click the No Frames icon in Design view (refer to Figure 10-4), and then proceed as though you're creating a regular Web page.

FrontPage's default No Frames message, "This page uses frames, but your browser doesn't support them," states the obvious but doesn't help the visitor solve the problem. A friendlier No Frames message offers an alternate method for exploring the site, such as providing hyperlinks to the site's content pages. A polite invitation to download a frames-capable browser (plus links that lead straight to the download sites) would be a nice touch, too.

Saving and Previewing a Framed Web Site

When you work with a framed Web site, it's easy to forget that you're working with several Web pages at the same time — the frames page plus its content pages. Because of this page-juggling, saving a framed Web site involves a couple of extra steps. Here's how to save a framed Web site:

1. **Click the Save button.**

   The Save As dialog box appears, as shown in Figure 10-7. The right side of the dialog box contains a diagram of the frames page. If the content pages are new, one of the frames in the frames diagram appears highlighted. The highlighted frame indicates which content page you are currently saving.

2. **Type a filename in the dialog box's File Name text box.**

3. **If you like, change the page's title by clicking the Change Title button to show the Set Page Title dialog box, typing a new title, and then clicking OK to close the dialog box.**

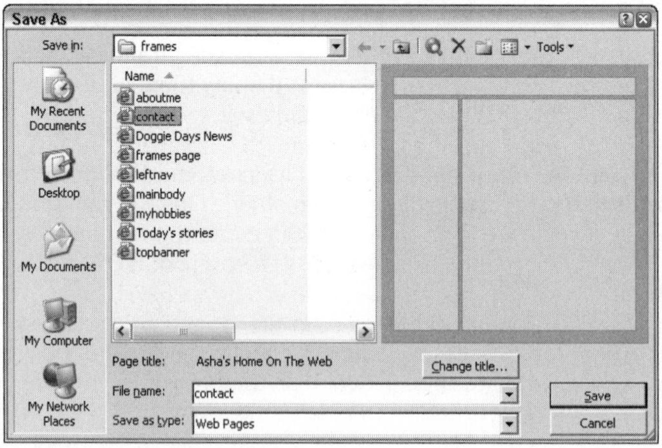

Figure 10-7:
The Save As dialog box.

4. **Click Save.**

   The dialog box closes, and FrontPage saves the content page. In a moment, the Save As dialog box appears again, this time with a different frame in the frames diagram highlighted.

5. **Repeat Steps 2 through 4 for each content page.**

   After you save the last content page, the Save As dialog box appears a final time, this time with the entire frames page diagram highlighted, indicating that you are now saving the frames page itself.

6. **Type a filename and choose (or change) a title for the frames page.**

7. **Click Save.**

   The dialog box closes, and FrontPage saves the frames page.

In the future, when you click the Save button, FrontPage saves all changes to the frames page and the content pages.

 After your site is in order, be sure to preview your site by checking out the Preview view or by clicking the Preview in Browser button. (For more information about how to preview your site, see Chapter 2.) Test the links in each frame to be sure they work the way you expect them to. When you preview your site by using a Web browser, change the browser window size to see how the frames rearrange themselves. If something is amiss, return to FrontPage and keep tweaking until everything works.

Using Inline Frames

Inline frames give your site some of the utility of regular frames without requiring a complete site overhaul. You can add an inline frame to any page, just as you would add a graphic or other effect.

Inline frames are useful when you want to make the content of another page available to your users without requiring them to leave the current page. For example, you could insert an inline frame to display another page that contains frequently updated content, such as news stories, sports scores, or featured products.

 If you like the notion of included content, but you don't want that content to appear inside a scrolling box, investigate the Included Content components, which I describe along with other Web components in Chapter 12. For a more systemic approach to included content, read Chapter 16 about Dynamic Web Templates.

To insert an inline frame into a page, place the cursor where you want the inline frame to appear, and then choose Insert⇨Inline Frame. An empty inline frame appears in the page.

For the most part, from here, working with an inline frame is similar to working with a regular frame, so I'll leave the step-by-step instructions to the earlier sections in this chapter. You begin by filling the inline frame with a content page (either a new or existing page). You can make changes to the content page directly from inside the inline frame, or you can open the content page in its own full-sized window. To do so, right-click the content page inside the inline frame and then choose Open in New Window.

To adjust the inline frame's properties, move your cursor over the inline frame's border until the cursor becomes a pointer. Then right-click, and choose Inline Frame Properties from the pop-up menu that appears. The Inline Frame Properties dialog box appears, as shown in Figure 10-8. Most of the options in this dialog box directly correspond to those in the Frame Properties dialog box (skim the earlier sections of this chapter for details).

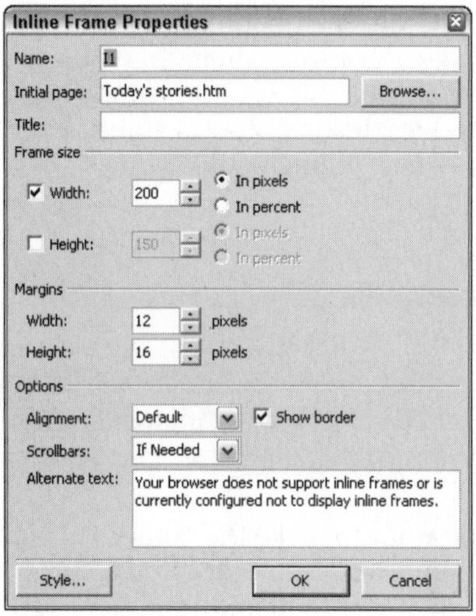

Inline Frame Properties

Name:	II
Initial page:	Today's stories.htm Browse...
Title:	

Frame size

☑ Width:	200	● In pixels / ○ In percent
☐ Height:	150	● In pixels / ○ In percent

Margins

Width:	12	pixels
Height:	16	pixels

Options

Alignment:	Default ▾ ☑ Show border
Scrollbars:	If Needed ▾
Alternate text:	Your browser does not support inline frames or is currently configured not to display inline frames.

Style...   OK   Cancel

Figure 10-8:
The Inline
Frame
Properties
dialog box.

WARNING!

One option in the Inline Frame Properties dialog box bears explanation: The Alternate Text box. In this box, you type a message that appears to visitors who are using browsers that are unable to display inline frames (similar to the No Frames message for regular frames). Make sure your message is meaningful, because inline frames are only visible in certain browser flavors and versions. You also might consider surrounding the message in brackets [ ] so that, for visitors unable to see the inline frame, the alternate next message doesn't run into adjacent text in the page, confusing its purpose.

Chapter 11

Adding Graphical Pizzazz with Themes

In This Chapter

▶ Decorating your Web site with a theme

▶ Modifying themes

▶ Making a custom theme

*Y*ou can probably tell the difference between a professionally designed Web site and a homegrown operation. Professionally designed sites look polished, with coordinating graphics and custom fonts. Web sites built by nondesigners are no less worthwhile, but they're sometimes, um, lacking in the looks department. Let's face it: Most people don't have the expertise to create graphics, the time to track down bits of clip art, or the money to pay a designer. Nor should someone need these things to create an attractive Web site.

To bridge this design gap, the creators of FrontPage got together with professional designers to create *themes*. Now, after a few mouse clicks, your Web site can have some of the style usually reserved for big-budget Web sites.

Applying a Theme to Your Web Site

Themes transform a Web site by applying a coordinated set of text and link colors, fonts, background graphics, table borders, link bar buttons, horizontal lines, and bullets to the site's pages. Each theme generates a different look and feel: For example, the Sumi Painting theme projects peace and serenity, and the Expedition theme creates an earthy, safari look.

For a hint at what themes can do, look at Figures 11-1 and 11-2. Figure 11-1 shows a rather dowdy page — perfectly functional but visually uninteresting. Figure 11-2 shows the same page after a theme makeover. Not bad. Themes won't do magic, but they can give you quick, easy access to home page decoration.

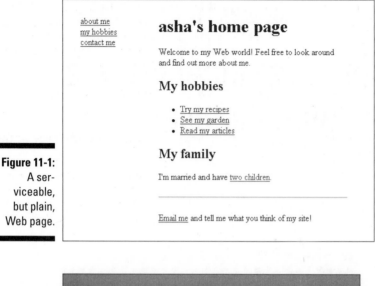

Figure 11-1:
A ser-
viceable,
but plain,
Web page.

Figure 11-2:
The same
Web page,
after the
application
of a theme.

When you apply a theme to your Web site, the theme changes your site's formatting (text styles and sizes, table border colors, and so on). You can always remove the theme later, but any formatting you've applied prior to adding the theme may go away. Just keep this reformatting in mind as you proceed.

Furthermore, when you use themes, FrontPage copies all the theme's graphics into your Web site's file system, which increases the amount of storage space your Web site takes up. This makes no difference to your visitors, but it may concern you if you have limited storage space available on your host

Web server. To find out how much disk space your Web site takes up, in the Windows Explorer, right-click the Web site's folder, and from the pop-up menu that appears, choose Properties. In the dialog box that then appears, the number following Size on Disk shows you how much disk space your Web site requires.

You can apply a theme to your entire Web site or to selected pages. To do so, follow these steps:

1. **Open the Web site. If you want to apply a theme to a single page in the Web site, open that page.**

   TIP

   To keep your site's look and feel consistent, I recommend applying the theme to the whole site in one go. To do so, in the Folder List, click the site's top-level folder (the first folder in the Folder List). This operation tells FrontPage to apply the theme to every page in the site, including open pages and pages inside folders, but not pages inside subsites.

2. **Choose Format➪Theme.**

   The Theme task pane appears (see Figure 11-3). Here, you get a glimpse of the themes included with FrontPage. Each theme contains a nicely coordinated set of text fonts and colors, bullets, a custom horizontal line, hyperlink colors, link bar buttons, a background graphic, and a page banner.

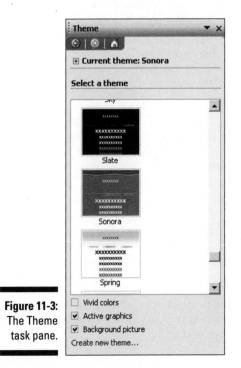

Figure 11-3:
The Theme
task pane.

If you're not familiar with some of the elements I just mentioned, flip through the following chapters for more information: Text color, text font, bullets, and horizontal lines are covered in Chapter 4; link bars and hyperlink colors are covered in Chapter 5; background graphics are covered in Chapter 6; and page banners are covered in Chapter 12.

 3. **In the Select a Theme area of the task pane, scroll down to peruse your choices, and then click the icon corresponding to a theme you like.**

    After you click an icon, the page open in Design view gets quite a makeover! (If you applied the theme to your entire site, all of your site's pages have been similarly endowed, whether or not they're open in Design view.)

    If you're not sure which theme you like, try one on for size. You can always click another icon to apply a different theme, or you can get rid of the theme by clicking the No Theme icon.

 4. **Depending on the options you want to use, near the bottom of the task pane, select one or more of the Vivid Colors, Active Graphics, and Background Picture check boxes. Then click the theme's icon again to apply the changes to your site.**

    These check boxes give you a little control (but not much) over the appearance of theme elements:

    • **Vivid Colors:** Select this option if you want to use a slightly brighter set of text, links, and graphic colors. De-select this check box if you prefer more muted colors.

    • **Active Graphics:** Active graphics add some spunk. In the Active Graphic set, FrontPage creates link bar buttons that change color or shape when clicked. Some themes also contain different page banners and bullets graphics.

      Note: Some of the active graphic effects in FrontPage are powered by JavaScript and, therefore, don't show up in older Web browsers. Visitors who use browsers that don't understand JavaScript see a static version of the active graphic.

    • **Background Picture:** This option enables you to turn on or off the theme's background graphic.

If you don't like what you see, return to the Theme task pane and customize the theme (read on to find out how). Or, if you want to remove the theme altogether, click the No Theme icon in the task pane's Select a Theme area.

The FrontPage/Office program CD comes with a bunch of additional themes; to install them on your computer, in the Select a Theme area, click the Install Additional Themes icon (it's the selection at the very bottom), and then follow the directions that appear on your screen.

If you apply themes to your site and then remove the themes later, the theme graphics and elements still take up file space in your Web site. FrontPage can remove unused themes for you. To do so, choose View➪Reports➪Site Summary to view the Site Summary Report. In the report, click Unused Themes. The Recalculate Hyperlinks dialog box appears, making sure you know what you're doing. Click Yes to close the dialog box and remove the unused theme files from your Web site.

Modifying Themes

You can easily customize the colors, graphics, and text styles of any of the FrontPage themes by using the Customize Theme dialog box. (The following sections describe how to use the dialog box to modify a theme.) To open the Customize Theme dialog box, follow these steps:

1. **Choose Format➪Theme.**

   The Theme task pane appears.

2. **In the Select a Theme area, scroll down until you see the icon for the theme you want to modify.**

3. **Move your cursor over the desired icon until a downward-pointing gray arrow appears on the right side of the icon, and then click the arrow.**

4. **From the drop-down list that appears, choose Customize.**

   The Customize Theme dialog box appears (see Figure 11-4). A representation of the theme elements appears in the dialog box's Preview of Theme box.

Figure 11-4:
The
Customize
Theme
dialog box.

You can also check out hundreds of ready-made themes on the Web (many are downloadable for free). A good place to start: `www.freefpthemes.com`.

Modifying theme colors

To change the theme's color scheme, follow these steps:

1. **Open the Customize Theme dialog box.**

   See the steps in the "Modifying Themes" section, earlier in this chapter, for instructions.

2. **Click the Colors button.**

   The contents of the Customize Theme dialog box change to display options for changing the theme's colors (see Figure 11-5).

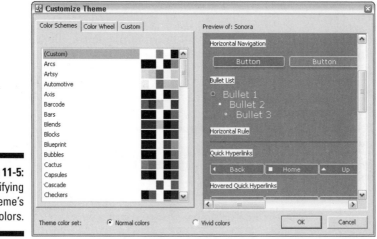

Figure 11-5: Modifying the theme's colors.

3. **To change the theme's overall color scheme, click the color scheme you like in the dialog box's Color Schemes tab.**

   After you click a color scheme, you can get an idea of how the theme will appear by looking at the Preview of Theme box. If you prefer a more vivid version of the color scheme, select the Vivid Colors option button at the bottom of the dialog box. (Frankly, the selections aren't much more vivid. What can I say?)

4. **To change the theme's hue or brightness, click the Color Wheel tab, and then change the settings of the color wheel or the Brightness meter.**

To use the color wheel, click the little circle pointer inside the wheel, and then drag the pointer to an area of the wheel that contains the hue you want. For example, if you want the theme to take on a yellowish hue, drag the circle pointer to the yellow area of the wheel. The Colors in This Scheme grid displays the color change, and, as always, the Preview of Theme box displays how the change looks inside the theme.

To change the theme's brightness, click the Brightness meter and drag it to the left (to decrease brightness) or right (to increase brightness).

5. **To change the colors of individual theme elements, click the Custom tab, and then choose options from the Item and Color list boxes.**

   For example, if you want to change the theme's Heading 1 color, choose Heading 1 from the Item list box, and then choose the color you want from the Color list box. Alternatively, you can choose More Colors to display the Color dialog box. (For details on how to use this dialog box, see Chapter 4.)

6. **Click OK when you're finished modifying colors (or click Cancel to stick with the theme's original color settings).**

   The general Customize Theme dialog box comes into view again.

7. **Click OK.**

   The Microsoft FrontPage dialog box pops open, asking if you want to save the changes you just made. If you don't, click No, and FrontPage will proceed as if nothing has changed. Otherwise . . .

8. **Click Yes.**

   The Microsoft FrontPage dialog box closes, and the Save Theme dialog box appears. Because each FrontPage theme is read-only, the dialog box prompts you to choose a new theme name.

9. **In the dialog box's text box, type a new theme name, and then click OK.**

   The Save Theme dialog box closes, and FrontPage saves and applies the theme changes.

If you later decide you want to return to the theme's original color scheme, follow the preceding directions, but in Step 3, click the color scheme associated with the theme, and then click OK.

Choosing different theme graphics

You can replace any of the theme's graphics with your own. Say you want a theme to display a page banner of your own design, or a custom horizontal rule graphic. No problem. You can also change the characteristics of the text that appears on top of page banners and link bar buttons. To do so, follow these steps:

1. **Open the Customize Theme dialog box by following the steps in the earlier section, "Modifying Themes."**

2. **Click the Graphics button.**

   The contents of the Customize Theme dialog box change, this time displaying options that control the theme's graphics.

3. **From the Item list box, choose the name of the graphic you want to replace.**

   Based on the graphic you choose, options pertaining to that graphic appear in the dialog box's Picture tab. Also, a sample of the graphic element you selected pops to the top of the theme preview, which is visible in the Preview of Theme box.

4. **At the bottom of the dialog box, click the option button that corresponds to the graphic set you want to modify.**

   You can modify either the Normal graphics set or the Active graphics set.

5. **In the appropriate text box(es), type the filename and location of the graphic you want to use, or click the Browse button to find a graphic by using the Select Picture dialog box.**

   If you're not sure how to use the Select Picture dialog box, see Chapter 6.

6. **To change the style of the text that appears on top of page banners and link bar buttons, click the Font tab, and then choose the options you want.**

   Note: If the options in the Font tab appear dimmed, then the type of graphic that is visible in the Item list box doesn't have associated text. To make the tab active, from the Item list box, choose an option that has associated text (such as Banner or Global Navigation Buttons) and proceed.

7. **Click OK to save your graphic changes (or Cancel to leave the theme graphics unchanged).**

8. **In the Customize Theme dialog box, click OK.**

   The Microsoft FrontPage dialog box prompts you to save the changes you just made.

9. **Click Yes.**

   The dialog box closes, and the Save Theme dialog box appears.

10. **In the dialog box's text box, type a new theme name, and then click OK.**

    The Save Theme and Customize Theme dialog boxes close, and FrontPage saves and applies the theme changes.

Changing theme text styles

You can easily change a theme's choices of body and heading text fonts. To do so, follow these steps:

1. **Open the Customize Theme dialog box.**

   To find out how, see the steps in the "Modifying Themes" section, earlier in this chapter.

2. **Click the Text button.**

   The contents of the Customize Theme dialog box change, this time displaying options that control text style.

3. **From the Item list box, choose the text element you want to change.**

4. **From the Font list box, click the name of the font you want to use for the element visible in the Item list box.**

   If you choose an unusual or custom font, keep in mind that only those visitors with that particular font installed on their computers can see that font. (To the rest, text will appear in the browser's default font.) As a backup, consider choosing a second, similar font that will display if the first font isn't present on the visitor's computer. To do so, in the Font text box, type the first font choice followed by a comma, and then the second font choice (for example, type **Arial, Helvetica**).

5. **Click OK to save your text changes (or click Cancel to leave the theme text styles unchanged).**

6. **In the Customize Theme dialog box, click OK.**

   The Microsoft FrontPage dialog box prompts you to save the changes you just made.

7. **Click Yes.**

   The dialog box closes, and the Save Theme dialog box appears.

8. **In the dialog box's text box, type a new theme name, and then click OK.**

   The Save Theme and Customize Theme dialog boxes close, and FrontPage saves and applies the theme changes.

You can, in fact, change any aspect of a theme's text style by clicking the More Text Styles button in the Text section of the Customize Theme dialog box. By doing so, you call forth the powerful Styles dialog box, which I talk about in Chapter 14.

Creating Your Own Theme

With a little creativity and a few custom graphics, you can create your own theme.

The steps are basically the same as modifying an existing theme: FrontPage gives you a boilerplate theme you use as your starting point, which you then modify to suit your own taste.

To create a new theme, choose Format➪Theme to display the Theme task pane. At the bottom of the task pane, click the Create New Theme link. The Customize dialog box appears with a generic theme (if you can call it that) visible in the Preview box. To choose your custom theme's colors, graphics, and text styles, follow the instructions in the "Modifying theme colors," "Choosing different theme graphics," and "Changing theme text styles" sections.

Chapter 12

With Web Components, Who Needs a Programmer?

- -

In This Chapter

▶ Finding out what Web components can do

▶ Integrating Web components into your site

- -

*U*sed to be, if you wanted your Web site to contain interactive features, you (or a programmer) had to do lots of mucking around with HTML and server-based programs, and you had to coordinate the whole process with your ISP or system administrator. With FrontPage, you can create similar effects with a few mouse clicks.

How? With *Web components*. Web components are gizmos that you insert into your Web page to simplify certain Web publishing tasks or to add interactive features to your site. FrontPage contains the following Web components, each of which performs a different task:

- ✔ **Interactive button:** Create a stylish button that, when clicked, works like a hyperlink.

- ✔ **Marquee:** Create scrolling text with this component. In my opinion, the effect was marginally cool in the mid-90s, when Microsoft created this Internet Explorer-only HTML tag. Now, marquees scream "tacky," and should be avoided. (Tell us what you *really* think, Asha.) If you don't agree, check out the FrontPage Help system (press F1) for a how-to on this Web component.

- ✔ **Web search:** Enable visitors to search your site for keywords with the help of this Web component.

- ✔ **Spreadsheets and charts:** Add functionality with embedded spreadsheets, charts, and PivotTables.

- ✔ **Hit counter:** Keep track of the number of visits a page receives with this handy tool.

- ✔ **Photo gallery:** Transform your site into an online digital photo gallery. I explain how to create a photo gallery in Chapter 6.

- ✔ **Included content:** Automate the inclusion of text and pictures into your site by using this group of Web components.

- ✔ **Link bars:** Help users navigate your site by including a row of text or graphic hyperlinks on each page. I explain how to create link bars in Chapter 5.

- ✔ **Table of contents:** Generate an automatically updated list of links to all the other pages in your site with this component. (I cover this Web component in Chapter 5.)

- ✔ **Top 10 list:** Display interesting information about the people that come to your site with this Web component, such as the top-10 browser types visitors use, the top-10 search phrases people use to get to your site, and more.

- ✔ **Additional Web components:** Use additional Web components that work with Microsoft Web-based services, such as Expedia (allowing you to link to a map), MSN (enabling visitors to search the Web or look up stock quotes), and MSNBC (letting you display the latest news and weather).

In this chapter, I show you how Web components can simplify your life, and I demonstrate how to put most of the critters to work. Web components aren't without their limitations, which I describe as well.

To work properly, some Web components must team up with a Web server that is outfitted with FrontPage Server Extensions. (I talk about what FrontPage Server Extensions are and what they do in Chapter 17.) I point out specialized server requirements as I go along.

Two additional Web components — List view and Document Library view — work only in Web sites published on Web servers that support Microsoft SharePoint Services. I talk briefly about SharePoint Team Web sites in Chapter 17.

Inserting an Interactive Button

An *interactive button* is an animated button that, when clicked, activates a hyperlink (see Figure 12-1). When the visitor moves the pointer over the button before clicking it, the button changes color or shape.

Figure 12-1:
Interactive
buttons add
oomph to
links.

By default, interactive buttons look like stylized rectangular boxes. If rectangles aren't your style, FrontPage gives you a bevy of button shapes to choose from, including capsules and tabs in several styles and colors.

Interactive buttons are produced using JavaScript, and therefore require that your visitors use JavaScript-capable browsers.

Adding an interactive button to your page

To create an interactive button, follow these steps:

1. **Choose Insert➪Interactive Button.**

   The Interactive Buttons dialog box appears with the Button tab visible, as shown in Figure 12-2.

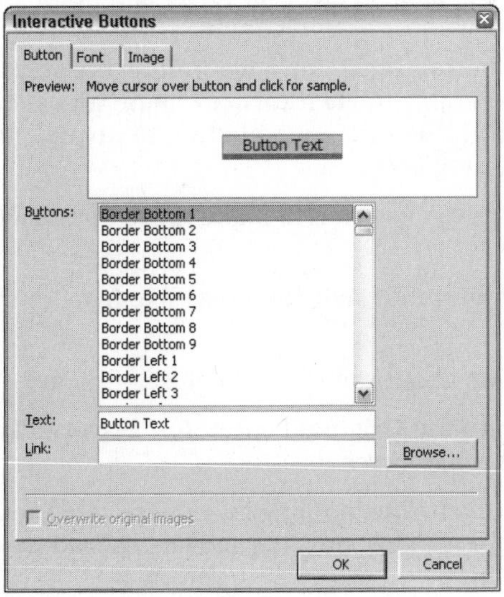

Figure 12-2:
The Button
tab of the
Interactive
Buttons
dialog box.

Interactive Buttons
Button	Font	Image
Preview: Move cursor over button and click for sample.
Button Text
Buttons: Border Bottom 1 / Border Bottom 2 / Border Bottom 3 / Border Bottom 4 / Border Bottom 5 / Border Bottom 6 / Border Bottom 7 / Border Bottom 8 / Border Bottom 9 / Border Left 1 / Border Left 2 / Border Left 3
Text: Button Text
Link: Browse...
Overwrite original images
OK	Cancel

2. **In the Buttons list box, click the type of button you want to create.**

Chances are that the cryptic list items won't necessarily make sense to you, so scroll down the list box and click an option that looks promising. A preview of the interactive button appears in the dialog box's Preview area.

3. **In the Text text box, type the word(s) that you want to appear on top of the button.**

4. **In the Link text box, type the filename or URL of the page you want to appear when the interactive button is clicked.**

Or click the Browse button to choose a link destination from the Edit Hyperlink dialog box. I describe how this dialog box works in Chapter 5.

5. **If you're happy with what you see, click OK to close the dialog box and insert the interactive button in your Web page.**

If you want to further tinker with the interactive button's text formatting and image style, don't click OK . . . read the next section of this chapter for more directions.

Changing an interactive button's text formatting

You're not stuck with the text formatting FrontPage provides when you create an interactive button. You can change text size, color, and more. Here's how:

1. **Insert an interactive button into your page (follow the steps in the previous section). Or, to change the text formatting on an existing button, in the page, double-click the interactive button to display the Interactive Buttons dialog box.**

2. **In the dialog box, click the Font tab to make those options visible, as shown in Figure 12-3.**

3. **Choose your desired font, font style, and text size from the appropriate list boxes.**

For detailed information about each font effect, see Chapter 4.

4. **Choose text colors from the Original Font Color, Hovered Font Color, and Pressed Font color list boxes.**

   - **Original Font Color:** When nothing is happening to the interactive button (the visitor isn't clicking it or moving the mouse over it), text appears in this color.

   - **Hovered Font Color:** When a visitor moves the cursor over the button without clicking it, text appears in this color.

- **Pressed Font Color:** When a visitor clicks the interactive button, text appears in this color *while the button is being clicked.* When the click is finished (about half-a-second later), text returns to its hovered color.

5. **To change how the text is aligned on the button, choose different options from the Horizontal Alignment and Vertical Alignment list boxes.**

   I won't waste your time describing each effect here. Just pick the effect that sounds like what you want. After you're finished creating the button, you can preview the page to see how the effect looks. If you don't like the effect, you can change this setting.

6. **When you're happy with what you see in the Preview area, click OK to close the dialog box and insert the interactive button in your Web page.**

   If you want to keep fiddling, don't click OK . . . read the next section of this chapter for more directions.

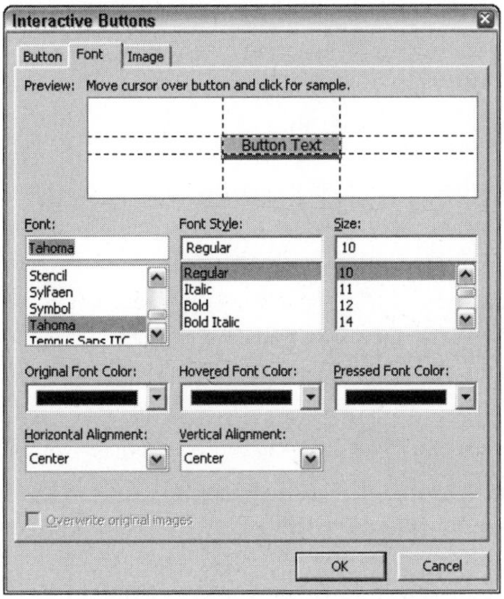

Figure 12-3:
The Font tab of the Interactive Buttons dialog box.

Altering an interactive button's image

You have a little wiggle room with the interactive button images FrontPage gives you. You can change their dimensions, as well as how they behave when clicked, by following these steps:

1. **Insert an interactive button into your page (follow the steps in the section, "Adding an interactive button to your page"). Or, to change how an existing button looks, in the page, double-click the interactive button to display the Interactive Buttons dialog box.**

2. **In the dialog box, click the Image tab to make those options visible, as shown in Figure 12-4.**

3. **To change the button's dimensions, enter new pixel values in the Width and Height text boxes.**

   Be sure the Maintain Proportions check box is selected so that the button image doesn't stretch in a funny way when you change its width or height.

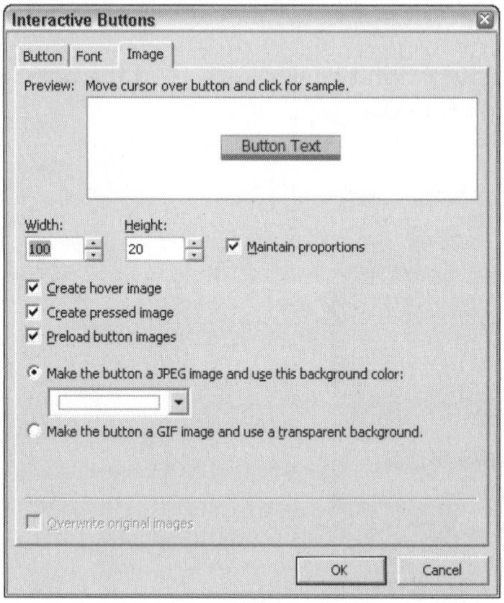

Figure 12-4:
The Image tab of the Interactive Buttons dialog box.

4. **If you want the button to look the same whether or not the visitor hovers the cursor over it, de-select the Create Hover Image check box.**

5. **If you want the button to look the same while the visitor clicks the button, de-select the Create Pressed Image check box.**

6. **Make sure the Preload Button Images check box is selected.**

   When this check box is selected, FrontPage inserts JavaScript into the page's HTML code that tells the visitor's browser to load the button's images in the background while the rest of the page text loads (the regular, hover, and pressed images are actually three separate graphic files). This way, when a visitor hovers the cursor over or clicks the interactive button, the images that create these effects are immediately available.

Incidentally, browsers that don't understand JavaScript simply ignore the script and display only the original button image.

7. **If necessary, choose the interactive button's background color.**

By default, the interactive button's background color is white. You can only see the interactive button's background color if you chose a rounded button — a capsule or a rounded tab — *and* if the page's background color is something other than white. If this is the case, you can either set the interactive button's background color to be the same as the page's (choose a color from the Make the Button a JPEG Image list box), or you can give the button a transparent background color (select the Make the Button a GIF image option).

8. **Click OK to close the dialog box and insert the interactive button in your Web page.**

Adding a Keyword Search to Your Web Site

A *keyword search* is to a Web site what a knowledgeable tour guide is to a big city: Both help visitors bypass the flotsam and get straight to the stuff they want to see. The Web Search component enables you to add a keyword search to your Web site in a few clicks.

With the Web Search component nestled in a page in your site, visitors type words or phrases into a text box and then click a button to activate the search. In a moment, a linked list of Web pages matching the search request appears. From there, your visitors just click a link to go to a particular page.

Using Office spreadsheets and charts in your site

FrontPage comes with three Web components that enable you to add Office functionality to your Web site in the form of working spreadsheets, charts, and PivotTables. These Web components are best reserved for use on an intranet site because they have specific server and browser requirements: The site must be published on a server that has FrontPage Server Extensions installed, and visitors must be using Internet Explorer (version 5.01 with Service Pack 2 and later) *and* have Microsoft Office (version 2000 and later) with Office Web components installed on their computers. If your publishing environment meets these conditions and you'd like to know more, visit the FrontPage Help system for details. To get there, in the upper-right corner of the FrontPage window, type **Office Web Component** in the Type a Question for Help list box, and then press Enter.

You can add a search form to an existing page or create a separate search page with the help of the Search Page template (the template gives visitors tips on how to search). See Chapter 2 if you're not sure how to create a new page based on a template.

Note: Don't let the name *Web Search* fool you into thinking you're adding an Internet-wide search box to your site. In this context, *Web* refers to your Web site. If you're looking for a way to add a World Wide Web-wide search to your site, check out the Web component called *Search the Web with MSN*. I show you how to use this component later in this chapter.

To use the Web Search component, you must publish your Web site on a host Web server that has FrontPage Server Extensions installed. For more information about FrontPage Server Extensions, see Chapter 17.

To use the Web Search component, follow these steps:

1. **Place the cursor in the page where you want the search form to appear, and then click the Web Component button on the Standard toolbar.**

   The Insert Web Component dialog box appears.

2. **In the Component Type list box, click Web Search.**

3. **In the Choose a Type of Search list box, double-click Current Web.**

   The Insert Web Component dialog box closes, and the Search Form Properties dialog box appears.

4. **In the Label for Input text box, type the text label that prompts visitors to type keywords.**

5. **In the Width in Characters text box, type the width (in number of characters) of the text box into which visitors type keywords.**

6. **In the Label for "Start Search" Button text box, type the text label that appears on the button that visitors click to start the search.**

7. **In the Label for "Reset" Button text box, type the label that appears on the button that visitors click to erase the contents of the keyword text box.**

8. **In the Search Form Properties dialog box, click the Search Results tab.**

9. **In the Word List to Search text box, leave the default value *All* alone.**

To hide pages from the Web Search component, stow them away in the _private folder. (In Chapter 15, I show you how to move pages into folders.) For example, you may not want the search to extend to pages that aren't yet complete.

10. **Select the check boxes next to the items you want to appear in the search results list.**

    After a visitor performs a search, the Web Search component returns a linked list of matching pages. You can display additional information in the results page by selecting one or more of the following check boxes: Display Score (Closeness of Match) sorts the pages according to the closeness of the match; Display File Date shows the date that the page was last modified; and Display File Size (in K bytes) shows the page's file size.

11. **Click OK to close the Search Form Properties dialog box.**

    A search form appears in your page.

To preview and test the search form, you must use FrontPage in conjunction with a Web server that is outfitted with FrontPage Server Extensions. To try out the keyword search, you must publish your Web site and then preview the *live* version of the site.

If, after you test the keyword search, the search results seem out-of-date, save all open pages in FrontPage and then recalculate your Web site's hyperlinks (choose Tools➪Recalculate Hyperlinks). Then republish your site and try your search again — it should be fit as a fiddle.

Tracking Visits with a Hit Counter

A *hit counter* is an odometer-like row of numbers that sits in your page and records the number of visits or *hits* that the page receives (see Figure 12-5). Each time someone visits the page, the number in the hit counter goes up by one. Hit counters let you brag to visitors about your site's popularity, and it's fun to watch the numbers increase every day.

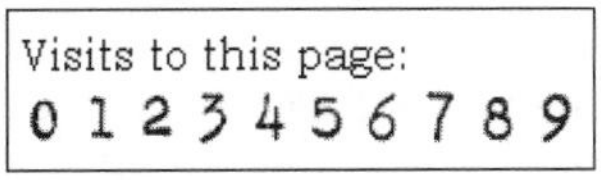

Figure 12-5:
A hit counter.

Visits to this page:
0 1 2 3 4 5 6 7 8 9

To use a FrontPage hit counter, you must publish your Web site on a host Web server that has FrontPage Server Extensions installed (version 2000 or later). For more information about FrontPage Server Extensions, see Chapter 17.

To insert a hit counter into your page, follow these steps:

1. **Place the cursor in the page where you want the counter to appear, and then click the Web Component button on the Standard toolbar.**

   The Insert Web Component dialog box appears.

2. **In the Component Type list box, click Hit Counter.**

   A list of available counters appears on the right side of the dialog box.

3. **In the Choose a Counter Style list box, double-click the graphic style you like (if you don't like any of the graphic styles, just double-click any one of the counters; I explain how you can substitute your own graphic for the FrontPage offerings in a moment).**

   The Insert Web Component dialog box closes, and the Hit Counter Properties dialog box appears.

   You can use your own image in place of FrontPage's preset counter graphics. To do so, click the Custom Picture option, and then type the image's filename and location in the accompanying text box. You must choose a single graphic that contains the numbers 0–9, and the numbers must be evenly spaced inside the image.

4. **Select the Reset Counter To check box, and in the accompanying text box, type the counter's starting number.**

   If your Web site is new, leave the number at 0. If your site has already been around for a while, you can start the counter with an approximation of the number of visitors who came by before your counter was installed. (Or you can artificially inflate the number of folks who have visited, but I know you weren't even considering that option.)

5. **If you want the counter to appear with a fixed number of digits, select the Fixed Number of Digits check box and then type the number of digits in the accompanying text box.**

   For example, if you type **5** in the text box, the counter displays hit number 1 as 00001.

6. **Click OK.**

   The dialog box closes, and a graphic placeholder appears in the page.

To preview and test the hit counter, you must use FrontPage in conjunction with a Web server that is outfitted with FrontPage Server Extensions. To see the hit counter in action, you must publish your Web site and then preview the *live* version of the site.

Letting Visitors Search the Web or Look Up a Stock Quote

These days, regular folks turn to the Web for quick information about every topic. Because there is no way to know where your visitors want to go after they are done visiting your site, give them a gracious exit: a way to search the Web or look up a stock quote right from your site.

FrontPage comes with two Web Components that do just that. They hook directly into the engines of MSN, Microsoft's comprehensive online portal/magazine/service (it's hard to sum up what MSN actually *is*).

To add a World Wide Web or stock quote search to your site, follow these steps:

1. **Place the cursor in the page where you want the search box to appear, and then click the Web Component button on the Standard toolbar.**

   The Insert Web Component dialog box appears.

2. **In the Component Type list box, click MSN Components.**

   You may need to scroll down the list box to find this item.

3. **In the Choose an MSN Component list box, double-click either the Search the Web with MSN option or the Stock Quote option.**

   The Insert Web Component dialog box closes, and the search box of your choice appears in your page.

You can test drive the search by using FrontPage's Preview view. (Remember, you must be connected to the Internet at the time.)

Linking to an Online Map

I have a terrible sense of direction. If there is one Web service I use more than any other, it's the ability to get driving directions to and from just about any destination. FrontPage enables you to plug this powerful functionality into your own site with a little help from another branded service, Expedia, Microsoft's own travel-related Web site.

You can choose to include a static picture of a map in your site, as shown in Figure 12-6, or you can include a hyperlink to a dynamic map that lets visitors get driving directions from whatever location they wish. Here's how:

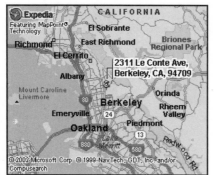

Figure 12-6:
Include a
map in your
site.

1. **Activate your Internet connection.**

   FrontPage must be able to connect to the Expedia Web site to insert either of the Web components.

2. **Place the cursor in the page where you want the map graphic or hyperlink to appear, and then click the Web Component button on the Standard toolbar.**

   The Insert Web Component dialog box appears.

3. **In the Component Type list box, click Expedia Components.**

   You may need to scroll down the list box to find this item.

4. **In the Choose an Expedia Component list box, double-click the type of map you want to use.**

   Link to a Map creates a hyperlink to a dynamic map on the Expedia Web site, while Static Map inserts a map graphic into your page.

   The Insert Web Component dialog box closes, and, depending upon which item you chose, the Link to a Map Properties dialog box or Static Map Properties dialog box appears. (The steps that follow apply to both dialog boxes.)

5. **Bypass the dialog box's introductory comments by clicking Next.**

   The contents of the dialog box change to enable you to select the location you want to map.

6. **In the What Would You Like to Locate section of the dialog box, specify the location you want to map.**

   You can choose either a street address or intersection (such as *1000 Main Street* or *Market and Beale*), or a place name (such as *Disneyland* or *Yosemite Falls*).

7. **Click Next.**

   (If you specified a place name in Step 6, Expedia may require you to choose a more specific form of the location name that it lists for you in a Best Matches list box. If so, choose an item from the list box and then click Next.)

   When Expedia is happy that it can fulfill your map request, the final screen appears.

8. **Click Finish.**

   The dialog box closes, and either a hyperlink or a picture of a map appears in your page.

Displaying the Latest News Headlines or Weather Report

If your site depends on up-to-the-minute information to keep visitors coming, let FrontPage give you a hand. FrontPage Web components hook into yet another Microsoft Web service, MSNBC NewsStand, to add a snappy graphic to your site that contains the latest headlines. The graphic is updated each hour, and you can choose what type of headlines the graphic contains (news, technology, sports, and more).

Here's how to add headlines to your site:

1. **Activate your Internet connection.**

   FrontPage must be able to connect to the MSNBC Web site to insert the Web component.

2. **Place the cursor in the page where you want the headline graphic to appear, and then click the Web Component button on the Standard toolbar.**

   The Insert Web Component dialog box appears.

3. **In the Component Type list box, click MSNBC Components.**

   You may need to scroll down the list box to find this item.

4. **In the Choose an MSNBC Component list box, double-click the type of headlines you want to insert in your page.**

   The Insert Web Component dialog box closes, and an official-looking MSNBC graphic appears in your page.

Note: If, in Step 4, you chose Weather Forecast, you need to take an additional couple of steps to specify the forecast ZIP code or city name, but the steps are self-explanatory.

After you publish your Web site, the MSNBC graphic will automatically refresh itself each hour.

Automating Content with Inclusions

Most Web sites contain some sort of repeating information, whether it's a copyright notice along the bottom of each page, or a list of important department announcements that appears on several pages in your site. You can minimize the time spent typing information more than once by taking advantage of *included content* components. When you place an included content Web component into your page, the component replaces itself with content from some source: either a list of entries that you define, another Web page, or a picture file. The beauty of this technology shines when you use included content in more than one page: You update the content source, and the change automatically appears wherever that content is included throughout your site.

Substitution

The Substitution component enables you to display placeholders in your page that replace themselves with bits of information called configuration variables. *Configuration variables* describe certain details about the page or contain snippets of information that you specify.

Displaying standard configuration variables

FrontPage maintains a standard set of configuration variables for each page:

- **Author:** The user name of the person who created the page.
- **Modified By:** The user name of the person who most recently edited the page.
- **Description:** A description of the page.
- **Page URL:** The current location of the page.

Some Web sites created using FrontPage's Web site templates contain additional standard configuration variables.

To see the values for each configuration variable in a page, in the Folder List, right-click the page's icon and choose Properties from the pop-up menu that appears. The Properties dialog box appears. In the dialog box, click the Summary tab. The author's name appears next to Created By. (If no name appears next to Created By, then the author did not use FrontPage to create the page.) The name of the person who last modified the page appears next to Modified By. The page description appears in the Comments text box. In the General tab, the page's current URL appears in the Location box.

To use the Substitution component to display standard configuration variables, follow these steps:

1. **Place the cursor in the page where you want the substitution to appear, and then click the Web Component button on the Standard toolbar.**

   The Insert Web Component dialog box appears.

2. **In the Component Type list box, click Included Content.**

   A list of available content types appears on the right side of the dialog box.

3. **In the Choose a Content Type list box, double-click Substitution.**

   The Insert Web Component dialog box closes, and the Substitution Properties dialog box appears.

4. **In the Substitute With list box, choose the name of the configuration variable that you want to display.**

5. **Click OK to close the dialog box.**

   The value of the configuration variable appears in your page.

If you use the Substitution component to display the Page URL configuration variable, the URL that appears corresponds to the computer on which the page is *currently* located. If you later publish the page on another Web server, the old, incorrect URL remains displayed inside the page.

To solve this problem, after you publish the Web site, open the Web site directly from the Web server on which the site is published (refer to Chapter 1 if you're not sure how) and then open the page displaying the Page URL configuration variable. Click the URL and press the Delete key to delete the Substitution Web component. Now reinsert the Substitution Web component and set it up to display the Page URL configuration variable. (Follow the steps outlined in this section.) The correct URL appears. Save the page to make the change visible to the rest of the World Wide Web.

Creating and displaying your own configuration variables

You can create your own configuration variables to use as placeholders for standard bits of information throughout the Web site. Say, for example, you want to list your mailing address in several Web pages. Instead of typing the address repeatedly, you can create a configuration variable named MyAddress. If you use the Substitution Web component to include the MyAddress configuration variable in your page, your address appears in its place. Even better, if you move, you simply need to update the configuration variable instead of editing your address in every single page.

To create your own configuration variables, follow these steps:

1. **Choose Tools➪Site Settings.**

   The Site Settings dialog box appears, with the General tab visible.

2. **In the dialog box, click the Parameters tab.**

3. **Click the Add button.**

   The Add Name and Value dialog box appears.

4. **Type the name of the configuration variable in the Name text box.**

   Choose a one-word name that is brief and descriptive, such as *MyAddress*.

5. **Type the value of the configuration variable in the Value text box.**

   FrontPage substitutes this text whenever you display the configuration variable in your page. For the MyAddress configuration variable, for example, you type your address here.

6. **Click OK to close the Add Name and Value dialog box.**

   The configuration variable's name and value appear in the box in the Parameters panel.

7. **To add more configuration variables, repeat Steps 3 through 6.**

   Modify or remove configuration variables by clicking their names in the list and then clicking the Modify or Remove buttons.

8. **After you finish creating configuration variables, click OK to close the Site Settings dialog box.**

To insert the newly created configuration variables in your Web site, follow the steps for displaying standard configuration variables in the previous section.

Include page

Include page is a Web component that simplifies the process of inserting the same information in more than one page in your Web site. After you insert an Include Page component into your page, the Web component is replaced by the contents of a second page.

Here's an example: Say you want to display a list of announcements in several pages in your Web site. Instead of typing the announcements into each page, you create a separate page that contains only the announcements. You then use the Include Page component to include the contents of the announcements page in the other pages in your Web site. If you want to change the announcements later, you update the announcements page, and the Include Page component reflects the update throughout the Web site.

The Include Page component works very much like shared borders (for more information about shared borders, see Chapter 5). However, you can insert an Include Page component in the body of your page, whereas shared borders stick to the page's margins.

If you find yourself using several Include Page components throughout your site, consider using a Dynamic Web Template instead. This feature (new to FrontPage 2003) enables you build an entire site using inclusions. If this sounds interesting, check out Chapter 16.

Inserting the Include Page Web component

To use the Include Page component, follow these steps:

1. **Place the cursor in the page where you want the inclusion to appear and then click the Web Component button on the Standard toolbar.**

   The Insert Web Component dialog box appears.

2. **In the Component Type list box, click Included Content.**

   A list of available content types appears on the right side of the dialog box.

3. **In the Choose a Type of Content list box, double-click Page.**

   The Insert Web Component dialog box closes, and the Include Page Properties dialog box appears.

4. **In the Page to Include text box, type the filename and location of the page in your Web site that you want to include.**

   Alternatively, click the Browse button to choose a page from the Current Web dialog box.

5. **Click OK.**

   The Include Page Properties dialog box closes, and the contents of the included page appear inside the current page.

Try passing your pointer over the included information; the pointer turns into a little hand holding a piece of paper. This special pointer reminds you that the text is there courtesy of the Include Page component.

Because the pages that you include by using the Include Page component are often just fragments of information that only the "host" page needs to access, you may want to hide included pages from Web browsers and from the Web Search component. To do so, store the included pages inside your Web site's _private folder. (Refer to Chapter 15 for descriptions of the different FrontPage folders and how to store pages inside them.)

The _private folder is private only if you publish the Web site on a Web server that supports FrontPage Server Extensions. For more information, see Chapter 17.

Updating included pages

To update a page that you've included inside other pages, simply open the included page in Design view, make your changes, and save the page just as you would any other Web page. When you save and close the page, FrontPage recalculates the site's hyperlinks, which updates the inclusion throughout the rest of your Web site.

When FrontPage recalculates hyperlinks, it refreshes the site, integrating any changes made to the site's system of hyperlinks. This process usually happens automatically as you update your site (you don't even notice), but you can also specifically tell FrontPage to recalculate your site's hyperlinks. To do so, choose Tools➪Recalculate Hyperlinks. The Recalculate Hyperlinks dialog box appears, warning you that recalculating hyperlinks may take several minutes. Click Yes to close the dialog box and proceed with the recalculation.

You can tell FrontPage to remind you when an included page has changed but hasn't yet been updated throughout the site. To do so, choose Tools➪ Options. The Options dialog box appears with the General tab visible. In the dialog box, select the Warn When Included Components Are Out of Date check box, and then click OK to close the dialog box.

Including a page or picture based on a schedule

The Scheduled Include Page and Scheduled Picture Web components work like included pages, except the inclusion appears only during a specified time period. The Scheduled Include Page component (like the Include Page component) inserts the contents of a page into another page, and the Scheduled Picture component inserts a single picture.

As an example of how the Scheduled Include Page component can help you, suppose that you use your Web site to announce upcoming events. Instead of keeping track of event dates and making sure that you update your Web site before the event occurs, you can create a separate page for the announce-ments. Then you can use the Scheduled Include Page component to include the contents of the page in other pages in your Web site, specifying the time period during which the announcements apply. After that time period is over, the announcements disappear.

The Scheduled Picture component is handy if, for example, you flag additions to your Web site with a "New!" icon. Because things are new only for a limited time, you can use this Web component to remove the icons after a week or so.

Both scheduled Web components work the same way, so I describe them together in the following steps:

1. **Place the cursor in the page where you want the included content to appear and click the Web Component button on the Standard toolbar.**

   The Insert Web Component dialog box appears.

2. **In the Component Type list box, click Included Content.**

   A list of available content types appears on the right side of the dialog box.

3. **In the Choose a Content Type list box, double-click either Page Based on Schedule or Picture Based on Schedule.**

   The Insert Web Component dialog box closes, and depending on your choice, either the Scheduled Include Page Properties dialog box or the Scheduled Picture Properties dialog box appears.

4. **In the During the Scheduled Time text box, type the filename and location of the page or picture that you want to include.**

   Or click the Browse button to choose a file from your Web site.

5. **If you want to include a different page or picture before and after the inclusion period, type the filename and location in the Before and After the Scheduled Time text box.**

   If you don't include an alternative page or picture, nothing appears at the location of the Web component before and after the inclusion period.

6. **In the Starting area, choose the date and time you want the inclusion to first appear.**

   Specify the date by selecting options from the Year, Month, and Day list boxes. To specify the time, click the time notation inside the Time scroll box and click the up- or down-pointing arrows at the right side of the box to adjust the time.

7. **In the Ending area, choose the date and time when you want the inclu-sion to disappear.**

8. Click OK.

The dialog box closes, and the specified page contents or picture appears at the location of the cursor. If the inclusion period begins at a later time, the message [Scheduled Include Page] or [Scheduled Picture] appears in your page — unless you specified an alternative, in which case the contents of the alternative page or the alternative picture appears. The message appears in FrontPage only to remind you that the Scheduled Web component is present. People who view the page with a Web browser can't see the message.

If your host Web server is located in another time zone (which is unlikely but possible if you publish your FrontPage Web sites by using an ISP or company server in another region), the times that you specify must apply to the server's time zone, not yours.

Inserting a page banner

FrontPage knows how to create a decorative *page banner* you can use in place of a page header. FrontPage superimposes the page's navigation structure label on top of the theme's banner graphic to create the banner, as shown in Figure 12-7. If you're not sure what a navigation structure is or how it works, refer to Chapter 15. To find out more about themes, see Chapter 11.

Figure 12-7:
A page banner produced by the Capsules theme.

about me

Here's how to insert a page banner:

1. Open the page into which you want to insert a page banner.

If you haven't already, in the Navigation view, add the page to the navigation structure. (See Chapter 15 for instructions on how to work with the Navigation view.)

2. Place the cursor in the page where you want the banner to appear, and then choose Insert➪Page Banner.

The Page Banner Properties dialog box appears.

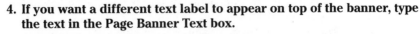

3. **In the dialog box, select the Picture option.**

   If you prefer a plain text banner, select the Text option.

4. **If you want a different text label to appear on top of the banner, type the text in the Page Banner Text box.**

   When you change a banner label, FrontPage changes the label in the site's navigation structure and also uses the label as the page title.

5. **Click OK.**

   The Page Banner Properties dialog box closes, and the banner appears in the page.

If the message [Add this page to the Navigation view to display a page banner here] appears in place of the page banner, the page in which the banner sits is not yet part of the site's navigation structure. To fix the problem, add the page to the navigation structure in the Navigation view, and then switch back to the Design view. The page banner now appears and displays the correct label.

If you were expecting a picture and a text banner appears instead, your page or site lacks a theme. To apply a theme to your site, choose Format➪Theme, and then choose a theme from the Themes task pane (for more information about how to work with themes, see Chapter 11).

To include a page banner in every page in your Web site automatically, take advantage of *shared borders*. I discuss shared borders in Chapter 5.

Inserting a top 10 list

I'm not talking about David Letterman or Billboard music charts here. In FrontPage lingo, a *top 10 list* is information about your site's visitors. Using the Top 10 List component, you can find out the following things:

- ✔ The ten most frequently visited pages in your site

- ✔ The top ten referring domains to your site (that is, the domains that your visitors are visiting just before they come to your site)

- ✔ The top ten referring URLs (the addresses of the Web pages that visitors are at just before they visit your site)

- ✔ The ten most common search phrases (or *strings*) entered into search engines to find your site

- ✔ The ten most frequent visitors to your site

✔ The ten most popular operating systems your visitors use

✔ The ten most popular browsers that your visitors use (great information when you're deciding which browser-specific effects to use in your site)

The Top 10 List component works by culling information from the host server's logs. When you insert a Top 10 List component into a page in your site, the list that the component creates is automatically updated as the server log changes.

To use this Web component, you must publish your site on a host server that supports FrontPage Server Extensions (version 2002 or later), which I discuss in Chapter 17.

To insert a top 10 list, follow these steps:

1. **Place the cursor in the page where you want the list to appear and then click the Web Component button on the Standard toolbar.**

   The Insert Web Component dialog box appears.

2. **In the dialog box's Component Type list box, click Top 10 List.**

   A list of top 10 list types appears on the right side of the dialog box.

3. **In the Choose a Usage List, double-click the list type that you want.**

   The Insert Web Component dialog box closes, and the Top 10 List Properties dialog box appears.

4. **In the dialog box's Title Text box, type a list title.**

   Or, if you're happy with FrontPage's default choice, skip this step.

5. **Select the Include Date Usage Processing Was Last Run check box if you want the date when the list was last updated to appear inside your page.**

6. **In the List Style area of the dialog box, click the box that represents the way you want the list to look, and then click OK.**

   The dialog box closes, and a placeholder for the top 10 list appears in your page.

To see the Top 10 List component in action, you must publish your site and then view the page with a Web browser.

If you're interested in the information a top 10 list provides but don't want to make the information public, insert a top 10 list into a page, and then store that page in the _private folder. I talk more about this handy folder in Chapter 15.

Chapter 13

Eye-Popping Extras: Multimedia and Dynamic HTML Behaviors

· ·

In This Chapter

▶ Including video in your site

▶ Adding sound effects

▶ Working with Flash animation

▶ Getting fancy with Dynamic HTML behaviors

· ·

Not so long ago, Web pages looked like flat, gray screens full of text, with a picture or two to liven things up. The most exciting design effect back then was the horizontal line. Needless to say, times have changed.

Unfortunately, cutting-edge design effects generally rely on advanced HTML knowledge and (sometimes) programming expertise, which puts these effects out of reach for many novice Web designers. Even accomplished designers must slog through meagerly documented HTML code with little direction and lots of willingness to experiment. Not a task for the faint of heart.

Once again, FrontPage steps in with a slew of design goodies, all usable with a few points and clicks. You can add sound effects and video clips to your Web site, you can add Flash animations to your site, and you can tap into the power of Dynamic HTML.

All Manner of Multimedia

Multimedia is the ubiquitous term that describes the jumble of electronically transmittable media formats. More often than not, when used on the Web, multimedia refers to video, animation, and sound. In the following subsections, I show you how to include all three in your Web site.

Keep in mind that only advanced browsers are able to display and play multimedia files. Some older browsers are able to work with multimedia by launching a separate program called a *helper application* to play the file, but other browsers are unable to deal with multimedia at all. Admittedly, only a small percentage of your audience would use browsers unable to handle multimedia, but you should be aware of this limitation all the same.

One last detail to remember: Because they pack so much information, multimedia files tend to be hefty and, therefore, take a long time to load. For an indication of how much load time each addition tacks onto your page, glance at the Estimated Time to Download box on the right side of the FrontPage status bar.

Fun with video

If a picture says a thousand words, a video clip . . . well, you know.

Even though Netscape Navigator is perfectly able to play multimedia files, the HTML tags that FrontPage adds to your page are specific to Internet Explorer. In the following sections, I describe cross-browser workarounds. The workarounds are tedious but worthwhile because they enable more visitors to enjoy your site in its full glory.

If you want to know more about the video-to-Web process (including how to work with streaming video formats such as RealVideo and Microsoft NetShow), see the Builder.com article, "How to Add Video to Your Site," at `builder.cnet.com/webbuilding/pages/Graphics/Video/index.html`.

You have two basic options for including video in your site: You can provide users with a hyperlink leading to the video file (causing the video to appear in its own window), or you can embed the video in the page, much like a regular picture.

To display the video in its own window, import the video file into your Web site and then create a hyperlink directly to the file. That way, only those visitors who want to see the video will click the link and wait for the download. Chapter 15 explains how to import files, and Chapter 5 shows you how to create hyperlinks.

To embed the video into your page, read on for instructions.

Inserting a video for Netscape Navigator and Internet Explorer users

To embed a video clip that is visible to users of both Internet Explorer (version 2.0 or later) and Netscape Navigator (version 3.0 or later), you must use one of FrontPage's Web Components (I talk in detail about Web Components in Chapter 12). The component I describe here works for all sorts of multimedia file types that have corresponding *plug-ins* (little programs built into the Web browser) that can play the file. If you insert videos using this method, you can use any video file format that either Web browser is able to display (popular formats include MPEG, AVI, and QuickTime).

1. **Place the cursor in the page where you want the video clip to appear, and then click the Web Component button on the Standard toolbar.**

   The Insert Web Component dialog box appears.

2. **In the dialog box's Component Type list box, scroll down to the bottom of the list, and then click Advanced Controls.**

   A list of advanced controls appears in the Choose a Control box on the right side of the dialog box.

3. **In the Choose a Control box, double-click Plug-In.**

   The Insert Web Component dialog box closes, and the Plug-In Properties dialog box appears, as shown in Figure 13-1.

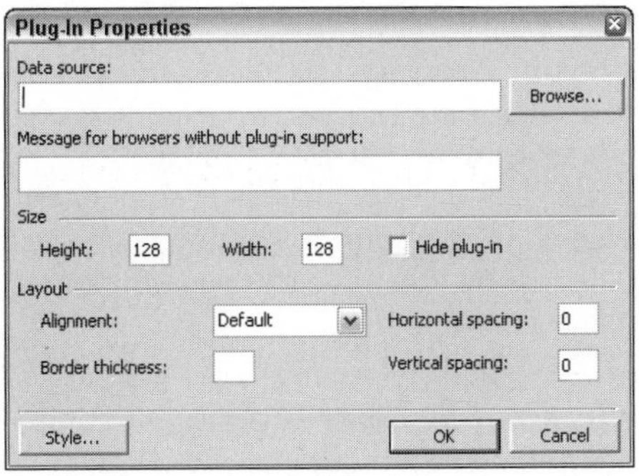

Figure 13-1: The Plug-In Properties dialog box.

4. **In the dialog box's Data Source text box, type the URL of the video file.**

   Alternatively, click the Browse button to locate the file in your Web site, elsewhere on your computer, or on the Web.

5. **If you want a message to appear in place of the video in browsers without support for that file type, type the message in the Message for Browsers without Plug-In Support text box.**

6. **To adjust the dimensions of the video display area inside the page, type new width and height values (in pixels) in the Height and Width text boxes.**

   By default, the original video file dimensions appear in the Height and Width text boxes.

7. **Select the Hide Plug-In check box if you don't want a plug-in icon to appear in your Web page.**

   When viewed with a Web browser, some plug-ins are displayed as icons before the actual plug-in file downloads and is visible. By selecting the Hide Plug-in check box, no icon appears.

8. **Choose an option from the Alignment list box.**

   Refer to Chapter 6 for a description of each alignment option.

9. **If you want the video to be surrounded by a black border, type the border thickness (in pixels) in the Border Thickness text box.**

   As of this writing, borders are visible only in Netscape Navigator and Internet Explorer (version 4.0 or later).

10. **In the Horizontal Spacing text box, type the number of pixels of blank space separating the video from text to its right or left.**

11. **In the Vertical Spacing text box, type the number of pixels of blank space separating the video from text above or below it.**

12. **Click OK.**

    The dialog box closes, and the plug-in icon appears in your page.

To see how the video looks in your Web page, preview your page in a Web browser. (You must have the appropriate plug-in program installed, and your Web browser must be configured to work with the plug-in.)

If the plug-in file is located elsewhere on your computer, the Save Embedded Files dialog box appears the next time you save the page. Refer to Chapter 2 for instructions on how to use this dialog box.

Inserting a video only for Internet Explorer users

The steps in this section explain how to embed a video clip visible only for users of Internet Explorer (version 2.0 or later). The only time you'd want to use such a browser-specific effect is if you're sure all your visitors use the same browser, as may be the case for a corporate intranet site.

Note: If you insert a video into your page using the following method, your video must be stored as an AVI, ASF, or RealMedia file.

1. **In the page, place the cursor where you want the video to appear.**

2. **Choose Insert⇨Picture⇨Video.**

   The Video dialog box appears. This dialog box works just like the Picture dialog box, which I explain in Chapter 6.

3. **In the dialog box, choose the video file you want to display and then click OK.**

   The dialog box closes, and the video appears in your page. The video doesn't move when viewed in Design view. To see the video play, preview the page using the Preview view, or use Internet Explorer.

After you insert a video into your page, you can tinker with some of its properties, such as how many times the video repeats and when the video begins playing. To adjust a video's properties, follow these steps:

1. **In the page, double-click the video.**

   The Picture Properties dialog box appears with the Video tab visible, as shown in Figure 13-2.

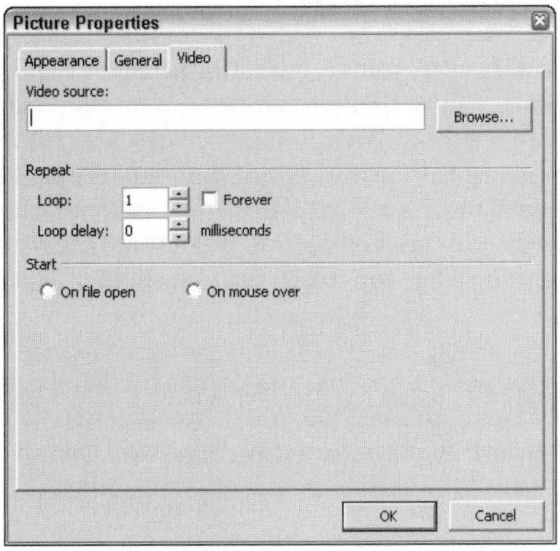

Figure 13-2: The Video tab of the Picture Properties dialog box.

2. **In the dialog box's Loop box, specify the number of times you want the video to repeat.**

   If you want the clip to keep playing until the visitor leaves the page, select the Forever check box.

3. **In the Loop Delay text box, specify the number of milliseconds you want the video to pause before repeating.**

   I know that it's hard to conceive of the length of a millisecond. Just do your best. For example, if you want the video to pause for 1 second before repeating, type **1000** in the Loop Delay text box.

4. **In the Start area, select the option button next to the event that you want to trigger the video to start playing.**

The On File Open option causes the video to play as soon as a visitor arrives. The On Mouse Over option causes the video to play as soon as the pointer passes over the video.

5. **Click OK to close the dialog box.**

To see the video in action, preview your page.

If the video file is stored outside the Web site, the Save Embedded Files dialog box appears the next time you save the page. Refer to Chapter 2 for instructions on how to use this dialog box.

Adding Flash animation

The first time you enter a Web site created with Macromedia Flash, a ground-breaking animation program, you're liable to wonder, "How did they *do* this?" Designers are able to create cartoon-like animations with Macromedia Flash, but because the animations are also programmable, many designers use the software to create entire user interfaces for Web sites. So instead of a static page full of text and pictures, you see a dynamic page that integrates video, sound, and design, with much of the functionality of a regular Web page. A good example: www.sonyclassical.com.

To view Flash animation, you (and your visitors) must be using a browser that knows how to display Flash animations. Most browsers have Flash support built-in, but others require that visitors download and install the free Macromedia Flash Player (available at www.macromedia.com).

While you're not likely to create your own animation with Macromedia Flash (the program carries a steep learning curve) — at least not yet — you may have the opportunity to embed a ready-made Flash animation into your site. FrontPage gives you the tools to do so with relative ease.

To embed a Flash movie into your site, follow these steps:

1. **In the page, place the cursor where you want the Flash animation to appear.**

2. **Select Insert⇨Picture⇨Movie in Flash Format.**

The Select File dialog box appears.

3. **Navigate to the location of the Flash file you want to insert, and then double-click it.**

The dialog box closes, and the Flash animation appears in your page.

4. In the page, double-click the Flash animation.

The Movie in Flash Format Properties dialog box appears with the Appearance tab visible, as shown in Figure 13-3. This dialog box enables you to control how the animation looks and behaves.

Movie in Flash Format Properties

Appearance | General

Movie

Quality: High

Scale: Default (Show all)

Background color: ☐ Automatic ▼   ☐ Transparent

Alignment: Default (Center)

Layout

Alignment: Default ▼   Horizontal spacing: 0

Border thickness: 0   Vertical spacing: 0

Size

☑ Specify size   Width: 550   Height: 400
   ⦿ in pixels   ⦿ in pixels
   ○ in percent   ○ in percent

☑ Keep aspect ratio

OK   Cancel

5. From the Quality list box, choose a quality setting.

By changing the Quality setting, you tell the browser how to prioritize the quality of the animation versus its playback speed (the higher the quality, the lower the speed, with Low being the lowest quality, and Best being the best). The Autolow and Autohigh settings attempt to balance quality and speed by changing how the animation appears, based on the visitor's processor and network speed. Autolow generally gives preference to playback speed, while Autohigh favors image quality.

6. From the Scale list box, choose how you want the visitor's browser to display the animation:

- **Default (Show All):** This options makes the entire animation visible inside the browser window. Borders sometimes appear on either side of the animation.

- **No Border:** This option crops the movie to fit inside the specified area (the size of which you can determine in Step 11).

- **Exact Fit:** This option squeezes the animation into the specified area, no matter what its size. If the width and height ratios don't match the animation's original dimensions, the animation appears distorted.

7. **Choose an option from the Alignment list box.**

   Refer to Chapter 6 for a description of each alignment option.

8. **If you want the animation to be surrounded by a black border, type the border thickness (in pixels) in the Border Thickness text box.**

   As of this writing, borders are visible only in Netscape Navigator and Internet Explorer (version 4.0 or later).

9. **In the Horizontal Spacing text box, type the number of pixels of blank space separating the animation from text to its right or left.**

10. **In the Vertical Spacing text box, type the number of pixels of blank space separating the animation from text above or below.**

11. **If you want to change the display area, in the Size area, select the Specify Size check box, and then enter pixel values in the Width and Height boxes.**

    By default, the display area for the animation equals the animation's dimensions.

12. **In the Movie in Flash Format Properties dialog box, click the General tab to make those options visible.**

    Leave most of the options in this section of the dialog box alone; FrontPage knows what it's doing when it fills in the text boxes. However, the options in the Playback section of the dialog box give you some control over how and when the Flash animation plays.

13. **If you don't want the animation to play automatically, deselect the Auto Play check box.**

    If this check box is deselected, the visitor must click the animation to see it play.

14. **If you don't want the animation to repeat continuously, deselect the Loop check box.**

15. **If you don't want a control menu to appear underneath the animation, de-select the Show Menu check box.**

16. **If your page contains JavaScript or Dynamic HTML, select the SWLiveConnect check box.**

    Flash animations and JavaScript don't play nicely together unless this check box is selected.

17. **Click OK to close the dialog box.**

    To see the Flash animation in action, preview your page.

If the Flash animation file is located elsewhere on your computer, the Save Embedded Files dialog box appears the next time you save the page. Refer to Chapter 2 for instructions on how to use this dialog box.

What about streaming media?

If you're into multimedia, you've probably heard about *streaming media*. As opposed to embedded video and sound, in which a page links to a static file that must fully download before the visitor can see or hear it, streaming video and audio can be viewed or listened to while the file downloads. This is great news for those who want to make big files, such as radio or television rebroadcasts, available on the Web. Unfortunately, adding streaming video or audio to your site isn't so simple. Besides acquiring the proper files, you (or your ISP) must have a streaming media server available to store and serve the files.

For a good overview of multimedia on the Web (including streaming media), see Adam's Multimedia Tutorial at hotwired.lycos.com/ webmonkey/multimedia/tutorials/ tutorial3.html.

Music to your ears

As with video, you can add music and other audio effects to your site by linking to audio files or by embedding audio files directly into a page.

To hear sounds, your visitors must have sound equipment (a sound card and speakers) installed on their computers, along with an advanced Web browser that's able to play sounds. The two most popular choices are Internet Explorer (version 3.0 or later) and Netscape Navigator (version 3.0 and later).

Don't have an audio file to add to your page? No problem. You can download any number of clips, from music to animal sounds to movie quotes to household noises. A Web-based sound archive, such as soundamerica.com, can get you started.

Most often, you include sound in your Web site by linking directly to the sound file. This way, users who want to hear the sound can click the link, and the rest can go about their business. To link to a sound, import the sound file into your Web site and then create a hyperlink directly to the file. Chapter 15 explains how to import files, and Chapter 5 shows you how to create hyperlinks.

Embedded sounds (also known as *background sounds*) play as soon as someone arrives. This feature is acceptable if — and *only* if — you choose a short, pleasant sound bite. Choose wisely, because loud, grating sound effects annoy visitors more than they entertain.

If, instead of a background sound, you want to attach a sound to, say, the click of a button, you can do so by using Dynamic HTML. Check out the section, "Playing a sound based on something a visitor does," later in this chapter, for details.

Though Netscape Navigator can play background sounds, the sound-related HTML tags that FrontPage adds to your page are specific to Internet Explorer. In the following sections, I explain how to insert sounds in two ways: The first method creates background sounds that can be heard using both browsers, and the second method is limited to an Internet Explorer-only audience. Choose the method that fits your target audience.

Inserting a background sound for Netscape Navigator and Internet Explorer users

For both Internet Explorer and Netscape Navigator users to be able to hear background sounds, you must first import the sound file into your Web site (see Chapter 15 for instructions). Be sure your sound file is saved using the WAV, AIFF, or AU format, because both Internet Explorer (version 3.0 or later) and Netscape Navigator (version 3.0 and later) can play these types of files.

Next, you must add a snippet of HTML code to your page. Just follow these steps:

1. **Place the cursor at or near the bottom of the page, and then click the Web Component button on the Standard toolbar.**

   (Placing the cursor at the bottom of the page enables users to see the page while the background sound file downloads.)

   The Insert Web Component dialog box appears.

2. **In the dialog box's Component Type list box, scroll down to the bottom of the list, and then click Advanced Controls.**

   A list of advanced controls appears in the Choose a Control box on the right side of the dialog box.

3. **In the Choose a Control box, double-click HTML.**

   The Insert Web Component dialog box closes and the HTML Markup dialog box appears.

4. **In the dialog box's HTML Markup to Insert box, type the following bit of code, but replace *sound.wav* with the name and location of your sound file:**

   ```
   <BGSOUND SRC="sound.wav"><EMBED SRC="sound.wav"
           HIDDEN="true" AUTOPLAY="true" AUTOSTART="true">
   ```

   Note: My example assumes the sound file is stored in the same folder as the Web page in which you're inserting the sound. If not (say the sound file is stored in a subfolder), indicate the file location by listing the name of the subfolder followed by a slash and then the filename (for example, `foldername/sound.wav`). Be sure to update this location in both the `BGSOUND` and `EMBED` tags.

5. Click OK.

The dialog box closes, and a little icon appears in your page to remind you where you inserted your bit of HTML code.

Be sure to preview the page using both browsers to make sure the sound plays properly. (This action works only if you have sound equipment installed on your computer.)

If you don't hear the sound when you preview the page, be sure your computer's volume is turned up and your speakers are on. If they are, return to the FrontPage Design view and check that you typed the HTML code properly. To do so, double-click the HTML icon in your page to display the code in the HTML Markup dialog box. Be sure the code looks just like the code snippet I provide, with all the angle brackets and quote marks in the right places. Be sure, as well, that you properly typed the filename and path of the sound file you are using. When you're done, click OK to close the dialog box, and preview again. All should be well.

Inserting a background sound only for Internet Explorer users

If you follow the steps in this section, the HTML FrontPage inserts into your page works only when the page is viewed using Internet Explorer. To insert a background sound using this method, follow these steps:

1. With the page open in Page view, choose File➪Properties.

The Page Properties dialog box appears. You specify the page's background sound using options in the Background Sound section of the General tab.

2. In the dialog box's Location text box, type the filename and location of the sound file you want to use.

Or click the Browse button to choose a sound file from the Background Sound dialog box.

3. If you want to control how many times the sound plays, de-select the Forever check box and type a number in the Loop text box.

I wouldn't use the Forever option. Playing a sound over and over drives visitors nuts.

4. Click OK.

The Page Properties dialog box closes.

To hear the sound, preview your page using the Preview view or Internet Explorer. (This action works only if you have sound equipment installed on your computer.)

If the sound file is located elsewhere on your computer, the Save Embedded Files dialog box appears the next time you save the page. Refer to Chapter 2 for instructions on how to use this dialog box.

Increasing Your Site's "Wow" Factor with Behaviors

Dynamic HTML (*DHTML* for short) isn't a "flavor" of HTML, per se. It's a combination of different technologies, including HTML, JavaScript, Cascading Style Sheets, and other techie goodies that work together to create interesting effects. For example, you can use DHTML to create a drop-down menu that contains hyperlinks to different locations. Or when a visitor clicks a picture, DHTML can cause a different picture to appear in its place.

As you can imagine, coding DHTML takes some geeky mojo. Good thing FrontPage comes with tools that do all the work for you.

In this section, I introduce you to the delights of DHTML (which FrontPage calls *behaviors*), and guide you through a few of its handier effects. You access FrontPage's DHTML tools in the Behaviors task pane, as shown in Figure 13-4. Several of the tricks this feature has up its sleeve (and, indeed, some of the fundamental workings of this task pane) wander into the intermediate-to-advanced realm, which goes beyond the scope of this book. Fortunately, the trusty built-in FrontPage Help system is always a click away, so be sure to use it if you decide to experiment with DHTML (and I encourage you to do so . . . you can always Undo and try again if things don't turn out as you expected).

Really getting to know DHTML (and, by extension, understanding FrontPage's DHTML features) requires knowing HTML, CSS, and JavaScript. If this describes you and you want to find out more, visit an excellent DHTML tutorial at hotwired.lycos.com/webmonkey/authoring/dynamic_html/tutorials/tutorial1.html.

Dynamic HTML effects are impressive. Unfortunately, the effects are visible only in a few browsers, the most popular being Internet Explorer 4.0 or later and Netscape Navigator 4.0 or later (a few behaviors require even later browser versions). Furthermore, Netscape's interpretation of Dynamic HTML differs from Microsoft's, resulting in browser-specific differences. If you use Dynamic HTML, be sure to preview using both browsers (and, if you can manage it, on more than one operating system platform) to make sure everything works as you expect.

Figure 13-4:
The
Behaviors
task pane.

The Behaviors task pane enables you to create a number of effects and behaviors. Some of the task pane's features insert standard bits of JavaScript into your page's HTML that control the page's behavior, such as Check Browser, Check Plug-In, and Preload Images. Other features create a look-at-my-cool-page effect, such as Change Property, Jump Menu, and Popup Message.

Here's a rundown of what the Behaviors task pane can do:

- **Call Script:** This option enables you to insert your own bit of script programming in your page (assuming you know how to write scripts using a language such as JavaScript or VBScript) and then choose an event, such as a click or a mouse-hover, that launches the script. Several ready-made scripts are available for download; if you're willing to experiment, check out the Earthweb JavaScript Archive at `webdeveloper.earthweb.com/webjs`.

- **Change Property:** Use this option to change how a piece of text looks. For example, when a visitor moves the cursor over a word, the word changes color or size.

- ✔ **Check Browser:** This standard script enables you to redirect visitors to different sets of pages, depending on the type of browser they are using.

- ✔ **Check Plug-In:** Another standard script that detects visitors' browser plug-in capabilities and directs them to appropriate pages.

- ✔ **Control Properties in Flash:** This script gives you additional control over any Flash animations you have inserted in your page.

- ✔ **Go To URL:** This item can basically turn anything in the page into a hyperlink to a location you specify.

- ✔ **Jump Menu:** This item creates a hyperlinked drop-down menu of items, and is generally used in place of or in addition to a navigation bar.

- ✔ **Jump Menu Go:** This item enables you to spruce up your Jump Menu with an associated graphical button that acts as the trigger for the jump. (With a regular Jump Menu, visitors jump to the selected location as soon as they choose an item from the drop-down list.)

- ✔ **Open Browser Window:** This option enables you to pop open a new browser window, the contents and setup of which you control.

- ✔ **Play Sound:** This option enables you to attach a sound to an event, for example, to play a bit of music when a visitor clicks a button.

- ✔ **Popup Message:** This option pops up a dialog box containing the message of your choice, based on the event you choose.

- ✔ **Preload Images:** Add this standard script to your page if you use the Swap Image and Swap Image Restore DHTML effects. This script loads the images used in the swap into the browser's memory so that they appear instantaneously instead of downloading when the image swap takes place (which would look terrible).

- ✔ **Set Text of Frame:** If you use frames in your site, this option sets the text inside a selected frame based on the event you choose.

- ✔ **Set Text of Layer:** This option sets the text of a layer based on the event you choose.

- ✔ **Set Text of Status Bar:** This option enables you to place a text message inside the visitor's browser status bar (the strip along the bottom of the browser window).

- ✔ **Set Text of Text Field:** This option enables you to control the contents of a text form field.

- ✔ **Swap Image and Swap Image Restore:** These options are most commonly used to create a dynamic button (similar to what the Interactive Button Web component can do; see Chapter 12 for details about Web components).

You control each DHTML effect or behavior by first selecting the object you want the DHTML to affect (for example, a chunk of text), and then choosing an event that triggers the effect (for example, moving the pointer over that chunk of text). An *event* is something the visitor does (such as press a keyboard button, click an item inside a page, or move the cursor over an item). Events can also refer to something a page or object inside the page does by itself (such as load inside a browser window).

Tables 13-1 and 13-2 list some of the more commonly used user- and page-initiated events. For a complete listing, visit the DHTML Events listing at MSDN (the Microsoft Developer Network): `msdn.microsoft.com/library/default.asp?url=/workshop/author/dhtml/reference/dhtml_reference_entry.asp`. The MSDN listing not only describes each event type, but includes an example so that you can see the event in action (which sheds light on the more technical descriptions).

Table 13-1	User-Initiated DHTML Events
Event Name	*Behavior Is Triggered When . . .*
onblur	An object in the page "loses focus," or is no longer the active object in the page (because the user clicks a different object, for example)
ondblclick	User double-clicks an object
onkeydown	User presses any key on the keyboard
onkeypress	User presses an alphanumeric key
onkeyup	User releases any key
onmouseover	User moves the pointer over an object
onmouseout	User moves the pointer out of an object's boundaries

Table 13-2	Page-Initiated DHTML Events
Event Name	*DHTML Is Triggered When . . .*
onerror	An error occurs while an item or object is loading inside the page
onload	The object loads in the browser

In the following sections, I show you how to slip a few of the more popular behaviors into your site.

 For quick access to a selection of text- and image-related behaviors, choose View➪Toolbars➪DHTML Effects to make the DHTML Effects toolbar visible. Using this toolbar, you can more simply apply DHTML to selected text and images than by using the Behaviors task pane.

Creating a drop-down menu of hyperlinks

If your page is short on space, *jump menus,* as they are called in FrontPage, are handy substitutions for rows of hyperlinks or navigation bars (which I describe in Chapter 5). Using a jump menu, visitors choose the location they want to visit by selecting an item from a drop-down menu of links.

Here's how to create a jump menu:

1. **Place the cursor in the page where you want the jump menu to appear.**

2. **Choose Format➪Behaviors.**

   The Behaviors task pane appears.

3. **In the task pane, click the Insert box, and from the menu that appears, choose Jump Menu.**

   The Jump Menu dialog box appears. You use this dialog box to specify the contents of the jump menu (the places visitors jump to when they select items from the menu).

4. **In the dialog box, click Add.**

   The Add Choice dialog box appears.

5. **In the Choice text box of the Add Choice dialog box, type the text you want to appear in the menu (for example, Google).**

6. **In the Value text box, enter the location that corresponds to the item you specified in Step 5 (for example, http://www.google.com).**

   Alternatively, click the Browse button to select a location from the Edit Hyperlink dialog box (which I describe in Chapter 5).

   You can specify external hyperlinks (such as to Google) or internal hyperlinks (to other pages in your site).

7. **Click OK to close the Add Choice dialog box.**

   The Jump Menu dialog box becomes visible again, with the menu item you just created listed in the dialog box's main area.

8. **Repeat Steps 4 through 7 until you have created all the menu items you want (see Figure 13-5).**

> **Jump Menu**
>
> | Choice | Value | |
> |--------|-------|--|
> | Google | http://www.google.com | Add... |
> | Ashaland | http://www.ashaland.com | Modify... |
> | Microsoft FrontPage Home | http://www.microsoft.com/frontpage | Remove |
> | | | Move Up |
> | | | Move Down |
>
> Open URLs in: Page Default (none) ▼
>
> ☐ Select first item after URL change
>
> OK   Cancel

You can change the order of a menu item by clicking the Move Up or Move Down button.

Prompt visitors to use the jump menu by creating a generic "Choose a destination" entry for the menu's first item. To do so, in Step 5, type **Choose a destination** (or **Go to . . .** or **Jump to . . .** or . . . you get the picture). In Step 6, leave the Value text box empty. In Step 8, click the Move Up button to bump this item up to the top of the list.

9. **From the Open URLs In list box, choose where you want the menu's destination pages to appear.**

You can tell the browser to load the pages in the same browser window (replacing the window's current contents) or in a new browser window.

10. **If you want the first item in the list to be visible each time a visitor returns to the page, select the Select First Item after URL Change check box.**

If you took my advice about the "Choose a destination" menu item, be sure this check box is selected.

11. **Click OK to close the Jump Menu dialog box.**

A jump menu appears in your page. If you click on the menu, a Jump Menu item appears in the Behaviors task pane. The event, onchange, tells the browser to activate the menu when a visitor selects an item from the menu.

Save and preview the page to watch the jump menu in action. (Be sure to preview using both Internet Explorer and Netscape Navigator to see how the effect looks in both browsers.) To edit the jump menu, double-click its listing in the Behaviors task pane (double-clicking the menu itself pops open the Drop-Down Box Properties dialog box, which does you no good in this case).

Swapping images

Most often, designers use this behavior to create dynamic graphical buttons, similar to the buttons FrontPage generates with the Interactive Button Web component (see Chapter 12). To do so, you need to have access to two image files. For the effect to look its best, the images should look similar, such as two button-shaped graphics that differ only in color or shading.

The first image sits in the page, and looks to all the world like a regular ol' button graphic. With the help of DHTML, the second image replaces the first based on event you choose (most often, onmouseover).

The following steps describe how to create your own interactive button:

1. **Import the two graphic files into your Web site.**

   If you're not sure how to import files, refer to Chapter 15.

2. **Insert the first image into the page.**

3. **Click the image, and then choose Format⇨Behaviors.**

   The Behaviors task pane appears.

4. **In the task pane, click the Insert box, and from the menu that appears, choose Swap Image.**

   The Swap Images dialog box appears. The main portion of the dialog box already contains the location of the selected graphic. You now must tell FrontPage which graphic you want to swap.

5. **In the Swap Image URL text box, type the URL or location of the second image.**

   Or click the Browse button to select the image from a list of files.

6. **Be sure the Preload Images and Restore On Mouseout Event check boxes are selected.**

   Preloading images for this effect ensures that they are immediately visible when the page loads . . . a key element of this illusion's success.

   By selecting the Restore On Mouseout Event check box, you tell FrontPage to insert DHTML that causes the original image to reappear when the visitor moves the cursor off the image, thereby completing the swap.

7. **Click OK to close the Swap Images dialog box.**

   The dialog box closes, and the Swap Images behavior appears in the Behaviors task pane. (If you don't see Swap Images, be sure the image in the page is still selected.)

Save and preview the page to watch the Swap Image and Swap Image Restore effects do their things correctly. (Be sure to preview using both Internet Explorer and Netscape Navigator to see how the effect looks in both browsers.) To change either effect, double-click their listings in the Behaviors task pane.

In this section, I've shown you how to use the Swap Image behavior to create an interactive button, but you can, of course, use the behavior however you like. For example, you can create a clickable "before and after" picture display in your Web site by using two photos that illustrate "before" and "after," and then attaching the Swap Image behavior to the onclick event. The possibilities are endless!

Playing a sound based on something a visitor does

When used sparingly, sound effects can add to your visitor's feeling of "doing something" as they move around your site. For example, with DHTML, you can cause a "click" to sound when a user clicks a link or a button, or a "whoosh" to signify when an image changes.

For a good selection of freely downloadable clunks, zings, and thwacks, visit www.flashkit.com/soundfx/Interfaces.

Here's how to insert a sound into your page using DHTML:

1. **Import the sound file into your Web site.**

   If you're not sure how to import files, refer to Chapter 15.

2. **In the page, select the item you want to associate with the sound.**

3. **Choose Format⇨Behaviors.**

   The Behaviors task pane appears.

4. **In the task pane, click the Insert box, and from the menu that appears, choose Play Sound.**

   The Play Sound dialog box appears.

5. **In the Play Sound text box, type the URL or location of the sound file.**

   Alternatively, click the Browse button to choose from a list of files.

6. **Click OK to close the Play Sound dialog box.**

   The dialog box closes, and the Play Sound behavior appears in the Behaviors task pane. The default effect, `onmouseover`, causes the sound to play when the visitor passes the pointer over the item you specified in Step 2. To change the event (to, say, `onclick`), in the task pane, click the Play Sound listing, and then click the down arrow that appears next to `onmouseover`. From the menu that appears, choose the event you want.

Save and preview the page to hear your sound. (You must have sound equipment installed to be able to hear sounds on your computer.)

Chapter 14

A Gentle Introduction to FrontPage HTML Tools

A nd you thought you'd sneak through this book without hearing anything about HTML, the coding language behind Web pages.

I find there are two types of people who want to publish Web sites: Those who want to peek "under the hood" to see how HTML works, and those who abhor the thought of dealing with something as geeky and (seemingly) complicated as HTML.

If you're in the first group, more power to you. If you're in the second group, you have no reason to feel ashamed. I was once a part of Group 2 myself until I discovered how far a little HTML knowledge can go — even for FrontPage users — and how easy basic HTML is to learn. Really.

In this chapter, I introduce you to FrontPage's HTML tools. If you already know HTML, these tools simplify accessing and working with your pages' underlying HTML code. If you don't know HTML, these tools give you a big boost as you learn it.

Of course, you can also disregard these tools altogether and still create a perfectly lovely Web site. It's up to you.

Can't I Just Ignore the HTML? Please?

You don't *have* to know HTML to publish fully functional, great-looking Web sites with FrontPage — that's probably why you bought FrontPage, after all. If you want to get serious about Web publishing, though, HTML fluency has no substitute. HTML evolves faster than Microsoft can crank out new versions of FrontPage, so knowing HTML enables you to integrate the latest Web design effects into your site right away.

You don't need programming experience to learn HTML because HTML isn't a programming language. HTML is a *markup language*. In other words, it's a series of codes that signal your Web browser to display certain formatting and layout effects. These codes, called *tags,* are easy to pick up.

Still don't believe me?

Figure 14-1 uses the FrontPage Split view to illustrate a Web page containing a single line of text, along with the page's underlying HTML. Ignore all the stuff at the beginning and end of the page, and focus on the HTML behind the line of text "*FrontPage For Dummies* is a masterpiece of technical literature." The HTML tags that define the text as a paragraph (<p> and </p>) surround the entire line of text. The tags that define italic text (<i> and </i>) surround only the words *FrontPage For Dummies.* In each case, the opening tags, <p> and <i> respectively, tell the Web browser where the layout or formatting begins, and the closing tag, </p> and </i>, indicate where the layout or formatting ends.

That's the basic premise behind HTML. Of course, there's more to HTML than that, but everything is based on the concept of opening and closing tags surrounding the content they affect. The rest is just memorizing the tags, and understanding how the tags interact with each other.

If my HTML teaser has piqued your interest, find out more by visiting an HTML tutorial on the Web (try my favorite, "HTML: An Interactive Tutorial For Beginners," at www.davesite.com/webstation/html). Or add *HTML 4 For Dummies,* 4th Edition (Wiley Publishing, Inc.), by Ed Tittel and Natanya Pitts, to your computer book library.

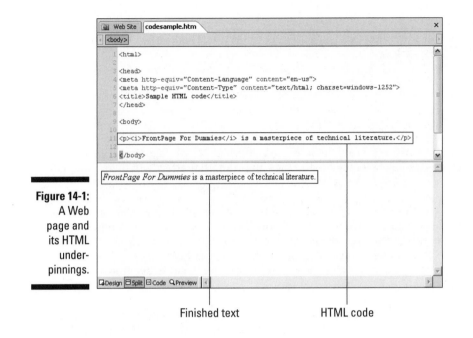

Figure 14-1:
A Web page and its HTML underpinnings.

Finished text   HTML code

Playing with the Code

One of the biggest criticisms about earlier versions of FrontPage was its tendency to block access to the HTML behind the pages it created. No longer. In FrontPage 2003, you can either dip your toe into the code using the Quick Tag Selector, or you can jump right in using Code view.

Using the Quick Tag Selector

As you add text and formatting to your page, notice the line of HTML tags growing near the top of the Design view window (see Figure 14-2; although you can't see my flashing cursor in the figure, I've selected the text *FrontPage For Dummies*). This handy tool is called the *Quick Tag Selector* because it gives you instant access to the page's HTML without having to switch to Code view. (If you don't see the Quick Tag Selector, choose View➪Quick Tag Selector.)

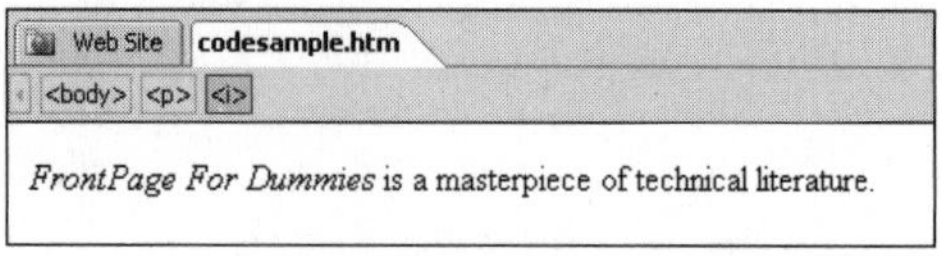

Figure 14-2:
The Quick
Tag
Selector.

Web Site	codesample.htm

`<body>` `<p>` `<i>`

FrontPage For Dummies is a masterpiece of technical literature.

To watch the Quick Tag Selector in action, click anywhere inside your page.
Click a word, a picture, a table, anything. The HTML tags that appear inside
the Quick Tag Selector are the tags, in order, that affect whatever you just
clicked.

If you already know HTML, the contents of the Quick Tag Selector probably
make sense to you. If you don't know HTML, or if you're just beginning to
learn, the Quick Tag Selector is an excellent tutor, because when you move
your cursor over a tag in the Quick Tag Selector, FrontPage highlights the
tag's contents in the page. In this way, you can begin to see how HTML
operates.

When you hover your cursor over a tag in the Quick Tag Selector, a little
down arrow also appears next to the tag. To edit that HTML tag, click the
down arrow to display a menu of options.

For the HTML-fluent, here are the options explained:

- ✔ **Select Tag:** Selects the opening and closing tags and their contents.
- ✔ **Select Tag Contents:** Selects only the contents of the tag.
- ✔ **Edit Tag:** Enables you to add attributes to the tag.
- ✔ **Remove Tag:** Removes the opening and closing tags, but leaves the tag
  contents alone.
- ✔ **Insert HTML:** Enables you to insert HTML at the location of the cursor.
- ✔ **Wrap Tag:** Enables you to insert HTML that surrounds (or *wraps around*)
  the selected tag.
- ✔ **Tag Properties:** Opens the Properties dialog box pertaining to the
  selected tag.

To see exactly how the Quick Tag Selector operates, use it while viewing your
page in Split view. Split view divides FrontPage's main viewing window
between Design view and Code view so that you can see what's happening
behind the scenes as you select options in the Quick Tag Selector.

If you want more information than the Quick Tag Selector provides, with a page open in Design view, choose View⇨Reveal Tags. An abbreviated version of the page's HTML appears in Design view. Alternatively, check out Split view, which divides the viewing area so that you can see the page's HTML along with its "finished" appearance at the same time. Think of Split view as Code view *Lite*. (Read on for details about Code view.)

Venturing into Code view

If you're comfortable working with HTML, the easiest way to access and edit your page's code is to switch to Code view (see Figure 14-3). Here, you find the HTML, nicely laid out, numbered by line, and color-coded so it's easier to read.

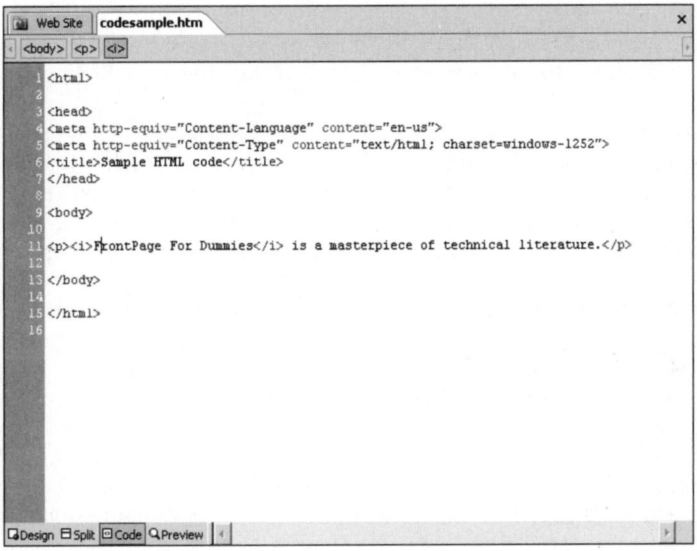

| Web Site | codesample.htm | | × |

`<body> <p> <i>`

```
1  <html>
2
3  <head>
4  <meta http-equiv="Content-Language" content="en-us">
5  <meta http-equiv="Content-Type" content="text/html; charset=windows-1252">
6  <title>Sample HTML code</title>
7  </head>
8
9  <body>
10
11 <p><i>FrontPage For Dummies</i> is a masterpiece of technical literature.</p>
12
13 </body>
14
15 </html>
16
```

Design   Split   Code   Preview

Figure 14-3:
Code view
shows only
the HTML
for the page.

As you type HTML tags, FrontPage helps by automatically closing all the tags you create. FrontPage also groups handy functions together in the Code View toolbar (choose View⇨Toolbars⇨Code View to make this toolbar visible).

FrontPage can also save frequently used bits of code as *snippets* so that you don't have to type them over and over. To create snippets, choose Tools⇨ Page Options, and from the dialog box that appears, click the Code Snippets tab. Follow the directions inside that portion of the dialog box to create and use code snippets. To insert a code snippet in your page's HTML, press Ctrl+Enter to display a list of saved snippets, and then double-click the snippet you want to use.

While in Code view, you can use FrontPage's Find and Replace function to automatically update HTML tags throughout the page (or even your entire site). To access HTML Find and Replace, choose Edit➪Find, and from the dialog box that appears, click the HTML Tags tab.

Controlling How FrontPage Generates HTML

Who cares how the HTML looks? If the page looks good when viewed with a Web browser, what does it matter if the HTML code is a little sloppy?

Although the formatting and layout of the HTML doesn't affect the look of the finished Web page (unless the HTML contains errors, of course), you're still wise to pay attention to the tidiness of your code. Neatly written HTML is easier to update, especially if the site eventually ends up in the hands of a different administrator (who may or may not use FrontPage to update the site).

And, believe it or not, a selection of your visitors won't just browse your site, they'll peruse your code as well. A site's HTML is visible to any visitor who chooses to look. (Every browser is able to display a page's underlying HTML; because the steps are different based on your browser version, I recommend that you check out your browser's help system to find out how to do this.) For many people, looking at others' finished pages is the best way to learn HTML. Others are simply part of the "under the hood" crowd and are curious how you built your site. Either way, messy code reflects badly on its author, so it pays to keep yours clean.

FrontPage helps by generating neat code to begin with. Even so, you may want to do a little tinkering.

The Page Options dialog box (available by choosing Tools➪Page Options) contains settings that control how FrontPage outputs HTML, and how FrontPage displays HTML inside Code view. Here's a quick rundown of the tabs inside this dialog box that deal with HTML output and formatting (for detailed information, turn to the FrontPage Help system):

✔ **General:** This tab enables you to choose how FrontPage generates particular bits of HTML, as well as the basic setup of Code view.

✔ **Code Formatting:** This tab lets you control how the finished HTML looks by choosing upper- or lowercase tags and attributes, line breaks, indentation, margins, and formatting details for individual tags.

✔ **Color Coding:** Here, you can tell FrontPage how to color-code the HTML inside Code view. Choose a color scheme that makes the code easiest for you to read as you work with FrontPage (the colors you choose have no effect on the finished look of the page, only how the HTML looks inside Code view).

✔ **IntelliSense:** This tab enables you to turn on and off FrontPage's automatic HTML features.

Finally, FrontPage does last-minute HTML cleanup when you choose Tools⇨Optimize HTML. The Optimize HTML dialog box enables you to select redundant or useless HTML that does little more than muddle your code. After you click OK, FrontPage erases the selected items.

Working with Style Sheets

Cascading Style Sheets or *CSS* (in FrontPage, referred to simply as *style sheets*) enable you to create new styles and to modify the standard HTML style definitions that come with FrontPage.

If you're a Microsoft Word user, styles may not seem like such a big deal. After all, word-processing styles have been around for years. Styles in Web pages, on the other hand, are relatively new. Until recently, Web designers were stuck with the standard effects produced by HTML. Style sheets open every HTML tag to modification, taking you beyond each tag's inherent abilities.

For example, if you're not satisfied with the staid appearance of the Heading 1 paragraph style (big, bold, plain text), you can use style sheets to define the Heading 1 style however you like. If you want all text formatted with the Heading 1 style to appear as magenta, 36-point, underlined, and blinking text, so be it.

Style sheets are especially useful if more than one author works on a site. Because the site's formatting instructions are stored in the style sheet, individual authors can concentrate on the page's content and can later apply the style sheet to take care of the stylistic details.

Style sheets are capable of much more than I demonstrate here. FrontPage gives you powerful access to style sheets, but to use style sheets to their fullest potential, you must be fluent in both HTML and style sheet syntax. So, think of the following subsections as an introduction to the wonders of style sheets . . . you may very well be seduced into finding out more.

For more information about style sheets, turn to the World Wide Web. Go to www.davesite.com/webstation/css (for starters). Also, be sure to look at the style sheet coverage in the FrontPage Help system (available when you choose Help➪Microsoft FrontPage Help or when you press F1). For the Dummies approach to CSS, see *Cascading Style Sheets For Dummies* by Damon Dean (Wiley Publishing, Inc.).

Creating and modifying styles in the current page

The Style dialog box (shown in Figure 14-4) enables you to embed a style sheet in the page currently open in Design view. You access the Style dialog box by choosing Format➪Style.

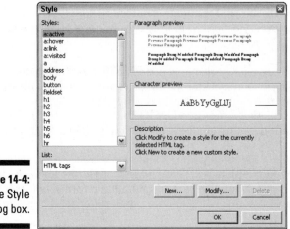

Figure 14-4:
The Style
dialog box.

In the dialog box, the Styles list box contains all the HTML tags you can modify using style sheet commands. I realize you don't necessarily know HTML, so, in Table 14-1, I list tags that control the elements you most likely want to change. For example, after you modify the style of the b tag (the tag that creates bold text), FrontPage refers to your style sheet for instructions each time you tell FrontPage to apply bold formatting to text.

Table 14-1	Quickie HTML Tag Reference
This HTML Tag . . .	*. . . Controls This Aspect of the Page*
a	Hyperlink color
b	Bold text
body	Default text color, page background color
h1-h6	Heading 1 through Heading 6 paragraph styles
i	Italic text
ol	Numbered lists (ordered lists)
p	Default paragraph text
ul	Bulleted lists (unordered lists)

To embed a style sheet inside the page currently open in Design view, follow these steps:

1. **With the cursor sitting anywhere inside the page, choose Format⇨Style.**

   The Style dialog box appears.

2. **Click the tag you want to modify in the Styles list box, and then click the Modify button. Or, to create a new style, click the New button.**

   When you modify an existing style, you change how the visitor's browser displays the results of a particular HTML tag. When you create a new style, you, in effect, create your own style instructions for the browser.

   Depending on which button you click, either the Modify Style or the New Style dialog box appears. Aside from their names, the dialog boxes are identical, so the instructions that follow apply to both.

3. **In the dialog box's Name (Selector) text box, type a one-word name. (If you are modifying the style of an existing HTML tag, skip this step.)**

4. **To define the style, click the Format button, and then choose the category of style change that you want to create from the menu that appears.**

You can choose from the following categories:

- **Font:** Affects typeface, font size, attributes, letter spacing, and font color
- **Paragraph:** Affects alignment, indentation, and word/line spacing
- **Border:** Affects borders, white space around paragraphs, and background and foreground colors
- **Numbering:** Affects the appearance of bulleted or numbered lists
- **Position:** Affects the item's position in the page

The category you choose determines the resulting dialog box that appears.

5. From the dialog box, select the options you want, and then click OK.

If you're not sure how to use the dialog box, see Chapter 4; these are the same dialog boxes that appear if you choose corresponding commands in the Format menu. (The Position dialog box requires additional explanation; see the FrontPage Help system for details.)

After you click OK, the dialog box closes, and the Style dialog box comes back into view.

6. If you like, define more styles by repeating Steps 2 through 5, or click OK to close the dialog box.

FrontPage applies the new style definitions to the current page.

If you later want to change the style definitions you've set up, choose Format⇨Style. In the Styles dialog box, choose User-Defined Styles from the List box. Then, click the style you want to change in the Styles list box, and follow Steps 2–6 in the preceding set of steps.

To apply a style to items in your page, first select the item, and then choose the style you want from the Style list box in the Formatting toolbar.

You can also apply style sheet effects to single instances of an object or effect. You may already have noticed the Style button sitting quietly in many of FrontPage's Properties dialog boxes. To apply a style sheet effect to a particular object, right-click the object, and from the pop-up menu that appears, choose the Properties command pertinent to that object (for example, if you right-click a hyperlink with the intention of changing its color, choose Hyperlink Properties). In the Properties dialog box that appears, click the Style button to bring up the Modify Style dialog box, and then follow the preceding steps (starting from Step 4).

Applying styles to more than one page in your site

The technique for applying a style sheet to more than one page in your site (or across the entire site) differs from embedding a style sheet inside a single page. In this case, you must create or have access to a separate style sheet file, which you then link to the pages to which you want the style sheet to apply.

Creating the style sheet

If you already have access to a style sheet file — say your company provides a standard style sheet to everyone building company-sponsored pages — import the file into your Web site, and skip to the next section (see Chapter 15 for details on how to import an existing file into a Web site).

If you don't have access to a ready-made style sheet, you don't have to start from scratch. FrontPage contains templates for several style sheets, all of which coordinate with different FrontPage themes. To create a new style sheet by using a template, follow these steps:

1. **Choose File⇨New.**

   The New task pane appears.

2. **In the New Page section of the task pane, click More Page Templates.**

   The Page Templates dialog box appears with the General tab visible.

3. **In the dialog box, click the Style Sheets tab to display the list of style sheet templates, and then double-click the template you want to use.**

   The dialog box closes, and the style sheet appears in Design view.

Don't be put off by all the style sheet's codes and brackets; you don't need to type anything into the page at all. You can modify the style sheet by using the Style dialog box. (To access the dialog box, choose Format⇨Style; see the "Creating and modifying styles in the current page" section, earlier in this chapter, for instructions on how to use the Style dialog box.) When you're done, save the page as part of your Web site (the process is the same as saving a regular Web page).

If you know HTML and style sheet syntax, the more straightforward course is to create a new blank page, type up your own style sheet, and save the page as part of your Web site (be sure to specify in the Save As dialog box that FrontPage is to save the file as a Hypertext Style Sheet).

Linking the style sheet to the rest of your site

Now that the style sheet is tucked away in your site, you must link the style sheet to those pages in your site to which you want the style sheet to apply.

To do so, follow these steps:

1. **In the Folder List, while pressing the Ctrl key, click the pages to which you want the style sheet to apply.**

   If you want to apply the style sheet to the entire site, skip this step. If the Folder List isn't visible, choose View➪Folder List.

2. **Choose Format➪Style Sheet Links.**

   The Link Style Sheet dialog box appears.

3. **If you want the style sheet to apply to all the pages in your site, select the All Pages option in the dialog box.**

   Otherwise, FrontPage applies the style sheet to the pages you selected in Step 2.

4. **Click the Add button.**

   The Select Style Sheet dialog box appears.

5. **In the dialog box, navigate your Web site's file list until you find the style sheet file, and then double-click the file.**

   After you double-click the file, the Select Style Sheet dialog box closes, and the Link Style Sheet dialog box comes back into view with the style sheet file listed in the dialog box.

6. **Click OK.**

   The dialog box closes, and FrontPage applies the style sheet to the pages you specified. Remember to save the page by pressing Ctrl+S.

You can apply more than one style sheet to selected pages. Here's where the *cascading* part of *Cascading Style Sheets* comes in: FrontPage applies the style sheet definitions, in order and starting with the most recently attached style sheet, to the page. Imagine, for example, that you have two style sheets. The first style sheet contains a background color and a typeface setting, and the second style sheet contains only a different background color setting. If you want to use features from both style sheets, you can apply both to your site. The background color setting from the second style sheet takes precedence (because that style sheet was most recently linked to the Web page), but the typeface setting from the first style sheet appears as well.

Part IV
Taking Your Web Site to a New Level

The 5th Wave   By Rich Tennant

BAIL BOND

"See? I created a little felon figure that runs around our Web site hiding behind banner ads. On the last page, our logo puts him in a non lethal choke hold and brings him back to the home page."

In this part . . .

After you build your Web site, you need to keep it in top working order. In this part, you discover how FrontPage helps you manage and maintain your site; how to control who can access your Web site; and also how to publish your site on the World Wide Web.

Chapter 15

Web Site Management 101

· ·

In This Chapter

▶ Familiarizing yourself with the different FrontPage views

▶ Creating a navigation structure

▶ Importing and exporting files and folders

▶ Creating, renaming, and deleting files and folders

▶ Working with subsites

▶ Moving your Web site to a different computer

▶ Backing up your Web site

· ·

*U*sing FrontPage, you can do just about anything to change, update, or repair your Web site (assuming something needs repairing).

In this chapter, you delve into the site-management capabilities of FrontPage. You become familiar with FrontPage's six Web site management views. You also discover how to use FrontPage to manage the files that make up your Web site.

Taking In the Views

No doubt you've been wondering about that mysterious *Web Site* tab lurking at the top of the FrontPage design window. The Web Site tab is your doorway to FrontPage's Web site management *views*. FrontPage contains six such views, each of which illuminates your site in a different way.

To switch between views, click the Web Site tab, and then click the appropriate icon at the bottom of window (see Figure 15-1). Or choose the name of the view you want to see from the View menu.

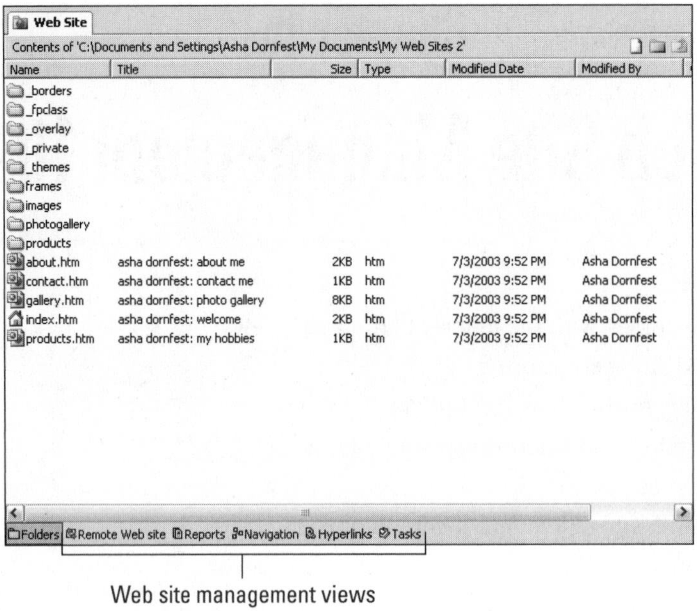

Name	Title	Size	Type	Modified Date	Modified By
_borders					
_fpclass					
_overlay					
_private					
_themes					
frames					
images					
photogallery					
products					
about.htm	asha dornfest: about me	2KB	htm	7/3/2003 9:52 PM	Asha Dornfest
contact.htm	asha dornfest: contact me	1KB	htm	7/3/2003 9:52 PM	Asha Dornfest
gallery.htm	asha dornfest: photo gallery	8KB	htm	7/3/2003 9:52 PM	Asha Dornfest
index.htm	asha dornfest: welcome	2KB	htm	7/3/2003 9:52 PM	Asha Dornfest
products.htm	asha dornfest: my hobbies	1KB	htm	7/3/2003 9:52 PM	Asha Dornfest

Contents of 'C:\Documents and Settings\Asha Dornfest\My Documents\My Web Sites 2'

Folders | Remote Web site | Reports | Navigation | Hyperlinks | Tasks

Figure 15-1:
The
contents of
the Web
Site tab.

Web site management views

Folders view

The Folders view, shown in Figure 15-1, displays your Web site as a group of files and folders to help you manage and organize your Web site's file system. This view serves the same purpose for your Web site as Windows Explorer serves for the files stored on your hard drive and local network.

The Folders view looks and works much like Windows Explorer:

✔ Click a folder in the Folder List to display its contents in the Contents area.

✔ To sort the list of files and folders in the Contents area, click the header label of your choice.

✔ To move a page into a folder, click the page icon, drag it on top of the folder, and then release the mouse button. FrontPage updates the page's hyperlinks to reflect the page's new location. (I talk more about how hyperlinks work in Chapter 5.)

Folders with globe icons on top denote *subsites,* which are complete Web sites that live inside a folder of the main or *parent* Web site. To view the contents of a subsite in the Folders view, double-click the subsite's folder to open the subsite in a new FrontPage window. I talk more about subsites in the "Working with subsites" section, later in this chapter.

Reports view

The Reports view tells you all sorts of interesting things about your Web site, as shown in Figure 15-2. For example, the Slow Pages report helps you monitor your site's estimated download speed, and the Older Files report reminds you which pages might benefit from an update.

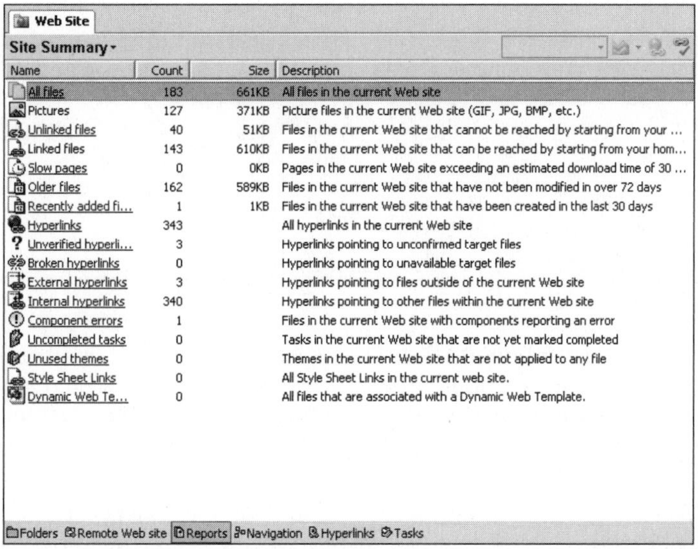

Figure 15-2: The Site Summary report in the Reports view.

When you first display the Reports view, you're greeted by the Site Summary report. This report rounds up useful tidbits of information, including how many hyperlinks and pictures the site contains, how many pages can and cannot be reached by following a link from the home page, and how many pages contain broken hyperlinks. This report contains much more information than I've listed here — see for yourself!

You can click any of the Site Summary report titles that appear blue and underlined to perform a relevant task or to display a more detailed report.

To switch between the reports in the Reports view, click on the report title, and from the drop-down menu that appears, select the category and name of the report you want to see. Most of the reports contain helpful information, but here are the reports I find most useful:

Weird FrontPage folders

When you switch to the Folders view, no doubt you notice some unfamiliar folders hanging about your Web site. All FrontPage Web sites contain a standard set of folders, and each folder has its own role:

✔ **_private:** Documents stored in this folder remain hidden from Web browsers and from the Web Search component. (Chapter 12 gives you the details about this Web component.)

✔ **images:** The images folder is where FrontPage stores images that appear inside

Web pages. I recommend keeping all your images in that folder, too, just so your Web site remains neat.

Additional folders appear in your Web site when you add navigation bars, themes, and some DHTML behaviors to your site. Good general rule: If the folder name begins with an underscore character (_), leave it alone. Folders FrontPage generates for its own purposes are earmarked with this character.

✔ **Problems/Unlinked Files:** This report lists files that fit all of the following criteria: They do not contain hyperlinks, they cannot be reached by following hyperlinks from the site's home page, and they are not "included" inside other pages using one of the Included Content Web components (see Chapter 12 for details).

Pages that appear in this report can safely be deleted because they are effectively cut off from the rest of the site. I show you how to delete pages later in this chapter (although you can probably guess how to do it . . . select the page and then press the Delete key).

If you delete a page using FrontPage, you can't later change your mind. FrontPage-deleted pages don't end up in the Recycle Bin — they go to Web page heaven. If in doubt, leave the page alone, or delete the page using Windows Explorer — that way, deleted pages go in the Recycle Bin and can be retrieved in a pinch.

✔ **Problems/Slow Pages:** Web surfers hate to wait for pages to download. This report helps you keep track of the potential slowpokes in your site. The report lists pages that take more than an estimated 30 seconds to load over a 56 Kbps modem. I say *estimated* because download speed depends on several factors, only one of which is page content. (Other factors include the speed of the host Web server, the amount of network traffic at that given moment, and the state of the phone and data lines that make up the Internet, to name a few.)

Keep in mind that the Estimated Time to Download box on the right side of the FrontPage status bar also gives you information about download speed based on different connection types. This report is helpful in that it puts all the information in one place.

✔ **Usage reports:** If you publish your Web site on a host server that supports the 2002 version (or later) of the FrontPage Server Extensions, you can use these reports to find out about who's visiting your Web site and how it's being used.

Because usage reports track information about how your visitors use your site, these reports are relevant only *after* the site has been live and accepting visitors for a while. So to view usage reports, you must first publish your Web site (see Chapter 17 for directions), and then wait a few days or weeks for the server to collect usage information in its logs. When you can no longer stand the suspense, open the *live* version of the site directly from the host server (see Chapter 1 for directions), choose View➪Reports, and then choose the name of the usage report that you want to see.

[Enlightening non sequitur follows.] Notice a similarity between the available usage reports and the available top 10 lists? (The Top 10 List Web component is covered in Chapter 12.) FrontPage gathers the data for both features from the same source: the host server's logs. Usage reports and top 10 lists are simply different ways of displaying the same information.

Navigation view

You may think that I started writing this book on Page 1, right? Wrong. I spent many hours putting together a table of contents before jotting down a single word. When it was time to write, my words flowed relatively easily because the information was already organized.

I relate this anecdote because building a Web site is not unlike writing a book. You have information to present to an audience, and you want that information to be clear and well-organized. Here's where the Navigation view comes in handy. Using this view, you can map out a navigation structure for your Web site. A *navigation structure* is a graphic representation of the "levels" of pages in your site. Similar to a company's organization chart, which provides a picture of the leadership hierarchy within the company, a navigation structure illustrates the organization of the information in your site.

Building a navigation structure is optional unless you want to take advantage of FrontPage *link bars* and *page banners,* because both features make use of information in the site's navigation structure. A link bar is a row of text or graphic hyperlinks that lead to other pages, allowing your visitors to get around easily. (I show you how to create link bars in Chapter 5.) Page banners are decorative banner graphics that add spice to your pages (see Chapter 12 for details).

Creating a navigation structure is easy. Just think about how you want your site to be structured, and then drag the site's pages from the Folder List into place in the Navigation view. Here's how:

1. **In FrontPage, open your Web site.**

2. **Make the Navigation view visible by clicking the Web Site tab, and then clicking the Navigation button.**

   The Navigation view becomes visible. The home page is already represented in the Navigation view. You construct a navigation structure by dragging pages from the Folder List and dropping them into the Navigation view. In this example, I illustrate creating a navigation structure for a simple personal Web site containing a home page, three second-level pages, and two third-level pages.

   If the Folder List isn't visible, click the Toggle Pane button on the Standard toolbar, or choose View⇨Folder List.

   Note: Web sites based on FrontPage site templates already have a navigation structure in place. Read on to find out how to add more pages to or change the setup of the navigation structure.

3. **In the Folder List, click the page you want to add to the navigation structure and, while holding down the mouse button, drag the page into the Navigation view.**

   As you drag the page into place, a line appears that connects the page you're dragging to the home page.

4. **Release the mouse button.**

   An icon representing that page appears in the navigation structure.

5. **Continue adding pages to the navigation structure until you've added all the pages to be represented in the site's link bars or page banners.**

   Figure 15-3 illustrates a complete navigation structure.

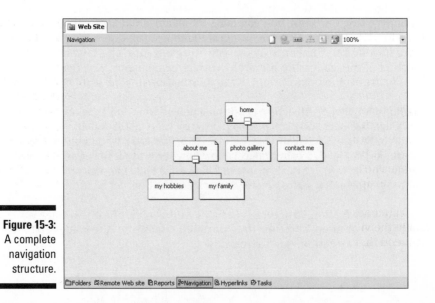

Figure 15-3:
A complete navigation structure.

You don't have to add every page in your site to the navigation structure — only add those pages you want to appear in the site's link bars or page banners. If you're not sure how you should arrange the pages, skim the information about link bars in Chapter 5. Understanding how link bars work may help you visualize the best way to lay out your Web site's navigation structure.

After you finish the navigation structure, you can easily rearrange it by clicking any icon and dragging it to a new spot. As you add new pages to your site, you can drag them into the navigation structure as well. The navigation structure can accommodate many different organizational schemes, including more than one top-level page. Experiment to figure out a structure that works for your site.

To remove a page from the navigation structure, click a rectangle in the map and then press the Delete key. The page disappears from the navigation structure (but the page file remains safely nestled in the Web site).

FrontPage keeps a condensed, outline-like display of the navigation structure in the Navigation pane (visible in Design view if you click the Navigation button at the bottom of the Folder List). This display is handy when you're building link bars because you don't have to keep switching back and forth between the Design and Navigation views to be able to see the site's navigation structure.

Hyperlinks view

The links between the pages in your Web site create a path that visitors follow when they explore the site. The Hyperlinks view is like a road map; it illustrates the Web site's navigational path so that you can make sure your Web site is easy to get around.

When you click a page in the Folder List, an icon representing that page appears in the Hyperlinks area of the view. Figure 15-4 shows how a Web site looks in the Hyperlinks view.

Small icons with blue arrows pointing to the central page icon illustrate *incoming hyperlinks,* or pages that contain hyperlinks leading to the selected page. Small icons to the right of the central page icon illustrate *outgoing hyperlinks,* or the destinations of hyperlinks inside the selected page. Broken hyperlinks appear as broken gray lines instead of blue arrows. (I show you how to find and repair broken hyperlinks in your site in Chapter 5.) If the selected page contains no hyperlinks and isn't linked to from any other page in the site, the page icon appears in the Hyperlinks area all by itself.

You can modify the Hyperlinks view diagram by right-clicking anywhere inside the view and then choosing one of the following options from the pop-up menu that appears:

✓ **Show Page Titles:** By default, the Hyperlinks view displays the page's filenames. Choose this option to display the page's titles instead.

✓ **Hyperlinks to Pictures:** Choose this option to display links to picture files.

✓ **Repeated Hyperlinks:** If the page contains more than one hyperlink to the same destination, the Hyperlinks view displays only one instance of the link. Choose this option to make repeated hyperlinks visible.

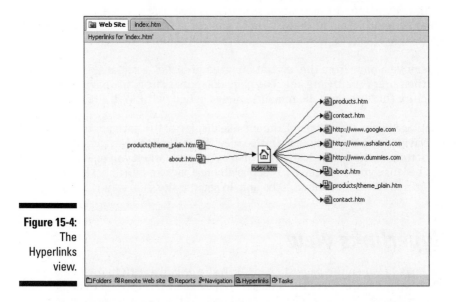

Figure 15-4:
The
Hyperlinks
view.

Tasks view

The Tasks view helps you keep track of the thousand-and-one details involved in putting together your site. You may find this integrated to-do list handy (especially if you are working with other site authors or have an especially complicated site), but I have never used it much. If you want to try it out, start tinkering; it's pretty intuitive. If you need assistance, lean on the FrontPage Help system.

Remote Web Site view

When you're ready to publish, back up, or move your Web site, here's where you'll do it. The Remote Web Site view contains all the tools you need to transfer your Web site's files and folders to a different location, be it a host Web server, another computer on your network, or whatever backup media you choose. I touch on the workings of this view later in this chapter, in the "Backing up and moving Web sites" section, and again in Chapter 17, when I show you how to publish your site on the World Wide Web.

Using FrontPage as a workgroup tool

Few Web sites are one-person operations. Even if you're the lucky staff member who got tapped to put together the company Web or intranet site, you probably need input and cooperation from other members of the team. If those team members are sitting in an office 500 miles away, collaboration can be tricky.

Fortunately, FrontPage is equipped to handle the job. Because FrontPage is able to work in conjunction with a Web server on which FrontPage Server Extensions are installed, any team member with access to an internal network or Internet connection and a computer outfitted with FrontPage can work on the company Web site. The process goes like this:

1. You work with the team to plan the site's content and design.

2. You create a core version of the site, which you then publish on a host Web server (either an ISP's Web server or a central company network server that's not accessible to the outside world).

3. All team members, using FrontPage on their individual workstations, log on to the central server to access the "live" site to add and change pages.

By using FrontPage to connect to a site stored on a central Web server, more than one person can work on the site simultaneously, making collaboration among far-flung team members possible.

Of course, keeping track of the team's workflow is potential chaos. Fortunately, FrontPage comes with several features that help rein in the production process, so everyone knows what's going on and what needs to happen next. FrontPage recognizes different levels of *permissions,* so you can assign different passwords and levels of site access to members of your team (more about permissions in Chapter 17). Using FrontPage, you can assign tasks to specific authors, and then track review status by using the Task view and the Review Status report. You can turn on FrontPage *source control* to require files to be checked in and out (thereby avoiding file conflicts if two people want to work on the same file at the same time).

Interested? Visit the FrontPage Help system, which details all of these features and more. Be sure to check out Chapter 16 as well, as it demonstrates how Dynamic Web Templates can also simplify workgroup operations.

Working with Web Site Files and Folders

FrontPage gives you easy access to the files that make up your Web site. Use FrontPage whenever you want to import, move, or delete files and folders in your Web site.

Adding existing files and folders to a Web site

The easiest way to add an existing file or folder to a FrontPage Web site is to move, copy, or save that file or folder inside the Web site's folder.

For example, say you have a document stored inside your `C:\My Documents` folder that you want to add to the Web site stored in the `C:\My Documents\My Web Sites` folder. Using Windows Explorer, simply copy or move the file from the My Documents folder to the My Web Sites folder. The next time you open the Web site in FrontPage, the new file appears in the Folder List. (If the Web site is currently open in FrontPage, click the Refresh button on the Standard toolbar to update the Folder List.)

Another option is to save a document directly inside a FrontPage Web site folder. For example, if you're currently working on a Microsoft Word document and you want to add that document to the Web site stored in the `C:\My Documents\My Web Sites` folder, save the document in Microsoft Word in the location `C:\My Documents\My Web Sites`.

If you prefer to do all your Web site work from within FrontPage, you can *import* files into your Web site instead. You can import files that are currently stored on your computer, local network, or the World Wide Web. When you import a file, FrontPage places a copy of the file inside the currently open Web site, leaving the original file and its location unchanged.

In this section, I show you how to add existing files to the Web site that's currently open in FrontPage. To import an entire Web site into FrontPage, take the Import Web Site Wizard for a spin (see Chapter 1 for details).

In the following steps, I show you how to import single files from your computer or local network into the current FrontPage Web site. At the end of this set of steps, I tell you how to import entire folders, and I also talk about how to import material that's currently stored on the World Wide Web.

1. **With a Web site open in FrontPage, choose File⇨Import.**

   (If the File⇨Import menu item is grayed-out, in the Folder List, click the Web site's top-level folder to select it, and then choose File⇨Import again.)

   The Import dialog box appears.

   (If you choose File⇨Import when no Web site is currently open, FrontPage thinks that you want to import an entire site and launches the Import Web Site Wizard.)

2. **In the dialog box, click the Add File button.**

   The Add File to Import List dialog box appears. You use this dialog box to poke around your hard drive or local network to find the files that you want to import.

3. **Navigate your hard drive or local network and select the files that you want to import.**

   To select multiple files, press and hold down the Ctrl key while clicking file icons in the Add File to Import List dialog box. To select a range of files, press and hold down the Shift key while clicking the first and last file icons. If you don't see the file that you want to import, from the Files of Type list box, choose All files (*.*).

4. **Click the Open button.**

The Add File to Import List dialog box closes, and the file appears in the import list in the Import dialog box.

5. **To add another file to the import list, repeat Steps 2 through 4. When you're finished, click OK to close the dialog box and import the file(s).**

If you would rather put off importing the files, click the Close button in the Import dialog box. FrontPage saves the import list and closes the dialog box, which you can later access by choosing File⇨Import.

To import a folder to your Web site, in Step 2 of the preceding list, click the Add Folder button. The File Open dialog box appears, enabling you to choose the folder that you want to import. Click the folder and then click the OK button. The File Open dialog box closes, and the folder's contents appear in the import list.

To import a single file or folder, you can also take the quick-and-dirty approach: Simply drag the file or folder from your desktop or Windows Explorer and drop it into the contents area of the Folders view.

To import a file or folder that's currently stored on the World Wide Web, in Step 2 of the previous list, click the From Site button. The Import Web Site Wizard launches. Refer to Chapter 1 for directions on how to use the Import Web Site Wizard.

Creating new folders

If your site contains lots of files and pages, folders help you keep the files organized.

Say, for example, your company's Web site contains four main sections — About Acme Consulting Company, Acme Services, Acme Staff, and Contact Acme — and each section contains several files. You can store each section's files in its own folder to keep your file system spic-and-span.

Don't confuse storing files inside folders to keep the files organized with creating a subsite. Although a subsite is indeed a group of files stored inside a folder in the current Web site, FrontPage sees a subsite as a distinct and fully functional Web site in its own right. I explain how to convert a folder into a subsite later in this chapter, in the "Working with subsites" section.

FrontPage gives you several ways to create new folders. Here's the easiest method:

1. **Right-click inside an empty area of the Folder List, and from the pop-up menu that appears, choose New⇨Folder.**

   A new folder appears. The folder name (New_Folder) is highlighted.

   If you right-click on a file in the Folder List, **New** doesn't appear inside the pop-up menu. Right-click anywhere inside an empty area of the Folder List, and then try again.

2. **Type a new, one-word folder name and then press Enter.**

   FrontPage renames the folder.

Renaming files and folders

I admit it. After all these years of using FrontPage, the power of the renaming feature still makes me weak in the knees. If, for any reason, you need to change the name of a file or folder in your Web site, FrontPage automatically updates all the file's associated hyperlinks. This is a big deal. Back in the days of hand-coding HTML, changing a file or folder name without updating associated links throughout the site resulted in broken hyperlinks. Not so with FrontPage! The program is smart enough to search your site for links containing the old file or folder name and to update the references for you.

Renaming the home page involves some extra considerations. The home page *must* be named index.htm or index.html (or whatever name the host Web server recognizes as the site's default page), or your site won't work properly. If you're not sure which home page filename your ISP's host Web server recognizes, give the customer service staff a call.

You can rename a file or folder several ways, but the easiest is by following these steps:

1. **In the Folder List, or in any Web site view except the Tasks view, click the icon for the file or folder you want to rename, wait a moment, and then click its filename.**

   A box appears around the filename, and the filename is highlighted. (If you don't wait a beat between clicks, FrontPage thinks you are double-clicking the file icon and opens the file, which you don't want. If this happens and the files opens, close the file and try again.)

2. **Type a new name.**

   Be sure to maintain the same filename extension so that FrontPage knows what kind of file you're renaming. Also, choose a one-word name (you can cheat a bit by using capital letters or the underscore character between words).

3. **Press Enter.**

   If the file contains associated links, the Rename dialog box appears, asking if you'd like to update the links to reflect the new name.

4. **In the dialog box, click Yes.**

   The dialog box closes, FrontPage updates the links, and all is well.

Working with subsites

Small, straightforward Web sites are easy to maintain in FrontPage. As the Web site grows, or the number of people involved in the site's creation and maintenance increases, however, keeping track of the Web site's exploding number of pages can turn into a major pain.

If your Web site is starting to resemble an ever-expanding amoeba, consider breaking the Web site into a core *parent* Web site with second-level tiers of information called *subsites.* A subsite is a complete Web site that lives in a folder inside the parent Web site.

The parent Web site/subsite setup works well when you are creating a large network of interrelated Web sites — for example, a main company site with subsites for each of the company's different products. The Microsoft Web site offers a good example; check out the Microsoft parent Web site at www.microsoft.com, and the FrontPage subsite at www.microsoft.com/frontpage.

Another example would be a company-wide intranet site, to which members of different departments contribute material. The entire operation exists inside a single parent Web site, but each department works on its own subsite. In this situation, you can take advantage of FrontPage *permissions* so that site authors from different departments must enter a username and a password to access their respective subsites. I talk in detail about how permissions work in Chapter 17.

The advantages to the parent Web site/subsite arrangement are as follows:

- ✔ A subsite is a complete FrontPage Web site in its own right. You can therefore open a subsite into its own FrontPage window and manage the Web site as you see fit. This is a good way to break an overwhelmingly big Web site into easy-to-manage chunks.

- ✔ If you're working in a collaborative environment, subsites can have different *permissions* from the parent Web site (handy when different groups of people are contributing to different parts of the Web site). I talk about permissions in Chapter 17.

- ✔ Because a subsite is distinct from the parent Web site, the subsite can have its own theme, keyword search capability, link bars, and shared borders. (You find out about all these features in Parts II and III of this book.)

Not surprisingly, the parent Web site/subsite arrangement also has its caveats, as follows:

- ✔ If you intend to *nest* subsites (that is, create a subsite inside a subsite), you must publish your Web site on a host Web server that has FrontPage Server Extensions installed (for details, see Chapter 17).

- ✔ If the pages inside the folder that you are about to convert contain FrontPage link bars or the Include Page component, these features may be affected by the conversion. (More about link bars in Chapter 5 and Web components in Chapter 12.)

You have two choices for creating a subsite: You can either convert a folder inside an existing FrontPage Web site into a subsite, or you can create a new subsite from scratch or by using a FrontPage Web site template or wizard.

To convert a folder into a subsite, follow these steps:

1. **With the parent Web site open in FrontPage, right-click the folder you want to convert into a subsite, and then choose Convert to Web from the pop-up menu that appears.**

   The Microsoft FrontPage dialog box appears, warning you that pages inside the folder will be affected by the conversion. If you change your mind and decide to maintain the status quo, click No. Otherwise . . .

2. **In the dialog box, click Yes.**

   The dialog box closes, and FrontPage converts the folder into a subsite. If the folder contains lots of files, the conversion may take a few moments. You can tell the conversion has taken place because a little globe appears on top of the folder icon.

If you change your mind and want to consolidate a parent Web site and its sub-sites back into a single Web site, you can convert subsites into regular folders. Just keep in mind that the conversion comes with a few consequences:

- ✔ If the parent Web site is decorated with a theme, the subsite's pages will take on that theme (presumably this is a good thing).

- ✔ The subsite's files will take on the permission settings of the parent Web site.

- ✔ Link bar hyperlinks leading from the parent Web site to the subsite will no longer work properly.

- ✔ The subsite's task list will be lost.

To convert a subsite into a folder, with the parent Web site open in FrontPage, right-click the subsite's folder, and then choose Convert to Folder from the pop-up menu that appears. The Microsoft FrontPage dialog box appears, listing the changes that will occur in the subsite's pages as a result of the conversion. If the changes are okay with you, click Yes to close the dialog box and convert the subsite into a folder.

To create a new subsite from scratch or by using a FrontPage Web site template or wizard, do this:

1. **With FrontPage running, choose File⇨New.**

   The New task pane appears.

2. **In the New Web Site section of the task pane, click More Web Site Templates.**

   The Web Site Templates dialog box appears.

3. **In the dialog box's Web Sites area, click the template or wizard you want to use.**

   To create a Web site from scratch, click One Page Web.

4. **In the Specify the Location of the New Web Site list box, enter the location of the new subsite, or click the Browse button to choose a location from a folder list.**

   Enter a file path that contains the location of the parent Web site followed by a backslash (\) and then the name of the new subsite's folder. For example, a new subsite named *joe* of the existing Web site *My Web Sites* stored in the My Documents folder on the C drive would have the following file path: `C:\My Documents\My Web Sites\joe`. If you're not sure how file paths work, refer to the sidebar "File path 101" in Chapter 1.

   The subsite folder name you choose should include all lowercase letters and should contain only one word. This makes the site's address easier for your visitors to type after you publish the site on the Web.

5. **After you've chosen the Web site's location, in the Web Site Templates dialog box, click OK.**

   The dialog box closes, and FrontPage creates the new subsite. If another Web site is already open in FrontPage when you create the subsite, the subsite appears in a new FrontPage window. In the parent Web site, the subsite's folder appears in the Folder List with a globe icon on top, as shown in Figure 15-5.

You can now update and work with the subsite just like you would any other FrontPage Web site.

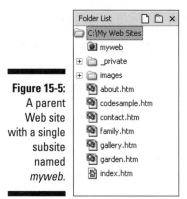

Figure 15-5:
A parent
Web site
with a single
subsite
named
myweb.

Deleting files and folders

If your Web site contains a file that has outlived its usefulness or is otherwise cluttering your Web site, you can boot the file out with one swift click. To delete a file or folder, do the following:

1. **In the Folder List or in any Web site view except the Tasks view, click the file or folder you want to delete.**

2. **Press the Delete key.**

   The Confirm Delete dialog box appears, making sure that you want to delete the file or folder.

3. **Click Yes.**

   If you are deleting more than one file, click Yes to All to delete them all in one step (instead of having the Confirm Delete dialog box pop up before deleting every single file). If you change your mind, click No or Cancel to close the dialog box without deleting the file.

Be careful: After you delete a file or folder using FrontPage, you can't later change your mind.

Also, if you delete a file that's the destination of a link from elsewhere in your Web site (whether that file is a Web page or a picture file), the link breaks. The damage isn't irreparable; you can always use FrontPage to find and fix broken hyperlinks. You should be aware of the problem all the same. The best way to avoid broken links caused by deleted files is to do your file cleanup using the Unlinked Files report (available by choosing View⇨Reports⇨Problems⇨ Unlinked Files). The pages and files listed in this report can safely be axed.

Backing up and moving Web sites

FrontPage enables you to copy your Web site to other locations, such as floppy disks or other backup media. By backing up your Web site, you not only have a clean copy in the event of a computer glitch, but also can maintain a working copy to use as a scratch pad, so that you avoid making permanent changes to the original. You can also use this method to transfer your Web site from one computer to another, should the need arise.

To back up your Web site, you follow similar steps to the ones you would follow if you were publishing your Web site:

1. **With the Web site open in FrontPage, choose File⇨Publish Site.**

   The Remote Web Site Properties dialog box appears. You use this dialog box to tell FrontPage where you want to back up or copy your Web site files.

   If you've already published your Web site on a host Web server, you can still follow these steps to back up or copy your site's files. By doing so, you don't affect the files already sitting on the host server's hard drive.

2. **In the Remote Web Server Type area, select the File System option.**

3. **In the Remote Web Site Location text box, type the path to the location to which you want to back up the Web site.**

   Or click the Browse button to select a location on your computer or network.

4. **If the Web site contains subsites, and you want to back up the subsites at the same time, at the top of the dialog box, click the Publishing tab, and then select the Include Subsites check box.**

5. **In the Remote Web Site Properties dialog box, click OK.**

   If the path you entered into the Remote Web Site Properties dialog box doesn't yet exist, FrontPage first prompts you to create a new folder there. Click Yes.

   The Remote Web Site Properties dialog box closes, and the Remote Web Site view becomes visible again with the contents of the currently open Web site displayed on the left side of the view, and the contents of the publish destination displayed on the right side, as shown in Figure 15-6.

6. **Click Publish Web Site.**

   A status indication appears at the bottom of the Web Site view to tell you what's going on. If any of the pages in the Web site contain features that require FrontPage Server Extensions to work properly (and the location to which you're copying the site doesn't support FrontPage Server

Extensions), the Publishing FrontPage Components dialog box will appear, warning you that the components won't work properly. That's okay, because you're simply backing up the Web site. If this dialog box appears, click the Continue button to make it go away.

After the work is done, an encouraging note appears at the bottom of the view, saying your Web site was published successfully. Don't be misled — your Web site isn't live. This is just the way FrontPage lets you know the copy process went smoothly.

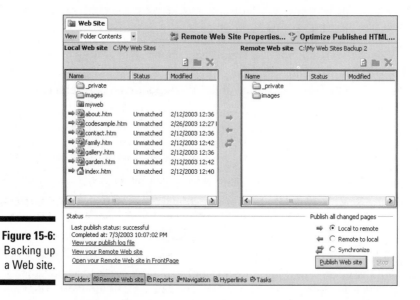

Figure 15-6:
Backing up
a Web site.

To move your Web site to a different computer that's not connected to yours with a local network, follow the steps in this section to copy the Web site to a floppy disk or other archive media (popular examples include Iomega Zip disks or Jaz drives). From the destination computer, launch FrontPage and then run the Import Web Site Wizard to copy the Web site from the disk or drive to the destination computer's hard drive. Chapter 1 explains how to import Web sites.

When you import a FrontPage Web site using the Import Web Site Wizard, the site's navigation structure is lost (and with it, the site's link bars and page banners). An article in the Microsoft Knowledge Base explains how to get around this problem. For help, go to support.microsoft.com and search for article number 198229. Furthermore, if the site originally was decorated with a theme, you may need to reapply the theme to the imported version of the site.

Chapter 16

Streamlining Site Updates with Dynamic Web Templates

Strangely enough, as your site grows in size and complexity, you may find yourself doing more and more repetitive work, especially when it comes to expanding your site. If your pages' layout and design are consistent, creating new pages generally involves cutting and pasting material from old pages, and then inserting new content. Not necessarily a difficult job, but certainly not an exciting one, and definitely time-consuming.

FrontPage cuts out some of the drudgery with *Dynamic Web Templates.* In this chapter, I demonstrate how Dynamic Web Templates simplify creating and maintaining a Web site (especially large sites or those with more than one author). I also show you how to create Dynamic Web Templates, and how to put them to work in your site.

Introducing Dynamic Web Templates

Before you jump into using Dynamic Web Templates, it helps to understand what you're getting yourself into. Dynamic Web Templates can save you a lot of time, but can also cause unnecessary hassle when used for the wrong type of site. Read on for details about what Dynamic Web Templates actually do, and for advice about how (or if) to use them in your site.

Separating static and dynamic content

Dynamic Web Templates enable you to place all the stuff that stays the same across pages (*static content*) into a template. Typical bits of static content include logos, page banners, and copyright notices, or design elements such as the page's background color. You then attach the template to separate pages containing unique content (*dynamic content*), and the static content appears in the page automatically.

Think of the Dynamic Web Template as your site's "letterhead" — a set of standard elements that appears in several pages, independent of the pages' content.

How Dynamic Web Templates differ from regular page templates

Dynamic Web Templates differ from regular page templates in three important ways.

You can keep several Dynamic Web Templates on hand

You can create several Dynamic Web Templates, and then radically change the look of a page by switching the Dynamic Web Template attached to that page. (You can use a regular page template only as a page's starting point; you can't later "detach" a regular page template.)

You can update several pages at once

You can attach a single Dynamic Web Template to many pages, and then change the static content in *all* the pages simply by updating and saving the Dynamic Web Template. (Regular page templates can only be used individually.)

You can "lock" static content so other authors can't edit it

When you attach a Dynamic Web Template to a page, you (and other site contributors) can type only inside the areas of the page you define in the template as editable regions. The rest of the page is "locked," and its content can't be edited. In this way, you can rest assured that the page's layout and design remains consistent, even when several people work on the site.

Editable regions are simply empty spaces inside the Dynamic Web Template that act as placeholders for each page's unique, or dynamic, content. After you apply a Dynamic Web Template to a page, you can place any type of content you like (text, graphics, tables, form elements . . . anything) into the page's editable regions.

Deciding if you should use Dynamic Web Templates in your site

To figure out whether Dynamic Web Templates would cut your workload or add to it, you must step back and take a look at your site's content. Sites that are good candidates for Dynamic Web Templates contain several pages with a consistent design and layout.

For example, if most or all the pages in your site use the same background graphic, have a company logo at the top of the page, and are laid out inside a layout table, it makes sense to place those static elements inside a Dynamic Web Template, so you don't have to rebuild these elements each time you add a new page to the site. With the help of the Dynamic Web Template, creating a new page becomes a matter of attaching the Dynamic Web Template to a new, blank page, filling the new page's editable region(s) with unique content, and then formatting that content however you like.

For a simple site, you might only use a single template for most or all of your pages. For a more complex site with different sections, each with its own design, you might want to use more than one Dynamic Web Template.

If you decide that Dynamic Web Templates aren't right for your site, FrontPage gives you a number of other ways to share content in your Web site. Here are your options:

- ✔ **Page templates:** Using regular page templates (as opposed to Dynamic Web Templates) makes sense when you want to create several pages from a common starting point, but you want to be able to edit (and let other authors edit) the static as well as the dynamic content in the page. I explain how to work with page templates in Chapter 2.

- ✔ **Shared borders:** Use shared borders when you want formatted content to appear in the top, left, right, and/or bottom borders of all (or selected) pages in your site. Shared borders also work hand-in-hand with features that take advantage of the FrontPage Navigation view, such as page banners and FrontPage-generated link bars. I talk about shared borders and link bars in Chapter 5 and page banners in Chapter 12.

- ✔ **Include Page Web Component:** This feature is essentially the opposite of Dynamic Web Templates, in which you link *dynamic* content (the included page) to another page. Use this feature when you want content that changes regularly (such as a list of announcements) to appear in more than one page in your site. When the time comes to update the dynamic content (you have a new announcement, for example), you update the included page, and FrontPage reflects the inclusion in all the pages containing the Include Page Web Component.

Creating a Dynamic Web Template

Creating a Dynamic Web Template involves three steps: building the template itself, defining the editable regions inside the template, and then saving the template.

Building the template

To create a Dynamic Web Template, take a look at your site's design and identify the elements (either content, such as a logo, or layout, such as a background color or a layout table) that remain the same in several pages in your site. These are the elements you want to place inside the Dynamic Web Template. Figure 16-1 illustrates elements a typical Dynamic Web Template might contain.

Company name

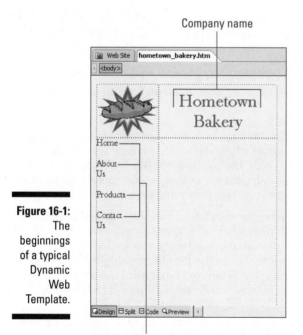

Figure 16-1:
The beginnings of a typical Dynamic Web Template.

Navigational links to other pages in the Web site

To build a Dynamic Web Template, follow these steps:

1. Create a new, blank Web page.

Just as if you are creating a regular page.

2. **In the new page, insert the elements you want to appear inside your Dynamic Web Template.**

   For example, insert the logo or layout table you want to appear in each of your content pages later on.

3. **Save the page as a Dynamic Web Template by choosing File⇨Save As.**

   The Save As dialog box appears.

4. **In the dialog box's Save as Type list box, choose Dynamic Web Template.**

5. **In the dialog box's File Name list box, enter a one-word filename.**

   FrontPage automatically adds the .dwt filename extension to the end of the filename after you save the page.

6. **In the dialog box, click the Save button.**

   The Save As dialog box closes, and FrontPage saves the Dynamic Web Template.

If you already have a page in your site that contains all the elements you want to appear inside your Dynamic Web Template, a quicker course of action may be to create a new page based on that existing page, and, in that new page, to delete whatever content you *don't* want to appear inside the template. I explain how to create a new page based on an existing page in Chapter 2.

Defining editable regions inside the template

After you've built your Dynamic Web Template, you must tell FrontPage which areas inside the template are editable. That is, you must define spaces in the template into which you (or other site authors) can later plop content after the template is attached to a regular Web page.

To define the Dynamic Web Template's editable regions, follow these steps:

1. **With the Dynamic Web Template open in Design view, place the cursor in the page where you want the editable region to appear.**

2. **Right-click the page, and from the pop-up menu that appears, choose Manage Editable Regions.**

   The Editable Regions dialog box appears (see Figure 16-2).

3. **In the dialog box's Region Name text box, enter an identifying label for that region.**

   Give the region a logical name that prompts the page's author to fill the region with the appropriate content. Good examples are **Article Text** or **Product Image**.

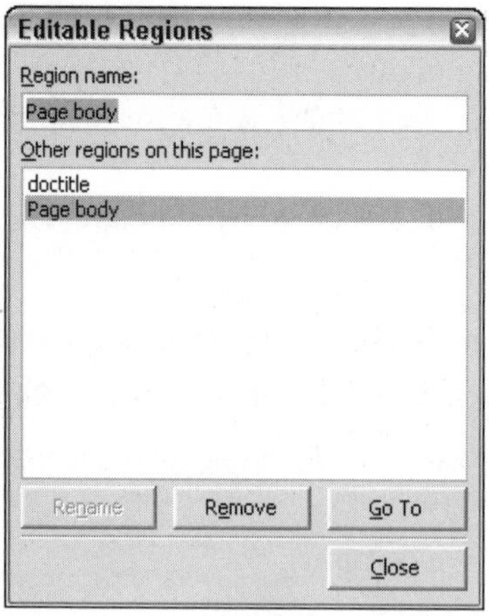

Figure 16-2:
The Editable
Regions
dialog box.

4. **In the dialog box, click the Add button.**

   The region name appears inside the Other Regions on This Page box. The region also appears in the template as a rectangular box with a small name label attached to its upper-left corner and a text placeholder inside it.

5. **In the dialog box, click the Close button.**

   The dialog box closes. Figure 16-3 shows what a Dynamic Web Template with one editable region looks like.

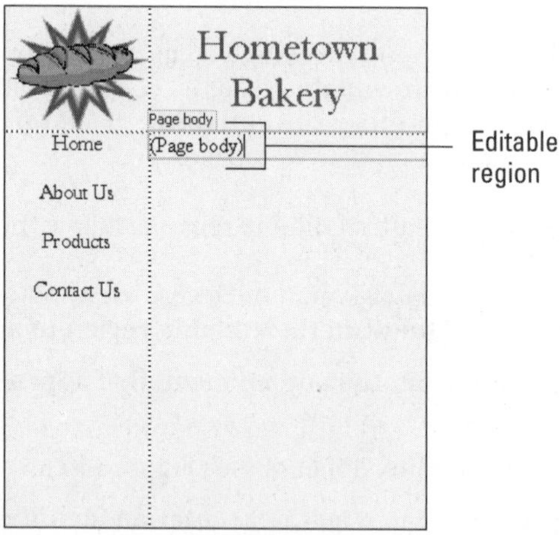

Editable region

Figure 16-3:
Adding an
editable
region to a
Dynamic
Web
Template.

Insert as many editable regions as you like into your Dynamic Web Template. To add another editable region, click elsewhere in the page and follow the steps in this section again.

If you're not sure where the editable region should go, just remember that these areas will eventually become the places where you add new stuff to a page formatted with this template. So you would place the editable region wherever you want the content to go. It's as easy as that.

Editable regions contain a basic text placeholder: the region name inside parentheses (refer to Figure 16-3). You can replace the placeholder with standard content (so the page looks good whether or not it's edited), or you can replace it with an HTML comment, which is invisible to the site visitor, but prompts the author to replace the comment with the appropriate content. To replace text with an HTML comment, highlight the entire placeholder (including the parentheses), and then choose Insert⇨Comment.

Saving the template

After you add editable regions to your Dynamic Web Template, save the page as you normally would (press Ctrl+S). If you created the Dynamic Web Template using an already-existing Web page, when you attempt to save the page, FrontPage pops open a dialog box reminding you that you are saving the page as a Dynamic Web Template. That's okay — just click OK to close the dialog box, and then proceed as usual to save the page.

If you intend to publish your site on a host server that supports FrontPage Server Extensions or SharePoint Services, you might want to save the Dynamic Web Template inside the _private folder so that it's kept hidden from Web site visitors. (For more about the _private folder, flip to Chapter 15.)

After you save the template, don't feel you're stuck with it — you can edit Dynamic Web Templates just as you would regular Web pages. Just make whatever changes you want, and then save the file again.

Attaching a Dynamic Web Template to Web Pages

After you create and save a Dynamic Web Template in your site, you *attach* it to a regular Web page (I'll call this regular page the *content page*). The content page you choose can be full of text and graphics, or it can be empty. Either way, after you attach a Dynamic Web Template to the content page, all of the elements in the template appear automatically inside the content page.

The results are more easily demonstrated than explained, so I encourage you to try the steps that follow to see what happens. At the end of this section, I show you a shortcut that accomplishes the same task, but I recommend following the first set of steps initially so that you become familiar with how Dynamic Web Templates work.

To attach a Dynamic Web Template to a content page, follow these steps:

1. **Open (or create) the content page to which you want to attach the Dynamic Web Template.**

   Figure 16-4 illustrates a simple content page. This page contains only text, but keep in mind that content pages can contain anything, from text and pictures to tables, form fields, and anything else a Web page can hold. Content pages can also start out empty.

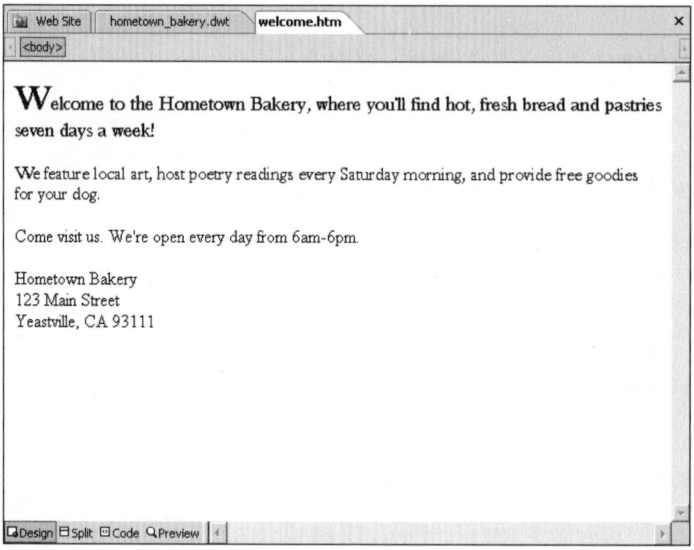

Figure 16-4:
An example of a typical content page.

2. **In the Folder List, click the icon for the Dynamic Web Template you want to use, and, while holding down the mouse button, drag and drop the icon anywhere inside the open content page.**

   Keep the following in mind when you attach the Dynamic Web Template:

   • *If the content page is empty,* the elements inside the Dynamic Web Template appear inside the content page automatically.

   The filename of the attached template appears in the upper-right corner of the page. (This notation is only a reminder for you; it doesn't appear when the page is viewed with a Web browser.) Also, the cursor blinks inside the content page's editable region (the first region in the page if there are more than one), prompting you to add some content to the page. Do so by typing some text, adding a graphic, or inserting whatever content you want. (You can skip the rest of the steps in this section.)

- *If the content page already contains text, graphics, or other content,* the Choose Editable Regions for Content dialog box appears, as shown in Figure 16-5.

Choose Editable Regions for Content

Please select which regions in the new page will receive content/regions from the old page:

| Current Page: | file:///C:/Documents and Settings/Asha Dornfest/My Documents/My Web Sites 2/welcome.htm |
| Dynamic Web Template: | file:///C:/Documents and Settings/Asha Dornfest/My Documents/My Web Sites 2/hometown_bakery.dw |

| Old: | New: | Modify |
| (Body) | Page body | |

[OK] [Skip Current Page] [Cancel]

Figure 16-5: The Choose Editable Regions for Content dialog box.

The first time you attach a Dynamic Web Template to a content page, you must tell FrontPage which editable region you want to hold the page's existing content (even if the page contains only a single editable region).

The main area of the dialog box lists the name of the first (or only) editable region in the page.

3. **Choose an editable region to hold the page's existing content by clicking that region's name in the dialog box.**

Existing content can only be funneled into a single editable region, even if the template contains more than one region.

If you're happy with FrontPage's default choice (the first editable region in the template), or if the template contains only one editable region, click OK. The Choose Editable Regions for Content dialog box closes, and a Microsoft FrontPage dialog box appears, confirming that the content page has been updated (click the Close button to close the dialog box). You're done!

If you're not happy with FrontPage's default choice, read on.

4. **In the main area of the Choose Editable Regions for Content dialog box, click the name of the editable region you want to change, and then click the Modify button.**

   The Choose Editable Region for Content dialog box appears (the dialog box names are similar, but the dialog boxes are indeed different).

5. **From the New Region list box, choose the name of the region you want, and then click OK.**

   Choose Editable Region for Content dialog box closes, and the Choose Editable Regions for Content dialog box becomes visible again.

6. **In the dialog box, click OK.**

   The Choose Editable Regions for Content dialog box closes, and a Microsoft FrontPage dialog box appears confirming that the content page has been updated (click the Close button to close the dialog box). The finished page appears, as shown in Figure 16-6.

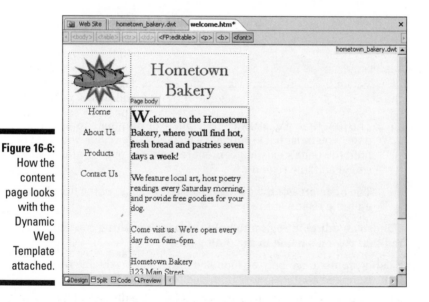

Figure 16-6: How the content page looks with the Dynamic Web Template attached.

You can attach the same Dynamic Web Template to as many content pages in your site as you like. In this way, you take greatest advantage of the benefits of Dynamic Web Templates: The more pages you format using templates, the more pages you won't later have to edit by hand when you simply want to change a single static element that appears in all of the pages (such as a new logo or an updated copyright notice).

I promised you a shortcut, and here it is: After you become comfortable with how Dynamic Web Templates work, use this shortcut for attaching templates to content pages:

1. **In the Folder List, select the file(s) to which you want to attach the template.**

   To select more than one file, while holding down the Ctrl key, click the files' icons.

2. **With the file icon(s) selected, choose Format⇨Dynamic Web Template⇨Attach Dynamic Web Template.**

   The Attach Dynamic Web Template dialog box appears.

3. **In the dialog box, double-click the template you want to attach.**

   The dialog box closes, FrontPage attaches the selected template, and a Microsoft FrontPage dialog box pops up, letting you know all is well (click the Close button to close the dialog box).

After you attach a Dynamic Web Template to a content page, you can only type or insert content into the page's editable regions; the rest of the page is "locked." If this isn't okay, and you need to make a change to a part of the page that lies outside an editable region, you can either detach the content page from the Dynamic Web Template (making the entire page editable), or you can add more editable regions to the attached template, and then save the template's changes (automatically updating any attached pages). I explain how to update a site based on Dynamic Web Templates in the next section.

Updating a Site That Uses Dynamic Web Templates

Here's where all your work creating templates and attaching them to content pages pays off.

After your site's static and dynamic content is neatly divided among Dynamic Web Templates and attached content pages, updating your site becomes a piece of cake. Depending on how you want to change your site, you can do so in one of three ways: make and save changes to the Dynamic Web Template itself; attach a different Dynamic Web Template to a content page; or detach the Dynamic Web Template from the content page altogether.

Updating the template itself

If you want to change any of the static elements in your content pages, you simply need to open the attached Dynamic Web Template file, make whatever changes you want to that file, and then save it. FrontPage keeps track of which pages the template is linked to and automatically reflects the changes inside those pages.

For example, imagine you have attached a Dynamic Web Template to 20 content pages in your site. The Dynamic Web Template contains a number of static design elements that form the visual backbone for your site's pages, including a rather dated logo that was designed in the early '80s. You decide to overhaul the company image by designing a new logo. To update all 20 pages in one go, you simply open the Dynamic Web Template file, replace the old logo with the new logo, and save the page. The new logo appears automatically in all of the linked content pages.

You can change the template in any way you want. You can add or delete elements, and you can move, add, or remove editable regions.

To open a Dynamic Web Template, you can either double-click its icon in the Folder List, or, with a linked content page open in Design view, choose Format➪Dynamic Web Template➪Open Attached Dynamic Web Template.

If your site uses several Dynamic Web Templates, and you can't remember which is linked to what, take a look at the Dynamic Web Template report, which rounds all the information up in a nice table. To view this report, choose View➪Reports➪Shared Content➪Dynamic Web Templates.

All Dynamic Web Templates must contain at least one editable region. If you delete an editable region in a template that, in linked pages, is filled with content, when you save the template's changes, FrontPage prompts you to move the content from the old region (the one you're deleting) to a different region in the page. If the region you're moving the content to already contains its own stuff, the two chunks of content merge together, sharing that region.

Swapping Dynamic Web Templates

For a more radical change of image, instead of making piecemeal changes to the attached template, you might want to create an entirely new template and swap it for the old template. Like changing outfits in a dressing room, changing Dynamic Web Templates enables you to "try on" different looks for a page without affecting the page's core content.

To swap Dynamic Web Templates, follow these steps:

1. **Create a new Dynamic Web Template (follow the steps earlier in the chapter).**

   Ideally, the new Dynamic Web Template should contain editable regions *with the same names as the old template.* That way, when you swap templates, FrontPage automatically funnels the content from the "XYZ" editable region in the old template to the "XYZ" region in the new template. If the new template contains regions that are named differently, or if the template contains a different number of regions, the swapping process becomes slightly more complicated.

2. **In the Folder List, select the file(s) to which you want to attach the new Dynamic Web Template.**

   To select more than one file, while holding down the Ctrl key, click the files' icons.

3. **With the file icon(s) selected, choose Format⇨Dynamic Web Template⇨Attach Dynamic Web Template.**

   The Attach Dynamic Web Template dialog box appears.

4. **In the dialog box, double-click the new template's icon.**

   One of the following three things then occurs:

   - *If the old and new templates contain equivalent editable regions,* the Attach Dynamic Web Template dialog box closes, FrontPage attaches the selected template, and a Microsoft FrontPage dialog box pops up, letting you know all is well. Click the Close button to close the dialog box. You're done!

   - *If the old and new templates contain different numbers of editable regions, or if the regions are named differently,* the Choose Editable Regions for Content dialog box appears, prompting you to map the regions between the old and new templates. If the regions in the old and new templates correspond properly, click OK. The Choose Editable Regions for Content dialog box closes, and a Microsoft FrontPage dialog box appears confirming that the content page has been updated. Click the Close button to close the dialog box. You're done!

   - *If the regions don't correspond properly,* you must map the regions listed in the Choose Editable Regions for Content dialog box by hand. Proceed to Step 5.

5. **In the main area of the Choose Editable Regions for Content dialog box, click the name of the editable region you want to change, and then click the Modify button.**

   The Choose Editable Region for Content dialog box appears.

6. **From the New Region list box, choose the name of the region you want, and then click OK.**

   Choose Editable Region for Content dialog box closes, and the Choose Editable Regions for Content dialog box becomes visible again.

7. **In the dialog box, click OK.**

   The Choose Editable Regions for Content dialog box closes, and a Microsoft FrontPage dialog box appears, confirming that the content page has been updated. Click the Close button to close the dialog box.

Detaching a page from a Dynamic Web Template

If you decide that a content page no longer benefits from its association with a Dynamic Web Template, detach it. The good news is that all the static content contributed by the template stays inside the content page and is now completely editable, so you don't have to rebuild the entire page to have it match up with all the other pages in your site. The bad news is that, if you later change the Dynamic Web Template (thereby updating all the attached pages in the site), you must update the detached pages by hand.

Keep in mind too that, after you detach a page from a Dynamic Web Template, you lose the distinction between the page's static content (the stuff provided by the template) and dynamic content (the stuff inside the page's editable regions). If you later decide to attach a different template to the page, you will have to delete all the content provided by the original template and start the process again from scratch.

To detach a content page from a Dynamic Web Template, do this:

1. **Open the content page you want to detach.**

2. **Choose Format⇨Dynamic Web Template⇨Detach from Dynamic Web Template.**

   FrontPage unlinks the two files, and a Microsoft FrontPage dialog box appears confirming the action.

3. **In the dialog box, click the Close button.**

Chapter 17

Making Your Worldwide Debut

In This Chapter

▶ Finding out what "publishing your Web site" involves

▶ Publishing your site on a host Web server

▶ Understanding how FrontPage Server Extensions affect the publishing process

▶ Spreading the word about your site

▶ Restricting access to your Web site using passwords

▶ Updating your site

*D*rum roll, please! It's the moment of truth . . . time to unveil your painstakingly prepared, lovingly built Web site and make it visible to the world.

In this chapter, I show you how to publish your Web site, I explain how to restrict site access using passwords, and I give you tips on how to update your site to keep it fresh and interesting.

What "Publishing Your Web Site" Means

Publishing your Web site means making the site visible on the World Wide Web for all to see (or, in the case of an intranet site, visible to members of the intranet). For your site to be accessible to visitors, you must store all the site's files and folders on a computer called a Web server. A *Web server* is a computer running special software that maintains a high-speed, round-the-clock connection to the Internet or internal network. (In Chapter 3, I give you an overview of how the Internet's client-server setup works.)

Most people gain access to a host Web server by getting an account with an Internet Service Provider (ISP) or a Web Presence Provider (WPP). Having an account at an ISP enables your computer and modem to establish a connection to the Internet. After you're connected, you can then use the Internet to send and receive e-mail, browse the Web, and transfer files between computers.

A typical ISP also provides a limited amount of publishing space on its Web server as part of your regular monthly fee. The amount of storage space varies. (Some ISPs provide as little as 5MB; others provide 50MB or more.) Check with your ISP for details.

Not sure how much file space your Web site takes up? Try this: In the Folder List, right-click the site's top-level folder and then choose Properties from the pop-up menu. The dialog box that appears displays the Web site's total file size. (The file size shown here doesn't including the size of any subsites; you must open subsites separately to check their sizes. For more information about what subsites are and do, see Chapter 15.)

Several companies provide Web server space for free. Assuming you already have Internet access, all you have to do is register at the company's Web site. Popular choices include Tripod (`www.tripod.lycos.com`) and Yahoo! Geocities (`geocities.yahoo.com`).

If you're building an intranet site, your company maintains its own Web server and network connection. Speak to your company's system administrator for details about your network setup.

The Skinny on FrontPage Server Extensions

Having access to a host Web server is only part of the publishing picture. For certain FrontPage-created features to work, the Web server must have a set of auxiliary programs called FrontPage Server Extensions installed. *FrontPage Server Extensions* are a special set of programs that act as translators between FrontPage and the Web server program.

Installing FrontPage Server Extensions on a Web server is a big job, which is why many ISPs and system administrators have yet to fully support FrontPage. However, the number of FrontPage-friendly ISPs is growing every day. (I give you tips on finding an ISP to host your FrontPage Web site in the sidebar, "Finding a FrontPage ISP.")

The good news is that you can publish a perfectly good FrontPage Web site on *any* Web server, with certain caveats. Repeat: You do *not* have to run out and sign up for a different Web hosting service if yours doesn't support FrontPage Server Extensions, as long as you're aware of some limitations. The following features will not work on a server that doesn't have FrontPage Server Extensions installed:

- ✔ The _private folder (you can use this folder, but it doesn't have any password protection)

- ✔ Nested subsites (that is, subsites within subsites)

- ✔ The following Web components: confirmation field, Web search, hit counter, table of contents based on categories, and top 10 list

- ✔ FrontPage workgroup features, including source control

- ✔ FrontPage discussion groups

- ✔ FrontPage user registration systems

- ✔ Usage reports

- ✔ File upload form field

- ✔ Custom link bars

- ✔ Shared border background properties

- ✔ Permissions and security

Additionally, if you want to open or create a Web site on a remote Web server, that server must have FrontPage Server Extensions installed.

If your site uses forms, remember that the built-in FrontPage form handler works hand-in-hand with FrontPage Server Extensions, but you can adjust the form handler to work on any Web server with a form handler installed. See Chapter 8 for details.

Finding a FrontPage ISP

The benefits of publishing your Web site with a FrontPage-friendly ISP are clear. To find a FrontPage ISP, check local computer magazines and newspapers, ask friends for recommendations, and lean on Microsoft for assistance. The Microsoft FrontPage site (www.microsoft. com/frontpage) contains a link to a database of Web presence providers who support FrontPage.

If you're happy with your current ISP, consider publishing your Web site at Tripod (www. tripod.lycos.com). Tripod provides free Web space to anyone who registers . . . and, best of all, Tripod supports FrontPage Server Extensions. Tripod doesn't support *all* the features FrontPage Server Extensions makes possible, such as permissions and the creation of subsites, but it is still a good option for a relatively straightforward site.

Creating an online meeting place with SharePoint

Microsoft SharePoint is a server-based technology (similar to FrontPage Server Extensions) that works hand-in-hand with Microsoft Office and FrontPage. With SharePoint Services installed on the host Web server, you can create a special type of team collaboration Web site that members can use as a meeting place, document library, bulletin board, calendar, contact resource, and more. The beauty of the resulting SharePoint Team Web site is its simplicity: Although you must use FrontPage to create and publish the site initially, the rest of the team needs only to use a browser to visit and contribute to the site.

SharePoint Services enables you to create even more complex Web sites with the use of *Web packages* (groups of related files you can import to use in a site) and *Web parts* (bits of code you drop into Web pages that change based on

connections to external sources of data). This stuff certainly falls in the intermediate-to-advanced category, but if you're looking to create dynamic, data-driven Web sites, SharePoint is worth exploring.

The easiest way to create a SharePoint site is to use the SharePoint Based Team Site template. Chapter 1 explains how to create a new Web site based on a template.

SharePoint has specific server requirements and is also a complex enough topic that I can't do it justice in a sidebar (or even a full chapter). Furthermore, the latest version of SharePoint Services differs in its capabilities from an earlier version (called SharePoint Team Services 1.0). I've only skimmed the surface here, but if you want to find out more, start with the FrontPage Help System (press F1).

If you attempt to publish a site that contains FrontPage Server Extensions-related features on a host Web server that doesn't have FrontPage Server Extensions installed, FrontPage pops open a dialog box that lists the pages that won't work properly and prompts you to change or remove the pages. FrontPage also lists these pages in the Component Errors report. To see the report, after publishing (or after canceling a publishing attempt), choose View⇨Reports⇨Problems⇨Component Errors.

Going Public

When you've finished creating your Web site in FrontPage, it's time to take your show on the road. In the following subsections, I show you how to publish your Web site.

Before the curtain goes up, give your Web site the white glove test. Rev up the FrontPage spell checker (choose Tools⇨Spelling), make sure your hyperlinks work properly (choose View⇨Reports⇨Problems⇨Broken Hyperlinks), and go through every inch of your site using a Web browser — preferably more than one browser model.

Consider, too, letting FrontPage check your Web site against accepted accessibility guidelines. For details, read the Chapter 4 section called "Checking your site against accessibility guidelines."

Excluding unfinished pages from publishing

If your site contains files (Web pages, graphics, or any other files) that aren't yet ready for public viewing, you can tell FrontPage to hold those files back while publishing the rest of the site. To do so, in the Folder List, right-click the file you want to hold back (or select multiple files by pressing the Ctrl key while clicking icons, and then right-click the selection), and choose Don't Publish from the pop-up menu that appears. A red X appears next to the file icon, letting you know that file won't be published the next time you publish the site.

For an overview of your site's publish status, take a look at the Publish Status report by choosing View➪Reports➪Workflow➪Publish Status.

If you exclude a page from being published that is linked to another page in the site, that link will not work properly in the live version of the site. Therefore, before you publish, be sure to dismantle any hyperlinks that lead to unfinished pages. For instructions on how to do this, see Chapter 5.

Publishing your Web site

After you've given your Web site a thorough once-over, the next step is to find out your publishing address. This address tells FrontPage where in the host Web server's file system to store your Web site's files. On servers that have FrontPage Server Extensions installed, the address may look something like `http://www.mydomain.com` or `http://www.server.com/~username`.

On servers that don't have FrontPage Server Extensions installed, you publish your site using FTP, or *file transfer protocol*, the conventional method for transferring files between computers on the Internet. Even though the address your visitors will eventually type to view your published Web site begins with `http://`, your publishing address most likely begins with `ftp://`.

You must have the correct publishing address in hand to publish your Web site. If in doubt, your ISP or system administrator can tell you your publishing address.

To publish your Web site for the first time, follow these steps:

1. **In FrontPage, open the Web site you want to publish.**

   If the site is already open in FrontPage, be sure to save any changes you have made to the site's pages (to do so, choose File➪Save All).

2. **Activate your Internet connection.**

3. **Choose File➪Publish Site.**

   FrontPage switches to the Remote Web Site view, and the Remote Web Site Properties dialog box appears. You use this dialog box to tell FrontPage where you want to publish your Web site.

4. **In the dialog box's Remote Web Server Type area, select the option that corresponds to the type of host Web server your ISP uses.**

   If your ISP supports FrontPage Server Extensions or SharePoint Services, select the FrontPage or SharePoint Services option button. If not, select FTP.

5. **In the Remote Web Site Location text box, type your publishing address.**

6. **If the Web site contains subsites, and you want to publish the subsites and the parent Web site at the same time, at the top of the dialog box, click the Publishing tab, and then select the Include Subsites check box.**

7. **If you want FrontPage to clean up your site's HTML code before publishing, at the top of the dialog box, click the Optimize HTML tab. In this section of the dialog box, select the When Publishing . . . check box, and then select the check boxes next to items you want FrontPage to remove.**

   For example, you can tell FrontPage to strip the published site of all HTML comments (most of which were probably meant for the site's authors, not its visitors). You can also have FrontPage tidy the code by removing unnecessary white space between HTML tags. By doing so, the look of your pages doesn't change — just the look of the HTML code for those visitors who care to check it out.

8. **In the Remote Web Site Properties dialog box, click OK.**

   The Remote Web Site Properties dialog box closes, and FrontPage contacts the server at the publishing address you specified. If the server contains security features (most do), the Name and Password Required dialog box appears.

9. **In the Name and Password text boxes, enter the user name and password that you chose when you established your account, and then click OK.**

The dialog box closes, and the Remote Web Site view becomes visible with the contents of the currently open (local) Web site displayed on the left side of the view, and the contents of the publish destination displayed on the right side, as shown in Figure 17-1.

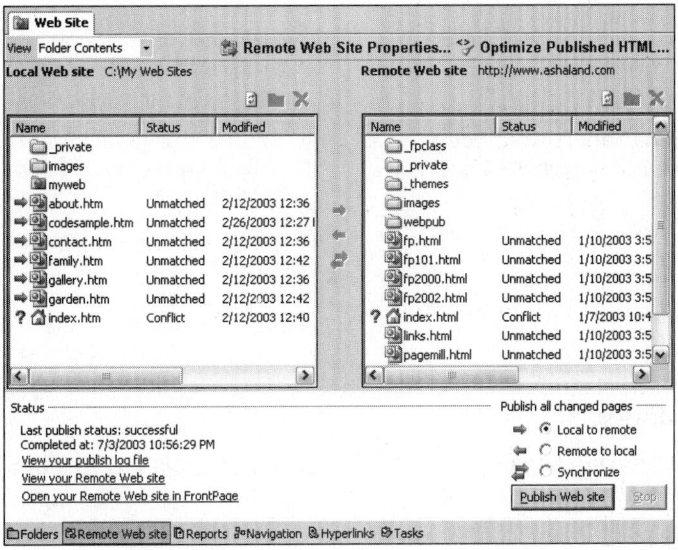

Figure 17-1:
The Remote
Web Site
view.

10. **In the lower-right corner of the FrontPage window, click the Publish Web Site button.**

FrontPage copies all your Web site files to the remote server. Depending on the size of your Web site and the speed of your Internet connection, this process may take a few minutes.

A status indication appears at the bottom of the Web Site view to tell you what's going on. If any of the pages in the Web site contain features that require FrontPage Server Extensions to work properly (and the location to which you're copying the site doesn't support FrontPage Server Extensions), the Publishing FrontPage Components dialog box appears, listing the offending pages and warning you that the components won't work properly. If this dialog box appears, click Cancel to halt publishing. Open the pages listed in the dialog box, remove the components in question, save the pages, and try publishing again.

On servers that have FrontPage Server Extensions installed, FrontPage takes care of file management and cleanup duties as it publishes your site. For example, if the host Web server contains files at the publishing address that are not part of the Web site you're publishing, FrontPage gives you the option of deleting those files from the host Web server.

Publishing a single page

You can save a page as part of a Web site that's stored on another Web server to which you're connected via your company intranet or the Internet. By doing so, you, in effect, publish the single page.

Note: To save a page as part of a Web site stored on a remote Web server, you must have authoring access to that Web site, and the host Web server must support FrontPage Server Extensions. I talk about FrontPage Server Extensions earlier in this chapter.

To save your page in a Web site stored on a different Web server, follow these steps:

1. **Activate your Internet connection.**

2. **Choose File⇨Save As.**

   The Save As dialog box appears.

3. **In the File Name list box, enter the Web address to which you want to publish the page, and then click Save.**

The Web address you specify must include the address of the server (it looks something like `http://www.server.com`) followed by a forward slash and the filename. If the file is to be stored in a folder or subsite on the server, the folder reference must precede the filename, like this:

```
http://www.server.com/
foldername/filename
```

Note: File paths on Web servers work just like file paths on your own computer, except that file paths on Web servers contain forward slashes, not backslashes. For a crash course in file path notation, see Chapter 1.

After you click Save, the Enter Network Password dialog box appears.

4. **In the dialog box, type your user name and password, and then click OK.**

   The dialog box closes, and FrontPage saves the page as part of the Web site.

If the host server has FrontPage Server Extensions installed and the host Web server recognizes a default home page filename other than `index.htm`, FrontPage changes the home page filename on the host Web server and updates any associated hyperlinks.

If the host server recognizes a home page filename other than `index.htm` and *does not* have FrontPage Server Extensions installed, you must manually change the home page filename in the local copy of your Web site and then publish the site again. (I explain how to rename files in Chapter 15.) If you're not sure which home page filename your host server recognizes, ask your ISP or system administrator.

After the work is done, an encouraging note appears at the bottom of the view, saying that your Web site was published successfully.

Congratulations — your site is now visible to the world!

Letting the World Know You're Ready for Visitors

Pass the bubbly! Your Web site has joined the Internet community, and you can now call yourself a true-blue Web publisher. Using your Web browser, visit your live Web site at its new URL and, just to be safe, give the site one last check. If all is well, heave a sigh of relief and enjoy a moment of satisfaction.

You might even want to line up a group of sympathetic testers who use different types of computers and browsers and ask them to give your site a run-through. Even if everything works perfectly when viewed with your computer and browser, a glitch might pop up when your site is viewed on a different platform.

If something doesn't work properly, fix the problem on the *local* copy of your Web site — the copy stored on your computer — and publish your Web site again. I show you how later in this chapter, in the "Keeping Your Web Site Fresh" section.

Now that your Web site is open to the public, you need to let everyone know you're accepting visitors. If you want your site to benefit from publicity, the following list gives some suggestions on how you can promote your site:

- ✔ **Search services:** List your site with popular search services, such as Yahoo! (www.yahoo.com) and Google (www.google.com). Each search service posts listing instructions on its Web site. Even if you don't actively list your site, many search engines use automated programs (called such creepy names as *spiders, webcrawlers,* or *bots*) to index the Web automatically, but doing a little legwork on your own never hurts.

- ✔ **E-mail signature:** Include your Web site address in the signature line of your e-mail messages. Most e-mail programs enable you to append a few lines of text to the bottom of every message.

- ✔ **Newsgroups:** Post a discreet announcement to newsgroups that discuss related topics. Keep your announcement low-key and respectful. If you blanket a newsgroup with advertising hype, not only will you irk the other newsgroup participants (hence, bad word-of-mouth), your publicity campaign will probably backfire.

- ✔ **Traditional print advertising:** Add your Web site address to business cards, letterhead, and print advertising.

- ✔ **Word-of-mouth:** Your best bet is to invite your friends and colleagues to visit your Web site and encourage them to spread the word to their friends, and so on, and so on. . . .

Password-Protecting Your Web Site

Not everybody wants the whole world to be able to look at their site. If you're one of those people, let FrontPage help you *password protect* your site so only the privileged few with passwords can get in.

Using FrontPage *permissions,* not only can you restrict who views your Web site, you can also specify who in your workgroup can create, update, and publish pages in the site. When each team member logs onto the central server to access the site, a FrontPage dialog box appears, prompting them to enter a user name and password, and FrontPage grants access based on the permissions you've specified.

To use FrontPage to access a server's permissions, the server must have FrontPage Server Extensions or SharePoint Services installed. What's more, the *version* of the FrontPage Server Extensions installed, the Web server program your ISP uses, and your own computer's network setup all affect permissions settings. The instructions in this chapter illustrate how permissions work for the 2003 version of the FrontPage Server Extensions installed with the Apache Web server, a popular UNIX-based Web server program that many ISPs use. If your host Web server uses a different Web server program or runs a different operating system, the steps are slightly different. (I discuss one difference in the sidebar, "Defining user roles," later in the chapter.) If you're in doubt about any of this information, check with your ISP or system administrator and refer to the FrontPage Help system by pressing F1.

Setting permissions

To control who may edit your Web site, you use FrontPage to specify administrators and authors. If you want your Web site to appear only to authorized visitors, you can also create a list of people with browsing access.

FrontPage provides for the following three levels of access:

- ✔ **Administer:** Giving someone Administer access makes them an *administrator,* and an administrator can create, edit, and delete Web sites and pages and adjust a Web site's permissions. Every Web site must have at least one administrator.

- ✔ **Author:** An author can create, edit, or delete pages but cannot create or delete Web sites or adjust the Web site's permissions.

- ✔ **Browse:** A person with Browse access can only view a Web site with a Web browser; that person can't edit the Web site or even open the site in FrontPage.

If the Web site for which you're setting permissions contains a subsite, the steps are slightly more complex. By default, all subsites have the same permissions as their *parent Web site* (the top-level Web site) and are visible to anyone with a Web browser. Therefore, if you adjust the parent Web site's permissions, you automatically change the permissions of all its subsites as well. (If you're not sure what a subsite is, refer to Chapter 1.) In the following steps, I show you how to change the parent Web site's permission settings, as well as how to give your parent Web site and subsites independent permission settings.

To set your Web site's permissions, follow these steps:

1. **Publish the Web site.**

   I show you how in the earlier section, "Publishing your Web site."

2. **Open the live version of the Web site directly from the host Web server by clicking the <u>Open your remote Web site in FrontPage</u> link in the lower-left corner of the Remote Web Site view.**

   The remote Web site opens in a new FrontPage window. You can now update and change the site just as if it were stored on your own computer.

   Just keep in mind that after you save your pages, any changes you make are immediately visible to the world, so proceed with care.

3. **Choose Tools⇨Server⇨Permissions.**

   The Permissions dialog box appears as follows:

   - If the Web site is a parent Web site, you see two tabs at the top of the dialog box: Users and Computers. Skip ahead to Step 5.

   - If the Web site is a subsite, the dialog box contains a third tab: Settings. The Settings panel enables you to change the permission setting, so that the subsite uses its own set of permissions instead of inheriting the parent Web site's permission settings.

Defining user roles

On SharePoint-powered sites, and on sites hosted on Windows-based Web servers running FrontPage 2002 (or later) Server Extensions, you have more sophisticated control over permissions. These server setups support the creation of *user roles* in which you can pick and choose the various access rights users have. For example, you can designate users with browse access (those who can view the Web site, but can not edit it) and contributor access (those who can view the Web site *and* participate in discussion groups, but cannot edit the site).

4. **If you want the subsite to have its own permission settings, select the Use Unique Permissions for This Web option button and then click the Apply button.**

   FrontPage adjusts the Web site's permissions.

5. **Click the Users tab.**

   The Users tab becomes visible.

6. **To add a user, click the Add button.**

   The Add Users dialog box appears.

7. **In the Name text box, type a user name.**

   User names and passwords are case sensitive, which means that FrontPage sees *gonzo* and *Gonzo* as two different names.

   If you are using permissions to password-protect your site from unauthorized visitors, you only need to set up one user name (such as *guest*) and one password. If you are using permissions to specify different levels of access among your workgroup, assign a unique user name and password to each individual in your group.

8. **In the Password text box, type a password.**

9. **Type the password again in the Confirm Password text box.**

10. **In the Allow Users To area of the dialog box, select the option button for the level of access you want the individual to have.**

11. **Click OK.**

    The Add Users dialog box closes, returning you to the Users tab of the Permissions dialog box.

12. **To restrict browsing access to authorized users only, select the Valid Username and Password Required to Browse This Web check box.**

    If you don't select this check box, anyone with an Internet connection and a Web browser can browse your Web site.

13. **Click the Apply button to activate changes and continue adjusting permissions, or click OK to activate changes and close the Permissions dialog box.**

Changing permissions

You can easily adjust your Web site's permissions. You can, for example, upgrade an author's access to administrator, or you can remove a user from the list of people authorized to browse the site. To edit a user's permissions, follow these steps:

1. **Open the live version of the Web site, and then choose Tools⇨ Server⇨Permissions.**

   The Permissions dialog box opens.

2. **If it's not already visible, click the Users tab.**

3. **In the user list, click the name of the user whose permissions you want to change, and then click the Edit button.**

   The Edit Users dialog box appears.

4. **In the Allow Users To area of the dialog box, select the option button for the user's new permission setting, and then click OK.**

   The Edit Users dialog box closes, returning you to the Users panel of the Permissions dialog box.

5. **Click the Apply button to activate changes and continue adjusting permissions, or click OK to activate changes and close the Permissions dialog box.**

To remove a user from the permission list, follow the same instructions, but in Step 3, click the Remove button rather than the Edit button.

Keeping Your Web Site Fresh

Stagnant Web sites are as appealing as day-old pastry. With doughnuts and Web pages, freshness counts, so keep your site vital by changing its content, updating its graphics, and adding new features regularly.

To update your site (or to correct any mistakes you find), you make changes on the local copy of your Web site and then publish the Web site again. To update the site's changed pages, a single button-click does the trick, as follows:

1. **In FrontPage, open the Web site you want to update and make (and save) whatever changes you want.**

2. **Activate your Internet connection.**

3. **Click the Publish Site button on the Standard toolbar.**

   If the host server supports security features, the Name and Password Required dialog box appears.

   Note: If you update your site several times during a single FrontPage session, this dialog box only appears the first time you publish or update the site.

4. **In the Name and Password text boxes, type your user name and password, and then click OK.**

   The dialog box closes, and FrontPage copies the changed pages to the host Web server. Your site is now fresh as a daisy.

If you prefer to choose which pages and files to update (as opposed to letting FrontPage simply publish all files that have changed), in the Folder List, right-click the file or folder you wish to publish (or select multiple files and folders by pressing the Ctrl key while clicking icons, and then right-click the selection), and choose Publish Selected Files from the pop-up menu that appears. The Remote Web Site Properties dialog box appears with the site's publishing address visible in the Remote Web Site Location text box. Click OK to close the dialog box and publish the selected file(s).

To republish the entire Web site (not just the changed pages) or to publish the Web site to a different location, follow the steps in the earlier section, "Publishing your Web site."

Part V
The Part of Tens

In this part . . .

In the following chapters, I share some tips that help you expand your Web-publishing consciousness. I list ten free (or almost free) add-ins that you can install to extend FrontPage's capabilities, and I point out ten Web sites you should plan to visit.

Chapter 18

Ten FrontPage Add-Ins to Try

In This Chapter

▶ Understanding what FrontPage add-ins can do

▶ Finding, downloading, and installing add-ins

▶ Familiarizing yourself with a selection of add-ins

*A*dd-ins are programs you download and install to add features and functionality to FrontPage. Generally written by third-party companies and programmers (that is, anyone who's not Microsoft), these snippets run the gamut from purely functional to patently flashy.

In this chapter, I show you how to find FrontPage add-ins on the Web, how to download them to your computer, and how to install them.

I also list ten add-ins you might want to explore. Some are free, and others are only downloadable as free demonstrations; you must pay the software creators for fully functional licensed versions. In each case, I list where you can download the add-in, and, if there is a fee, I tell you so.

Most of these add-in programs were written for previous versions of FrontPage. As such, the add-ins will only work reliably *after* their creators update the programs to work with FrontPage 2003. When this book was published, most of the add-in creators were in the process of updating their programs; be sure to check their Web sites for the latest system requirements.

Finding, Downloading, and Installing FrontPage Add-Ins

Where do you find add-ins? First stop, Microsoft. The keeper of FrontPage keeps track of many (but not all) add-ins on its own site. Go to the Microsoft FrontPage home page (www.microsoft.com/frontpage) for a link to the

Add-In Center. At the Add-In Center, you find information about hundreds of add-ins, indexed by type and author. You also find user ratings, download links, and links to the add-in creators' Web sites.

Next, search for the phrase "FrontPage add-ins" at Google, my favorite search utility (www.google.com). Google always manages to unearth more interesting finds.

When you find a promising add-in, download it to your computer. Each add-in site has a "download now" type of link: Just click the link to tell your computer to save the add-in file on your own hard drive or network.

If you don't already have one, I suggest creating a Downloads folder on your hard drive, and then saving all downloaded files there, so you can easily find the files later.

After you download the add-in, you must install it, just like any other piece of software. The add-in's Web site, in addition to providing a download link, should give you step-by-step instructions for installing the add-in on your computer.

In some cases, the download comes in the form of a ZIP file (a group of files that has been compressed for faster download). You must "unzip" the file before you can install the add-in. My favorite zip utility is WinZip, which is available at www.winzip.com. If you must unzip a file, download and install WinZip (you can try out a free evaluation version), and then double-click the ZIP file to decompress it.

After you install the add-in, you can access it from inside FrontPage. Each download site explains how to work with the add-in after it is installed.

In general, when you download programs and install them on your computer, you risk contracting a computer *virus*. Viruses aren't as common as people might think, but if you're the unlucky person who must deal with one, you're in for a hassle. Viruses, if you don't already know, are a naughty programmer's idea of a practical joke. These harmful bits of code "infect" your hard drive and can cause minor annoyance (by flashing a rude message on your screen) or major damage (by erasing files or corrupting your hard drive).

For safety's sake, I recommend that you purchase and install virus protection software such as Symantec Norton AntiVirus (www.symantec.com) or McAfee VirusScan (www.mcafee.com). Be sure to update the software regularly to keep on top of the latest viruses.

J-Bots Plus

Webs Unlimited, creators of J-Bots, has been in the FrontPage add-in business for years, and for good reason. This collection of components adds to FrontPage's already-impressive collection of DHTML behaviors and Web components. Examples include a digital image clock, a pullout menu, and an "e-mail a friend" link.

Download site: `www.microsoft.com/frontpage/downloads/addin/searchdetail.asp?a=79`

Download type: Free 14-day trial. After that, if you want to keep using J-Bots, you must purchase the software.

For more information: `www.websunlimited.com`

1-2-3 PayPal Purchase Button Wizard

Want to sell stuff on your Web site? Consider using PayPal, a trusted method for sending and receiving money online (see `www.paypal.com` for more information). If you decide to use PayPal, this add-in simplifies creating a shopping cart, adding payment buttons to a Web page, and accepting credit card payments.

Download site: `www.microsoft.com/frontpage/downloads/addin/searchdetail.asp?a=137`

Download type: Free download. If you decide to use this add-in, consider sending a donation to the add-in's creator, Patrick Husting, who updates this add-in on his own time. Donations take just a moment, using PayPal at his Web site, of course.

For more information: `www.auctionmessenger.net/paypal`

FrontFX Picture Splitter

A favorite graphic trick among Web designers is to chop large graphics into several smaller graphics, and then reassemble the pieces on the page (generally inside a table) to increase the page's download speed. This clever add-in enables you to easily split your own graphics without the help of a complicated graphics program.

Download site: www.microsoft.com/frontpage/downloads/addin/
searchdetail.asp?a=133

Download type: Free download.

For more information: www.xzmedia.com/frontfx/index.asp

Webstyle Web Graphics

This eye-candy add-in gives you plenty of graphic buttons, banners, headings, and bullets to play with.

Download site: www.xara.com/products/webstyle

Download type: Free 15-day trial. More effects are available (for a fee) at the company Web site below.

For more information: www.xaraonline.com

Meta Tag Maker

Meta tags are bits of HTML that describe the content of your site. Search engines often use the information contained in meta tags to index and classify sites in their own databases. This add-in enables you to access and change your site's meta tags without venturing into the HTML code.

Download site: www.microsoft.com/frontpage/downloads/addin/
searchdetail.asp?a=80

Download type: Free 14-day trial. After that, if you want to keep using Meta Tag Maker, you must purchase the software.

For more information: www.websunlimited.com

FrontPage Web Template — Project Management Site

This Web site template guides you in the creation of a Web site devoted to project management. If you're pretty comfortable with FrontPage, check it out — this template is geared toward intermediate users.

Download site: www.microsoft.com/frontpage/downloads/addin/
searchdetail.asp?a=262

Download type: Free download.

For more information: www.vividoffice.com

Office Power! Add-Ins

Office Power! makes available add-ins that increase your productivity as you work with FrontPage. SiteTagger helps optimize your site for search engines, QuickWorks simplifies handy tasks such as creating printer-friendly pages (plus much more), and MyHelp enables you to create your own list of commonly used programs and files so that you can keep them within easy reach from inside FrontPage.

Download site: www.office-power.com/products/downloads/index.htm

Download type: Free 14-day trial. After that, if you want to keep using Office Power! add-ins, you must purchase the software.

For more information: www.office-power.com

Case Changer

This simple add-in enables you to easily convert all the file and folder names inside the currently open Web site to all lowercase letters. It may not be exciting, but this little feature saves your visitors lots of awkward pressing of the Shift key when typing your site's URL into their browsers.

Download site: www.microsoft.com/frontpage/downloads/addin/
searchdetail.asp?a=13

Download type: Free download.

For more information: www.jimcoaddins.com

FrontLook Page Effects

Previously called *FrontLook FX*, this add-in enables you add flashy splash pages, animated effects, and cursor effects to your site.

Download site: www.microsoft.com/frontpage/downloads/addin/searchdetail.asp?a=107

Download type: Free limited-function sampler. Fully functional software available for a fee.

For more information: www.frontlook.com/pfx/pfx.asp

Sothink Glanda

This oddly named add-in enables you to create Flash movies with no graphics experience. Glanda comes with templates that get you started creating animated buttons, banners, text effects, and motion backgrounds.

Download site: www.microsoft.com/frontpage/downloads/addin/searchdetail.asp?a=121

Download type: Free 30-day trial. After that, if you want to keep using Glanda, you must purchase the software.

For more information: www.sothink.com/webtools/glanda/index.htm

Chapter 19

Ten Web Sites Worth a Closer Look

In This Chapter

▶ Finding out about FrontPage, HTML, and Web design on the Internet

▶ Searching the Web and newsgroups with Google

▶ Downloading stuff from Download.com

*T*hroughout this book, I point you to Web sites that I find particularly helpful. In this chapter, I highlight ten sites you really shouldn't miss.

Microsoft FrontPage Home Page

`www.microsoft.com/frontpage`

This site is the place to go for all things FrontPage. Here you find FrontPage tips and information, free accessory downloads, and links to related resources. You can also access online support and FrontPage help, including FrontPage newsgroups, a list of frequently asked questions, and much more.

Microsoft Product Support Services

`support.microsoft.com`

Got a question? Come here first. This mammoth online database contains thousands of articles that answer common software questions or explain annoying bugs. The Knowledge Base contains articles pertaining to all Microsoft products, including FrontPage.

OutFront

`www.outfront.net`

This excellent site contains FrontPage tips, tutorials, forums, plus a number of FrontPage-related products. Be sure to check it out.

HTML: An Interactive Tutorial for Beginners

`www.davesite.com/webstation/html`

The surest way to beef up your Web publishing savvy is to learn HTML, the language behind every Web page. Plenty of good books on the subject are out there, but if you're itching to get started *now,* check out this straightforward, easy-to-take introduction to HTML basics. Be sure to browse the entire site for info on style sheets, Web design, and more.

Builder.com

`builder.com.com`

(Yep, there are two *dot-com*'s in that URL.)

If you like to keep on top of Web publishing happenings, make this Web site one of your regular stops. Builder.com contains practical how-to articles for all sorts of Web tricks.

Webmonkey

`hotwired.lycos.com/webmonkey`

The attitude-filled folks at Webmonkey offer advice about all things Web design. Enthusiastic Web publishers can spend hours here; the site contains information on everything from basic Web page creation to advanced design and programming.

Learn the Net

`www.learnthenet.com`

If you just want to know how the Internet works, visit this well-organized Web site. You can find tons of good, well-written information, but not so much that you're overwhelmed. Be sure to check out the section devoted to Web site building.

Google

`www.google.com`

Among bazillions of other topics, the Web contains information about the current political climate, pictures of African wild dogs, and several online dating services — the trick is finding sites specific to the topic you're interested in. I've tried most of the search engines out there, and I keep coming back to Google. This engine always chug-a-chugs me in the right direction.

Another Google boon: You can search newsgroups as well as Web sites. Go to Google, and then click the Groups tab just above the search box. You end up at the gateway to hundreds of discussion forums (collectively known as *Usenet newsgroups*) about every topic under the sun, including FrontPage. Type **frontpage** in the Search box on the Google Groups page, click the Google Search button, and then click the `microsoft.public.frontpage.client` forum link on the resulting page. The `microsoft.public.front page.client` forum has many discussions with and help from other FrontPage users around the world. If you're stumped by a FrontPage problem, chances are someone there can give you a hand.

Download.com

`download.com.com`

Before you trudge to the computer superstore to pick up new software, find out what shareware and freeware is available on the Net. A software repository such as Download.com contains thousands of software titles, from handy, little utilities to fully fledged programs, all freely downloadable. Most software authors ask that you pay a shareware fee if you decide to keep and use the software, but some programs are free for the taking.

Dummies.com

www.dummies.com

If you can't wait to get your hands on your next good read, check out the Dummies.com Web site. Find out which new books are about to hit the shelves, pick up some savvy tips, or order a title online.

Index

• *Y* •